THE LIFE AND WORK OF
GOETHE

PORTRAIT OF GOETHE
After J. K. Stieler, 1828

THE
LIFE AND WORK OF
GOETHE
1749—1832

BY

JOHN G. ROBERTSON

 BOOKS FOR LIBRARIES PRESS
FREEPORT, NEW YORK

First Published 1932
Reprinted 1971

INTERNATIONAL STANDARD BOOK NUMBER:
0-8369-6665-1

LIBRARY OF CONGRESS CATALOG CARD NUMBER:
79-179536

PRINTED IN THE UNITED STATES OF AMERICA
BY
NEW WORLD BOOK MANUFACTURING CO., INC.
HALLANDALE, FLORIDA 33009

TO

THE ENGLISH GOETHE SOCIETY

IN MEMORY OF
AN ASSOCIATION OF NEARLY FORTY YEARS
WITH ITS ACTIVITIES

CONTENTS

vii

CONTENTS

PART III

OLD AGE

LIST OF ILLUSTRATIONS

PREFACE

A BOOK published at the Centenary of the death of a great personality necessarily takes on the character of a retrospect. To myself the writing of this volume and its amplification in its present form have been in a peculiar degree such a retrospect. Very much of my work has been associated with Goethe since early days when, under the influence of our greatest British apostle of Goethe, Carlyle, I first devoted myself to the study of the poet; the elucidation of his work and thought has always stood in the forefront of my teaching as professor of Modern German Literature in the University of London; and I have a particular satisfaction in the fact that this "Goethejahr" has provided the opportunity of rounding off my academic activity with a series of public lectures at University College in honour of the poet.

My original intention was to make this Centenary book a collection of special studies on Goethe written at various times in the past thirty years; but Messrs. Routledge have been good enough to fall in with my alternative suggestion that some of these might be incorporated in an enlarged edition of the life of Goethe which they published for me six years ago. That work, in accordance with the plan of the series in which it appeared, was mainly biographical, and the literary criticism it offered was scanty and summary. I welcome the opportunity of supplementing it with a fuller treatment of Goethe's writings.

In dedicating the volume to the English Goethe Society I would express my indebtedness to that body for the sympathetic encouragement it has shown to my efforts to revive the serious study of Goethe in this country, and my gratitude for the honour it has done me in electing me its President.

J. G. ROBERTSON.

UNIVERSITY OF LONDON,
January, 1932.

PART I

YOUTH

1749–1775

THE LIFE AND WORK OF GOETHE

CHAPTER I

EARLY YEARS IN FRANKFORT AND LEIPZIG

THE biography of Goethe is in itself an epoch of
European intellectual history. No man of our
race " bestrode like a Colossus " so enormous a span
of human development, a span the width of which is
not to be measured in terms of years—although in
this respect Goethe was favoured beyond the common
lot—but by the epoch-making events and conflicts
these years encompassed, by the kaleidoscopic changes
they brought over the face of Europe. Goethe was
born into the age of Frederick the Great; his boyhood
felt the quiver of that pride of race with which the
great king imbued, not merely his Prussians, but the
German people; the best years of his manhood were
passed amidst the elation and the disillusionment of
the great Revolution; he watched the star of Napoleon
rise and set; he was a witness of the Holy Alliance and
the new Europe created by the Congress of Vienna;
and before he died he saw France once more in the
throes of revolution. In its spiritual aspect the age
was even more eventful. Goethe began life in the
stagnant complacency of the epoch of Enlightenment;
and his student years in Leipzig were as frivolous and
inept as those of any *petit-maître*. But this period was
hardly at an end, when he experienced the full brunt

3

of the spiritual awakening that was ushered in by Rousseau ; and, indeed, he became the apostle of that awakening in Germany, and led it to a higher consummation than it reached in France itself. Yet Goethe was by no means a one-sided disciple of Rousseau ; he could never forget that he was at the same time the heir of the great classical eighteenth century, and for the first thirty years of his life, he had been the contemporary of Voltaire. The persistent dualism which runs through all Goethe's spiritual life—the " two souls within his breast "—might thus be regarded as a reflection of the dualism of the age in which he lived. And, once his impetuous " Storm and Stress " was behind him, he set himself to hold the balance—and no man was ever a greater adept at holding balances than Goethe—between the rationalistic tradition and the new individualistic impulses. Goethe's later years, again, fall in the period when the constellation of German Romanticism was in the ascendancy ; he was the disapproving spectator of the triumph of the Romantic over the Classic ; but he lived long enough to see the fairy castles of the Romantic dreamers crumble to dust before, not a reviving Classicism, but a ruder realism than the eighteenth century had ever known, a realism grown arrogant under the advance of scientific discovery and the democratic industrialization of the new Europe. The poet who in his young years had been nurtured on Rousseau, lived to hail in Byron the herald of the modern spirit. No doubt it was something of a disadvantage that Goethe had to pass his life in the seclusion of a small provincial court; but this did not prevent him participating to the full in the rich and varied intellectual life of his time. Nothing that his contemporaries thought or did was uninteresting to him ; and he stood face to face with the greatest personality of his time, Napoleon, and received his homage. Paris, London, Vienna, it is true, he never saw ; and Berlin he disliked ; but he had been

4

for many months a citizen of what to him was the capital of the world, Rome.

Johann Wolfgang Goethe was born at Frankfort-on-the-Main at midday on August 28th, 1749. The constellations, he tells us, were favourable: " The sun stood in the sign of the Virgin, and had culminated for the day ; Jupiter and Venus had a friendly aspect, Mercury not an adverse one ; Saturn and Mars were neutral ; only the moon, which was just full, exercised her counteracting power, the more so as her planetary hour had begun ". Speculative critics have liked to elaborate this astrological fancy by showing us that Goethe came into the world at the precise moment which enabled him to carry out the mission with which Providence had entrusted him ; but it is idle to dwell on the fitness of any particular year for a great man's birth. Might not one with equal justice claim it as the prerogative of all great men to master the Time-spirit, and by making it subservient to their will, create the illusion of the fit moment ? It is a greater temptation to trace a higher purpose in the fact that this, the greatest and most representative of German poets, sprang, not from the north, and not from the south, but from the very heart of Germany, where north and south meet and mingle.

In point of fact, this mingling of north and south is to be seen in Goethe's ancestry which has been traced back through three generations ; his father's family came originally from Thuringia, his mother's from the south. The grandfather on his father's side was the son of a farrier, and became a tailor ; he then drifted to Frankfort where he married, as his second wife, Cornelia Schelhorn, proprietress of the inn " Zum Weidenhof ", and thus gave up tailoring for inn-keeping. This grandfather, however, was dead many years before the poet came into the world. His father, Johann Caspar Goethe, born in 1710, had had a legal training at Giessen, Strassburg and Wetzlar, and then paid a visit to Italy, on the discomforts of which a diary that has been preserved is eloquent; in after life, however, only the happy memories remained. The roomy and comfortable old house in the Grosse Hirschgraben, which he inherited, was adorned with the pictures of Rome and the collections which he had brought back with him from his travels. But he was a disappointed man, his native town having refused him the preferment he felt entitled to, or, at least, refused to accept his services on terms which were acceptable to him. He had, however, ample means—the innkeeping had prospered in its day—which made it unnecessary for him to practise his profession; and in 1742 he acquired from the Emperor Charles VII the title of " kaiserlicher Rat " (Imperial Councillor) which gave him a good social position in Frankfort, even if he was never regarded, in those days of strict caste, as belonging to the town's aristocracy. He consolidated his position still further by marrying in 1748, Katharina Elisabeth Textor, eldest daughter of the " Stadtschultheiss ", the highest dignitary of the city. Goethe's mother was little more than a girl—not quite seventeen—when she became the bride of Rat Goethe, more than twenty years her senior. The marriage was, of course, an arranged affair; there was affluence on the one side and social position on the other. That there could be any real bond of sympathy between husband and wife was hardly to be expected; but Frau Rat was one of those happy natures who are able to get full satisfaction out of life in any situation. The poet was their first-born; and so difficult was his birth that it was something of a miracle that he and his mother lived at all. Five children followed, but of these four died in infancy; and Wolfgang grew up in the sole companionship of a sister, Cornelia.

From parents so opposed in temperament and mentality—but are not such parental antitheses always an essential condition for the birth of a child of genius?—

Goethe inherited that dualism of character which meets us at every turn of his life. From his father came staidness, order, balance—" des Lebens ernstes Führen "—and also that punctiliousness which, unfortunately, in later life degenerated into a chilling stiffness so discouraging to the younger generation; while all that made Goethe the poet—imagination, sensitiveness, alacrity of spirit—came, as is usually the case with men of genius, from his mother. Young enough herself to be almost a child with her children, Frau Rat was, one feels, the right kind of mother for a poet. She had not had much education, the defects of which her husband endeavoured to make good; but her innate gaiety, her healthy naturalness and unwillingness to see the dark side of things, bathed her two children in sunshine; and the stories young Wolfgang listened to at her knee were the first stimulus of his imagination. From his mother Goethe received, indeed, his " Frohnatur ", his happy nature; from her, too, came that inherent faith in the goodness of the world, tinged, it may be, with fatalism, a fatalism perhaps inherent in the pietism in which she had been brought up, which provided the foundation for the confident optimism of her son's mature years. Her letters, ungrammatical and badly spelled as they are, are a delight to read; and one cannot but feel some resentment that Goethe should have so grudgingly repaid the debt he owed her. His visits to Frankfort in later life were few and far between.

The education of the two children was the father's affair; and it lacked nothing in manysidedness and thoroughness; but his methodical pedagogy was heavy-handed, Cornelia naturally suffering more under it than her brother, who in due time escaped to the university. As the children grew up, private tutors were engaged, but Rat Goethe did not give the reins out of his own hands; he was determined that his son should not be contaminated by attending a public school. Languages, Latin and Greek, French, Italian and English, to which was added, in the boy's case, Hebrew, formed the main constituents of this schooling; and Goethe tells us how, to sugar the pill of grammar, he himself invented a novel in which members of a family in various parts of the world wrote letters to each other in different tongues and styles. Some sprightly Latin dialogues, humorous and dramatic, written in his seventh or eighth year, bear witness to a good deal more than the child's progress in Latin. Looking back on his earliest years, Goethe has less to tell us of the knowledge he acquired than of the factors which awakened and moulded his literary sense. He recalls the Bible stories and fairy-tales his mother read to him; and Bettina von Arnim—not, it is true, always a very creditable witness, but likely to be trustwothy here—records a charming scene which Frau Rat had described to her:

> There I sat, and he devoured me with his large black eyes; and when the fate of one of his favourites was not according to his mind, I saw the angry veins swell on his brow, and how he was repressing his tears. He often interrupted with: " But, mother, the princess won't marry the hateful tailor, even if he does kill the giant. . . ." When I guided the threads of fate according to his plan, and said to him: " You have guessed rightly: that is how it happened," then he was all afire, and one could see his little heart beating underneath his collar.

The deepest impression of all was left by a puppet-theatre, a present from his grandmother, which was shown to the children at the Christmas of Goethe's seventh year. Here a *David and Goliath* was performed in which the boy declaimed the rôles with great gusto; and soon his father's library was ransacked for more ambitious plays. In later life Goethe vividly recalled these memories in his *Wilhelm Meister*. Thus the boy grew up in pleasant surroundings; his childhood was

exceptionally happy ; he knew nothing of that lot of
poverty which formed the stern school of the majority
of German poets in the eighteenth century. His young
mind unfolded graciously in the old patrician house
which his father largely rebuilt in 1754, with its wide
view from the higher windows over the town and the
fertile Main valley. The busy commercial life of
Frankfort, which was then a town of some 33,000
inhabitants, its river lively with shipping, and its
biennial international fairs, early gave him a glimpse of
the great world beyond ; and it was full enough, too,
of old monuments and memories, going back to the
Carlovingians, to awaken his historical sense. But
there were also shadows on this fortunate childhood,
although Goethe does not allow them to darken unduly
the retrospect of his Autobiography. The boy had
more than his share of childish illnesses, including
smallpox ; and at an early age religious questionings
seem to have been a disturbing factor. He reminds us
that he was just emerging into mental consciousness
when the great Lisbon earthquake of 1755 upset the
complacent deism of the eighteenth century, and sent
a shudder through Europe. But perhaps in his
retrospect he attaches too much importance to such
things at this stage ; it is, at least, difficult to think of
so young a child discovering the Rousseau-like solution
to his religious difficulties which Goethe ascribes to
himself.

The campaign of Frederick the Great against Saxony
and Austria and their French allies which constituted
the Seven Years War, was also a disturbing factor. It
plunged Frankfort into confusion, especially after the
Battle of Bergen in the Easter week of 1759 ; for over
three years the city was occupied by French troops.
The Goethe household was, moreover, divided against
itself by this internecine conflict, his father being an
ardent admirer of the Prussian king, while the sympathies of his mother and her family lay with Austria.

For the child, who was on his father's side, the war was, however, hardly a calamity. A Count Thoranc from Provence, a "lieutenant du roy", was quartered on the house in the Hirschgraben, and, in spite of much irritating provocation on the part of the head of the house, he acted with great consideration towards the family. An art connoisseur, Count Thoranc arranged an atelier in the house, and gathered round him the Frankfort painters, commissioning them to paint pictures for him. This made a lasting impression on young Wolfgang, in whom the count took a particular interest, and sowed the seeds of that love of art which remained with him through life. The French brought, too, their theatre with them, to which Goethe, as the grandson of the "Stadtschultheiss", had free access, his father's grudging approval being won over by the consideration that Wolfgang would thereby improve his French. An acquaintance struck up with a boy connected with the troupe led to him being even admitted behind the scenes. Thus the enthusiast for Shakespeare of only a few years later, the poet of *Götz von ·Berlichingen* and *Faust*, absolved his apprenticeship to the theatre of the alexandrine and the unities. All this, however, led to a welcome relaxation of the hours of instruction.

An outstanding event at the beginning of 1764 was the election and coronation of Joseph II as German Emperor, which, in accordance with ancient tradition, took place in the Frankfort town-hall or "Römer". This glittering pageant in which notabilities from all parts of the Empire took part—not to speak of the motley crowd of sightseers, showmen and jugglers who thronged to the city—made a deep impression on the boy's imagination. But it was also associated with an incident which led to his Frankfort days ending in discord. Wolfgang had found a circle of associates that were none too desirable. One of these—Goethe calls him his Pylades—discovered his talent for writing

verses and induced him to help him and his friends to
write their love-letters. A chance remark by one of
the objects of these addresses, that it was a pity he
did not write them on his own account, seems to have
been the spark that kindled. For the first time the
god Eros, who was to lead Goethe so many a dance
in the course of his long life, gave him a taste of his
power. Goethe's earliest love, his Frankfort Gretchen,
is dwelt on a little obviously in the Autobiography;
the old poet clearly liked to link up the object of this
boyish passion with her immortal namesake in *Faust*;
it is even possible that *Dichtung und Wahrheit* may not
be quite true here, and that Faust's Gretchen may have
lent her name to the Frankfort episode which Goethe
describes. The affair, which reached its culmination
on the night of the coronation, did not get beyond the
single kiss which Gretchen at parting imprinted on his
brow. It was not very serious; but Gretchen's subsequent statement, which came to Goethe's ears,
that she had never regarded him as anything but a
child, took time to live down. Wolfgang's interest in
her came to light in an unpleasant way, for he had
been induced to use his influence with his grandfather
to obtain a municipal post for one of her friends
who was subsequently convicted of embezzlement.
Young Goethe, to his great relief, escaped being
compromised; when the matter was gone into by the
authorities, his innocence and Gretchen's were completely established. The disconcerting ending to his
boyhood was, however, soon forgotten, when he
found himself a student in the intellectual metropolis
of Leipzig. He would himself have preferred Göttingen; but his father had studied at Leipzig, and to
Leipzig Wolfgang had to go to be drilled into a jurist.

The biographer eagerly scans these early years for
signs of the poet's awakening genius; but unfortunately little has come down to us. Goethe, however,
early learned to use his pen; and indeed in 1763 he

boasted that he could present his father with a respectable quarto volume of his poems every year. Besides
the novel in different tongues already mentioned, we
hear of an epic on the Bible story of Joseph, the supposed discovery of which created a passing flutter in
recent years ; and Goethe himself gives us an example
(*Der neue Paris*) in his *Dichtung und Wahrheit* of the kind
of fairy tale he liked to tell. But the drama—from his
first efforts to supply his puppet-theatre with a repertory,
to ambitious Biblical tragedies intended for the French
theatre—attracted him most. As a student in Leipzig,
however, he committed all his youthful efforts to the
flames ; and nothing has been preserved but a bundle
of school exercises, a couple of childish poems to his
grandparents and a rhetorical ode, first written in 1762
and remodelled three years later, *Poetische Gedanken über
die Höllenfahrt Jesu Christi*. The echoes of Klopstock
in this poem recall to mind Goethe's amusing account in
the Autobiography of how the *Messias* was smuggled
into the Goethe household by a friend of the family in
defiance of Rat Goethe's antipathy to the new unrhymed
poetry : Wolfgang and his sister's excited declamation
of a violent passage upset the equanimity of his father's
barber to such a degree that he upset over him the basin
of soap-suds !

Not only does a new chapter open in Goethe's life,
when he became a student at the university of Leipzig
in the autumn of 1765 ; it is the beginning of a new
Goethe. Leipzig was a much more modern town than
Frankfort, and with its great university and central-
ized book-trade pre-eminently a centre of culture and
refined manners. And it gave Wolfgang his first
taste of freedom. He did not take long to cast the
skin of his provincial boorishness, to get rid of his
home-made clothes which elegant Leipzig laughed at,
and to adapt himself to his new surroundings. It is,
indeed, with difficulty that we recognize again the
Frankfort boy in the powdered young dandy who

strutted the Leipzig streets. Scandalized at the change that had come over him, one of his Frankfort friends wrote in the summer of 1766 :

> Goethe is still the arrogant, fantastic fellow he was when I came here. If you were only to see him, you would either rage with anger or have to split with laughter. I cannot see how a person can so quickly change himself. All his ways and his whole present behaviour are miles apart from his former ways. In his pride he is also a dandy, and all his clothes, fine as they are, are in such a grotesque *goût* that they make him conspicuous in the whole university. But this is all indifferent to him, you may point out his folly to him as much as you like.

He tossed off graceful and for the most part vacuous anacreontics, in which the usual motives of wine-drinking and gallantry jingled to light music; he schoolmastered his sister in informative letters home, written sometimes in bad French and quite impossible English; and in boyish fervour he clutched new friends to his heart, choosing by preference, as always in later life, antithetic natures, like Ernst Wolfgang Behrisch, some eleven years older than himself, a lanky, mocking individual who lived in Leipzig as tutor to a nobleman's son, and, with his sword dangling at his side, cut an odd enough figure in the Leipzig streets. Goethe was much impressed by his first introduction to the academic world, and he began his studies industriously enough. One of the introductions which he had brought with him was to Hofrat Böhme, professor of history; and to him he ingenuously confessed his preference for literary pursuits to the study of jurisprudence, only to receive a discouraging rebuff. Frau Böhme, however, took a motherly interest in him. Before his first term was very far advanced we find him writing home in a tone of superior sarcasm about the academic authorities. Lectures on jurisprudence or anything else did not, after the first few weeks, engage him very seriously; and for Christian Fürchtegott Gellert—

13

famous alike as poet and professor—did he alone feel any warmth and respect.

There is no glossing it over: the Leipzig Goethe was a young rake, and was too much preoccupied by his initiation into " life " to have much time for study of any kind. Before long he had his " Mädgen ", a very different kind of affair from the shy calf-love of Frankfort. Her name was Anna or Annette Käthchen Schönkopf, daughter of the host of the wine-house where Goethe took his midday meal. He seems to have met her in April 1766. She was a lively little creature, three years older than Goethe, not over pretty, and probably less so in the unbecoming coiffure of the day than she might have been, but with ingratiating manners. They saw each other daily and acted together in private theatricals. This coquettish personification of the Leipzig rococo was exactly the partner for the young elegant, the appropriate muse of his new mood. There is a difficulty in gauging how much depth there was in his passion for Annette; indeed, it is not easy with any of Goethe's loves, for one can never say how much Goethe's erotic fancies were inflamed by the actual person, and how much by a transfigured idea of her; at all times, Goethe, as is the poet's way, let his imagination contribute more to his passions than they to his imagination. In this particular case it is difficult to disentangle the reality, for rococo love-making was largely flirtation and protestation; a deeper note of passion, one feels, might have shattered the Dresden china ; and, in point of fact, something like this did happen. The lyrics which Annette inspired— only discovered and published as late as 1895—are too much concerned with Amor's ingenuity in circumventing coyness and with the other anacreontic conventions of the day, to reveal the truth. But if we turn to Goethe's letters to his friend Behrisch, we see that his feelings did become more involved than was required by the philandering spirit of the day. He took upon himself the blame that the course of his love did not run smoothly; he tells us that he tormented Käthchen with jealousy; but one cannot help suspecting that she, on her part, had a pleasure in teasing her young admirer, and was not so seriously anxious as he professed to be, that their love-making should be guided into the still waters of matrimony. Goethe's deeper nature was stirred; he fell into fits of melancholy; and the passion reverberated in him until long after Leipzig was a turned page in his life. Indeed, the sting still rankled when Käthchen ultimately, in 1770, gave her hand to a Dr. Kanne. Thus his Leipzig romance ended in that disillusionment to which all Goethe's serious love-affairs inevitably led. The process of disintegration was hardly different now from that of Goethe's later passions; but he was still too young to understand that behind the disintegration was his subconscious self, dimly feeling its power, refusing to let itself be fettered, and urging safety in flight.

The pin-pricks of this love that would not run smoothly have left their mark on Goethe's comedy in well-turned alexandrines, *Die Laune des Verliebten*, which had possibly in some form been already planned before Goethe came to the university at all. Two happy lovers, Lamon and Egle, are contrasted with another pair, Eridon and Amide, whose harmony is disturbed by the swain's jealousy. As Amide cannot be induced to make a stand against her lover's unreasonableness, her friend Egle lures him into kissing her, whereby he is put to shame and reformed. This still readable little play is in the conventional pastoral mould, and is Goethe's tribute to the *genius loci* of Leipzig, his contribution to the Saxon comedy of would-be French elegance. A more significant reflection of Goethe's emotional distraughtness is to be read out of another piece written at this time, *Die Mitschuldigen*, even if it is not so intimately a reproduction of

15

its author's experiences. *Die Mitschuldigen*—after his return to Frankfort Goethe expanded it into three acts—is an enigmatic and unpleasant play. Its theme is a somewhat sordid anecdote of how Söller, the good-for-nothing son-in-law of the landlord of the Black Bear, robs Alceste, a guest of the inn, and former lover of his wife Sophie. As, however, on the same night Alceste has arranged a rendezvous with Sophie in his room, and her father, curious about a letter which Alceste has received, also betakes himself there, all feel themselves guilty and the theft is condoned.

One resents the cynical attitude the young poet takes up to these delinquencies and the lack of seriousness with which he handles them. The inference seems to be that Goethe had been drawn in Leipzig into waters that were too deep for him; his moral convictions had been shaken and unsettled. These dramatic essays, to which must be added the lost plan of an ambitious five-act tragedy, *Belsazar*, are not, however, of much importance; and, as we have seen, his lyric beginnings, however sympathetically we may view them, show little promise of what was to come. Indeed, much the most pleasing products of Goethe's pen in these student days are the vivacious letters he wrote to his home and friends; there is a truer ring of genius here than in his poetry. Goethe's literary horizon in Leipzig was definitely bounded by the rococo. Wieland, among his contemporaries, stood highest in favour; and his ambition now, and until he went to Strassburg, was to follow in that poet's footsteps. Lessing, on the other hand, did not interest him sufficiently to induce him to seize the one opportunity life ever gave him of meeting face to face the greatest and manliest of his predecessors. Still, we must not make too much of these things. And it has not to be forgotten that Shakespeare—even if only through the medium of Dodd's *Beauties of Shakespeare*—was already familiar to him as a Leipzig student, far as he still was from finding the key that was to unlock for him Shake-speare's heart.

In the last year of his stay in Leipzig Goethe found a more engrossing interest than the university had been able to provide. He made the acquaintance of Adam Friedrich Oeser who presided over an academy of painting, housed in the Leipzig Pleissenburg. Here Goethe applied himself assiduously to learning to draw and etch. Oeser was a disciple of Winckelmann ; and for the Goethe that was to be, it was surely more valuable that he, with Oeser's help, should have got a glimpse, beyond the narrow horizon of Leipzig, into that promised land of a chaster classic beauty which Winckelmann had revealed, than that he should have become an adept in Justinian. Three years later he wrote of Oeser : " His instruction will have conse-quences for my whole life. He taught me to see the ideal of beauty in simplicity and repose ". His art interests were deepened and widened by a furtive visit early in 1768 to the Dresden gallery.

Goethe's first student years came to a sudden and unforeseen end. He paid the penalty of his youthful excesses—and possibly also of the rigorous treatment of cold baths to which he subjected himself as a counter-balance—with serious illness, the rupture of a blood-vessel in the lung. He woke up one morning with his mouth full of blood, and many weeks elapsed before, on his nineteenth birthday, he was sufficiently recovered to venture on the journey home.

As we look back on this period of Goethe's life, the most urgent thought that presses on us is that he—the great European Goethe—should have passed his first apprenticeship to life and poetry in the stuffy atmo-sphere of provincial Leipzig, and in the leading-strings of an artificial taste. It is tempting to find irony rather than purpose in such a beginning for a poet who had the rôle to play in the world that Goethe played. On the other hand, his initiation into poetry, such as it was,

lengthens out the span of his life enormously : his
literary achievement is linked up with the pastoral and
pseudo-classic poetry of the century before him, indeed,
with the very beginnings of our modern literature.
The poet who was to put its final stamp on the classicism in modern literature which was initiated by the
Renaissance, himself passed, like the embryo, through
all its developmental phases. Leipzig provided the
stimulus and the starting point for his first positive
mission in his nation's poetry, namely, to discredit the
mincing artificiality with which the German Muse had
been tripping it for generations, and to lead her back to
sincerity and truth.

Chapter II

BACK IN FRANKFORT. STRASSBURG

Goethe's father had little enough reason to be satisfied with his son's progress at the university of Leipzig. It was clear that Wolfgang had not made much effort to prepare himself for that legal career which the stern old disciplinarian had mapped out for him. But the boy came home an invalid, and there were probably no serious recriminations. Mother and sister, of course, welcomed him effusively. His recovery progressed, and he spent his time mainly in drawing and etching. He did not take kindly to the dullness of his native town after the motley freedom he had enjoyed in Leipzig, and in correspondence with the Leipzig friends he endeavoured to retain something of the old rapture. His love for Käthchen was still very much alive; he wrote once a month to her and sent her little presents. In December there was an alarming return of the hæmorrhage from the lung, apparently aggravated by the fumes of the acids he had been using in etching. His life was this time almost despaired of, but his mother drew consolation from the text at which she opened her Bible: " Thou shalt yet plant vines upon the mountains of Samaria: the planters shall plant and " (in the Lutheran text) "play the pipe". The timely administration of an alchemistic salt behind the physician's back brought miraculous relief, thus strengthening still further his mother's confidence in the Providence that watched over him. Recovery was slow, and all through the spring months of 1769 he was more of an invalid than he had been in the weeks following his return from Leipzig.

This, Goethe's twentieth year, was a crucial year in his development, although no particular weight is laid upon it in the Autobiography; life was shaping itself earnestly for him. Leipzig, with its light-hearted frivolity and gallantry, was receding into the past. He still clung to his love for Käthchen, but he had the instinctive feeling—even before he had knowledge, in May, of her formal betrothal—that she had to be forgotten. This was a very disrupting thought: his first experience of that " Entsagung " which so often and in so many guises was to throw its shadow across his life. Abysses of despair yawned before the young poet, who but a year or two earlier, had been making his first experiments in poetry by commuting his light-hearted dance of life into the alexandrines of *Die Laune des Verliebten*, in the poetry to " Annette ", and the *Neue Lieder*, which appeared—Goethe's first published work—in the autumn of 1769, with his friend Breit-kopf's music. Chameleon-like, as so often in the crises of his life, Goethe assumed a new colour; haunted by upsetting presentiments, he found refuge in that pietism, which has always been present in German hearts beneath the veneer of rationalism or materialism. Into this atmosphere of religious brooding he was initiated by Susanna von Klettenberg, a relative of his mother's who was associated with the Moravian Brethren; and in communion with this " beautiful soul "—for it was she Goethe had in mind when he wrote the sixth book of his *Wilhelm Meister*—Goethe turned away from the glittering surface of things and probed the depths. Through pietism he found his way back to the head-springs of German mysticism in the works of Helmont and Paracelsus; he studied the *Aurea Catena Homeri* and that dreary folio of pietistic heterodoxy, Arnold's *Unpartheyische Kirchen- und Ketzergeschichte*; he spent hours over Thomas à Kempis and Tauler, and made the acquaintance of the great Swedish mystic of his own time, Emanuel Swedenborg. With the help of Welling's *Opus Mago-Cabbalisticum* and Boerhaave's *Elementa Chemiae*, he acquired, too, a knowledge of chemistry, then, of course, still largely alchemy; a furnace and retort were erected in his little attic, and his days and nights were spent in experimenting—all this, no doubt, with but little approval from his father. A more complete conversion and metamorphosis of the young anacreontic rhymer it would be difficult to imagine; but one could not have a better testimony to the elasticity of his temperament and his capacity for spiritual growth. In those days and nights Goethe must have thought many searching thoughts, poring over the mysteries of matter and spirit amidst his books, retorts and crucibles, seeking to discover:

> was die Welt
> Im Innersten zusammenhält.

We have no documents of these explorations, for the young poet did not so easily find utterance for his thoughts; and his letters of the time are inclined to veil them in humour and irony. But there is little doubt that Goethe, wrestling with the dark powers in these months of convalescence in Frankfort, experienced the first of the great spiritual crises which punctuated his life.

When health ultimately did return, the practical question had to be faced: what next? Rat Goethe again took control, and decided that his son should complete his professional training in France, at the Academy of Strassburg, and afterwards acquire a final polish in Paris. These plans were the more welcome to Goethe, as the dreaded date of Käthchen's wedding approached. He could not bring himself to congratulate her, or to provide the epithalamium she wished him to write for her; and when the marriage was postponed until Easter, he still clung to the hope that she might be his after all. Yet he writes to her asking her to break off the correspondence: " It is a sad request, my best one, the only one of your sex I may not call friend ". And in his last letter of January 1770, in which he tells her of his plans of going abroad, there is an underlying note of finality:

> You are and always have been the loveable girl, and you will also be the loveable wife. And I—I shall still be Goethe. You know what that means. When I name myself, I name all of myself, and you know that, ever since I saw you, I have been only a part of you.

No city, except Rome, meant so much for Goethe as Strassburg, this old Alemannic focus of spiritual light which has contributed more to the culture of the German race than any other of its centres. With its 48,000 inhabitants it was a larger town than either Frankfort or Leipzig; but it could not compare with the latter as an intellectual centre. Moreover—and notwithstanding that the French of those days frankly recognized Alsace as a " German " province of France—there was a division of allegiance in the town which lessened the significance of its larger population. In Strassburg Goethe's crisis found its solution; here the meaning of the days of brooding in Frankfort became clearer. His delight in Alsace—unexpected, perhaps, in one who came from the more picturesque Main valley—was unbounded; and no land, except Italy, was flooded with brighter sunshine in his memory. Again we are tempted to dwell on the chameleon in Goethe. Could there be a greater contrast than the rococo dandy of Leipzig and the serious, handsome youth who, in the spring of 1770, rode across the Rhine bridge into Strassburg? Only the eyes—those wonderful eyes into which no one, man or woman, could ever look and forget—were the same.

Goethe arrived on the 2nd of April; he took rooms in the Fischmarkt under the shadow of the cathedral,

and he dined at the house of two maiden ladies called
Lauth, who provided a midday meal for paying guests
in the Knoblauchsgasse. This company was presided
over by a Strassburg actuary, Johann Daniel Salzmann,
the oldest of the circle, who took a particular interest in
Goethe, introducing him to his friends and enlisting
his co-operation in a literary society. Goethe soon
slipped into easy intimacy with his fellow-diners, who
were mostly medical students; of these Franz Lerse
and a theologian, Friedrich Leopold Weyland, became
his particular friends. Later, Heinrich Jung-Stilling,
that extraordinary product of German pietism, joined
the company; still later, the poet Jakob Lenz came to
Strassburg and attached himself with embarrassing
affection to Goethe, and another young dramatist,
Heinrich Leopold Wagner, a student of law and fellow-
townsman of Goethe, became one of his intimates.
Goethe devoted himself more seriously to his legal
studies than in Leipzig, for a practical end had this
time to be achieved; and he even succeeded in discovering that jurisprudence had its attractive sides.
But he also found time to dabble in medical studies, and
his Frankfort interest in chemistry was not forgotten.
Pietism visibly lost its hold over him. A note-book
of this time, which he labelled *Ephemerides*, has been
preserved, and bears witness to a quite extraordinary
range of reading. On holiday rides through Alsace
and Lorraine—to the Odilienberg and to Saarbrücken
—he gained a wide knowledge of the land and its
people.

In Strassburg Goethe discovered his genius and found
his soul. Affectionately as he has in his Autobiography
dwelt on all that that city meant to him, we cannot but
regret that just here so much calm and mellow retrospect
has crept into its pages. There was surely more unrest
and more impatience of control in the Strassburg
Goethe than Goethe, the elderly chronicler, would have
us believe; his letters and poetry reveal, indeed, a very

different Goethe. That his rebellious spirit was led
into productive channels was almost entirely due to the
influence on him of the pioneer of the new outlook on
life and poetry, associated with the " Storm and Stress ",
Johann Friedrich Herder. It was, indeed, a memor-
able moment, not only in Goethe's life, but in the intellectual history of the German people, when these
two young men met on the stairs of the old Strassburg
inn, " Zum Geist ". Goethe was twenty-one, Herder
twenty-six. Well might Goethe see in it, as in so much
else in his wonderful life, the hand of a " divinity that
shapes our ends ". Herder was then only known to
the young poet as the author of the *Kritische Wälder*—
the *Fragmente über die deutsche Literatur* he did not read
until later—but this was enough. He was hungering
for new spiritual food ; and Herder, as no other of his
contemporaries, had this food to give him ; Goethe
welcomed him with open arms.

Herder had come to Strassburg as travelling tutor
to the young prince of Holstein-Eutin ; but on the way
thither, in Darmstadt, he had met his future wife, Caroline Flachsland, and had been offered a fixed position
by the Prince-Bishop of Bückeburg. Thus he was not
unwilling to find an excuse for resigning his tutorship ;
and he took advantage of his stay in Strassburg to
undergo an operation for a stoppage in the lachrymal
duct of the eye. The treatment was long and tedious,
and in the end ineffectual, but one part of the cure was
that he was obliged to spend his days in a darkened
room ; and here Goethe bore him company for hours
at a time.

From Herder Goethe received in their long intimate
talks the foundations on which the first and most
prolific epoch of his literary life was reared. Herder
expounded to him his inspiring conception of human
evolution ; taught him to see the beginnings of our
race in primitive poetry, especially in the Hebrew literature of the Bible ; showed him the virile strength in

the medieval past of his own people. He opened his eyes to the beauties of Homer, Pindar and Ossian; and he revived Goethe's early interest in Klopstock. Most significant of all, he revealed to him the greatness of Shakespeare. Before this master of the northern soul Goethe felt like his Faust writhing before the Earth Spirit. Later, after his return to Frankfort, he put what that revelation meant to him into words:

> Do not expect me to write much or to write sedately; tranquillity of soul is no garment for a festival; and even still I have thought little about Shakespeare; to divine him, feel him in great passages, is the highest to which I have been able to attain. The first page I read in him, made me his for life, and when I had reached the end of the first play, I stood like one born blind, on whom in a moment a miraculous hand has bestowed sight. I recognized, I felt most intensely, that my being had been infinitely widened; everything was new to me, unknown, and the unwonted light gave me pain in my eyes. Gradually I learned to see, and, thanks to my receptive nature, I still feel intensely how much I have gained.

The break with the rococo was complete; French literature filled him with aversion, and Wieland was a broken idol. Herder showed him, too, that the eternal spring of poetry was not to be found in dusty compendiums of literary rules, still less in dainty gilt-edged volumes of drawing-room poetry, but in the heart of the people. A handful of simple Volkslieder vanquished for ever the jingling anacreontic insincerities in Goethe's own poetry, and in that of his country. At the Volkslied his own matchless lyric genius was kindled; and with Herder's encouragement he set about collecting songs from the lips of the Alsatian peasants. Goethe's own remoulding of such poetry, as in his splendid *Heidenröslein*, shows the hand of a master:

Sah ein Knab' ein Röslein stehn,
Röslein auf der Heiden,
War so jung und morgenschön,
Lief er schnell es nah zu sehn,
Sah's mit vielen Freuden.
Röslein, Röslein, Röslein rot,
Röslein auf der Heiden.

And as the background to this quivering excitement towered—in its Gothic beauty a symbol and an inspiration—the great Strassburg Minster attributed to Erwin von Steinbach. For Goethe this noble pile was the very incarnation of the Germanic soul.

Can one wonder that the young poet was dazzled by the light that broke over him in Strassburg? No later experience of Goethe's life created so revolutionary a turmoil within him. Intoxicated, carried off his feet, it would, indeed, have not been surprising had he lost his balance altogether; he might have raged and rollicked, as so many a " Stürmer und Dränger " of these days and the aftertime, glowing with the new wine of freedom, saturated with the genius of Shakespeare and the fermenting yeast of Rousseau, and—ended in mere empty sound and fury. But Herder acted not merely as a stimulus; he was also a corrective, a brake on the wheel. He had something in him of a Swift or a Mephistopheles, and Goethe stood in awe of his sharp tongue. Still more, there came to Goethe's aid that mental equilibrium which never deserted him in the crises of his life. This was what enabled him, almost alone of his generation, to make the " Storm and Stress " a positive and productive factor in his country's literature.

Such were the forces which were rapidly moulding Goethe into a poet. But before the metamorphosis of the Leipzig gallant was complete, his emotional nature had to experience another upheaval. Goethe's Strassburg love, Friederike Brion, supplemented the intellectual revolution in him which Herder had initiated. As

THE HOUSE IN WHICH GOETHE WAS BORN, 1755
(Before the Alterations)

[*face p.* 26

befitted the new world he had entered, Friederike was no coquette versed in the allures of the rococo, but a simple country girl of unassuming manners, of no great education, but with a great well of sentiment waiting to be tapped. She was the second eldest of the un-married daughters of the pastor of Sesenheim, a village lying some twenty miles to the north of Strassburg. Goethe had been introduced to the family by his friend Weyland, who was related to them; and as a youthful joke he had himself, on the first visit, introduced to them as a poor dependant. This was in October, 1770. The delightful vignette of this meeting in *Dichtung und Wahrheit* bears witness to the vividness of Goethe's memory, even if it be retouched with the mature art that has given us Hermann's Dorothea:

At this instant she actually appeared at the door; and then indeed, a lovely star arose in this rural firmament. Both daughters still wore German dress, as it was then called, and this almost obsolete national costume became Friederike particularly well. A short, white full skirt, with a flounce, not too long to reveal the neatest little feet and ankles; a tight white bodice and a black taffeta apron—thus she stood on the boundary between town and peasant girl. Slender and light, she tripped along with buoyant step, and her neck seemed almost too delicate to bear the weight of the thick, fair plaits on the neat little head. The look of her merry, cheerful blue eyes was frank and free, and her pretty turned-up nose peered as freely into the air as if there could be no care in the world; her straw hat hung on her arm, and thus, at the first glance, I had the delight of seeing and appreciating her at once in her full grace and loveliness.

A couple of days after his return he needs must write to her telling her of his regrets at parting from her. The actual letter we do not possess, Friederike's sister having destroyed all that Goethe wrote to her; but we have Goethe's rough draft of it. He began:

DEAR NEW FRIEND,

I do not hesitate a moment to call you so; for if I know anything at all about eyes, then mine read at the first glance the hope of this friendship in yours; and for our hearts I would swear. You, gentle and good as I know you are, must you not be just a little bit kindly in return to me who love you so?

And then, thinking better of it, he began over again:

DEAR, DEAR FRIEND,

Whether I have anything to say to you or not does not come into question; but whether I just know why I am actually writing to you and what I would like to say, that is another thing. This much I perceive in a certain inward restlessness: that I should very much like to be with you; and in that case a little scrap of paper is a true consolation, a winged horse for me here in the midst of this noisy Strassburg—as it may also be for you in your quiet, if you really feel the parting from your friends. . . . You would not believe that the bustle of the town, contrasted with your sweet country joys, could be distasteful to me. In truth, Mamsell, Strassburg never seemed so empty to me as it does now. I hope, indeed, it will be better when time has dimmed a little the remembrance of our pleasant little amusements, when I no longer feel so much how good and charming a friend I have. Yet could I or would I forget that? No, I will rather keep my little heartache and write often to you.

Repeated visits to Sesenheim during the winter ripened the intimacy, without, it would appear, awakening any misgivings in Friederike's parents; and with the coming of the spring Goethe's new passion reached its zenith. Then in summer Friederike fell ill, and Goethe spent several weeks at the parsonage, partly in happy dalliance, but partly also troubled, as may be read in and between the lines of a letter to his friend Salzmann, by thoughts of the future. The inevitable rift in the lute had begun to show itself. Rarely in the course of his long life was love to mean to Goethe more than a fleeting happiness, to be more than a poppy flower that he had but to grasp and the bloom was shed. The inevitable end approached, and more swiftly than it had come in Leipzig. On June 20th they parted. As from his horse he gave her his hand, " tears stood in her eyes and I, too, was deeply unhappy ". And the letter from her which he received in reply to one of his, rent his heart; it was " written in a moment when it almost cost her her life ". Such was the course of the most moving of all Goethe's love experiences. To Friederike it was indeed a tragedy; perhaps a deeper tragedy than, on our slight evidence, we have any right to hint. In the old sentimental phrase, it broke her heart; and the sting of the parting rankled in Goethe for years after his flight. In Strassburg, Goethe tells us, he took lessons in dancing from a French dancing-master who had two pretty daughters who helped in teaching him to waltz. He was attracted by the younger; the elder had set her heart on him. The little affair ended in a passionate scene of jealousy in which Lucinde threw her arms round the young poet, kissed him violently and pronounced a curse on whoever should again kiss his lips. Goethe was never averse from believing in omens and pre-monitions.

The story of Goethe and Friederike in *Dichtung und Wahrheit* has always been regarded as a pearl of Goethe's prose, one of the beautiful love stories of literature. And yet there is perhaps no episode in Goethe's retro-spect of forty years, where the " truth " is more suffused with idealizing " poetry " than just this. He frames it, for instance, in an ingratiating literary analogy with *The Vicar of Wakefield*. But Goethe did not know Goldsmith's story when he first saw Friederike, and even if he had known it, it is doubtful whether the impetuous, unreflective passion which she stirred in him would have been patient of so sedate a parallel. Moreover, to fit the Sesenheim family into the literary

29

picture he had to do some violence to the facts ; he has no room for Friederike's third sister ; and he deliberately heightens the beginning of the romance by transferring it to the springtime. But it is the placidity of the retrospect, beautiful as it is, that is the greatest sin against the truth : it was not thus that the Strassburg Goethe loved. The best of proofs is the handful of wonderful lyrics Friederike inspired, lyrics in which the artificialities of Goethe's earlier poetry fade completely before the onrush of an emotional sincerity that knew nothing of literary conventions. The truth of Goethe's passion is enshrined, not in *Dichtung und Wahrheit*, but in poems like *Willkommen und Abschied*, especially if we read them, not as they are to be found in his collected works, but as he originally wrote them) :

Es schlug mein Herz, geschwind zu Pferde,
Und fort, wild, wie ein Held zur Schlacht !
Der Abend wiegte schon die Erde,
Und an den Bergen hing die Nacht.
Schon stund im Nebelkleid die Eiche
Wie ein getürmter Riese da,
Wo Finsternis aus dem Gesträuche
Mit hundert schwarzen Augen sah.

Der Mond von einem Wolkenhügel
Sah schläfrig aus dem Duft hervor ;
Die Winde schwangen leise Flügel,
Umsausten schauerlich mein Ohr.
Die Nacht schuf tausend Ungeheuer ;
Doch tausendfacher war mein Mut.
In meinen Adern welches Feuer !
In meinem Herzen welche Glut !

Der Abschied, wie bedrängt, wie trübe !
Aus deinen Blicken sprach dein Herz :
In deinen Küssen welche Liebe !
O, welche Wonne, welcher Schmerz !
Du gingst, ich stund und sah zur Erden,
Und sah dir nach mit nassem Blick.
Und doch, welch Glück geliebt zu werden !
Und lieben, Götter, welch ein Glück !

And the beautiful *Mailied*:

Wie herrlich leuchtet
Mir die Natur!
Wie glänzt die Sonne!
Wie lacht die Flur!

Es dringen Blüten
Aus jedem Zweig
Und tausend Stimmen
Aus dem Gesträuch,

Und Freud' und Wonne
Aus jeder Brust.
O Erd', o Sonne!
O Glück, o Lust!

O Lieb', o Liebe!
So golden schön,
Wie Morgenwolken
Auf jenen Höhn!

Du segnest herrlich
Das frische Feld,
Im Blütendampfe
Die volle Welt.

O Mädchen, Mädchen,
Wie lieb' ich dich!
Wie blickt dein Auge!
Wie liebst du mich!

Dichtung und Wahrheit attempts to soften and exonerate the young poet's break with Friederike. We
are told there how it was only necessary for her to pay
a visit to Strassburg for her to stand stripped of her
magic, to appear the mere peasant girl she was. It
brought home to Goethe that his castle was only built
on sand; the patrician home in Frankfort rose up
before his eyes, his unbending father, who had already
unpleasantly enough let him feel the weight of his
authority. No doubt these thoughts did pass through
the young man's mind; but perhaps Goethe in later

life gave undue prominence to them. Was there, after
all, any reason why Friederike should have been a
bride less acceptable at home than the daughter of a
Leipzig victualler? And Goethe had once seriously
enough thought of braving his father and marrying
Käthchen. Moreover, his professional education was
now approaching its end, and there was every reason
to believe that a short time would see him established
and independent in his native town. Behind Goethe's
faithlessness lay rather, now as in Leipzig, the vaguely
understood, but imperative craving of his genius for
freedom. The guardian angel, whose hand Goethe
saw watching over him at all the turning-points of his
life, stepped in and barred the way; insisted once more
on that renunciation which was for Goethe always the
key to the effective life. This was the real exoneration, and the only exoneration that mattered. In his
Autobiography he tells us how he entertained the
Sesenheim sisters by telling them the fairy-tale of *Die
neue Melusine*, which he ultimately incorporated in one
of his very last works, *Wilhelm Meisters Wanderjahre*.
Very likely the association of the story with Sesenheim
is only " Dichtung " and not " Wahrheit "—but it is
" Dichtung " with a very real meaning; for *Die neue
Melusine* is the tale of a young man who, to win a
dwarf king's daughter, must himself become a dwarf;
finally he breaks the ring that binds him under the
spell; regains his true form and his freedom. Friederike was Goethe's Melusine.

Goethe's biographers are perhaps inclined to attach
undue importance to Friederike's share in the poetic
creations of his next few years. It is doubtful, indeed,
if she may be regarded, in any literal sense, as the model
for the Maries of his *Götz von Berlichingen* and *Clavigo*;
the process of Goethe's transmutation of the reality into
poetry was not, even in his young days, the simple
thing we used to think it was. An experience had to
pass through many stages and subtle metamorphoses

before it became the " great confession " of imaginative creation ; and in the end the emotional experience,
as often as not, ceases to be recognizable. Such was
the case with Goethe's love for Friederike Brion. It
is enough that, when the breach came, the young poet
once more passed into the outer darkness, now more
difficult to endure than when he left Käthchen Schönkopf in Leipzig ; for the responsibility for all the un-
happiness lay this time, he felt, on his shoulders alone.
Remorse mingled with the bitterness ; and it was this
remorse, not herself, that Friederike contributed to her
lover's imaginative creations. From the darkness
Goethe emerged a deeper and a greater poet ; and at
the same time his confidence in his guiding genius was
strengthened.

In the last Strassburg months Goethe was busy with
many poetic plans. He contemplated writing a drama
of Julius Cæsar ; and, if we are to believe *Dichtung und
Wahrheit*, the Swabian robber-knight Gottfried von
Berlichingen had already attracted him as " a well-
meaning self-helper in a wild anarchic time ". Faust,
too, early familiar to him from the grotesque associa-
tions of Auerbach's wine-cellar in Leipzig, and again
from his own Faust-like studies and broodings during
his Frankfort convalescence, began in Strassburg to grip
his imagination in earnest. The Faust motive, as it
first shaped itself, was, however—apart from the ex-
traneous Gretchen tragedy—probably mainly concerned with his own disgust with academic routine and
pedantry. His first impulse was to make it a satire on
the dull learning of the schools. " I, too, had wandered
amidst all learning, and early enough its vanity had
been brought home to me. I, too, had experimented
with life in many ways, and had always returned more
unsatisfied and tormented." It was in this form—a
ringing of the changes on the lines :

> Grau, teurer Freund, ist alle Theorie,
> Und grün des Lebens goldner Baum——

that the saga of the wonder-working magician, which was never again to leave him, first emerged.

Goethe had hoped to obtain the doctor's degree from Strassburg ; but either his thesis was not regarded as adequate, or, more probably, was not sufficiently ortho-dox—we only know that the two first words of its title were " De legislatoribus "—and he was not per-mitted to dispute it. Instead, he presented fifty-six " Positiones juris ", the successful defence of which gave him his licentiate. The disputation took place on August 6th, and his friend Lerse, whom one can hardly think of as very formidable in this capacity, was his opponent. So ended Goethe's university years. He returned home by way of Mannheim, where the collection of models of antique sculpture awakened a lively interest in him. Before the end of August he was again in Frankfort.

CHAPTER III

WETZLAR

THE period that lay between Goethe's return from Strassburg, and his departure for Weimar in the autumn of 1775 is, for the biographer, fuller than any other similar span of the poet's life. These years are packed with the most varied and interesting experiences; and so indelible was the memory which Goethe's magnetic personality left on all with whom he came in contact that we find abundant light thrown upon him from many sides. Above all, his imaginative production was spontaneous and overwhelming. We have still *Dichtung und Wahrheit* to guide us through the maze of this rich experience; but the veil of poetry drawn across the truth by the old man's remoteness from the facts becomes increasingly distorting as that work progresses. Twenty years lay between the publication of the first volume of the Autobiography and the last, and we have but to compare the picture of Friederike and Lotte Buff with that of Lili Schönemann to see how much we have lost by that consideration for the feelings of the living which did not allow Goethe to give the last volume out of his hand until Lili was dead.

On his return to Frankfort this time Goethe could reckon on a friendly welcome; for he returned with the qualifications which permitted him to enter at once on his profession as an advocate; he was entitled by courtesy to call himself " doctor ". The old councillor could not but be satisfied with his son, and he was—for a time at least; but, no doubt, he heard little about Herder, and nothing at all about Friederike. It was

now a question of settling down to a steady professional
career; his application for admission to the roll of
advocates was presented and granted without delay;
and Rat Goethe was ready to lend his son a helping
hand in the preparation of his briefs. Settling down
was not, however, in the young Titan's books; routine
of any kind was distasteful to him, and business meant
at first little more than drafting dull legal documents.
Actual practice was slow in coming; indeed, in the
first half year only two cases were entrusted to him, and
his excessive zeal and impetuosity in the conduct of one
of them brought upon him a reprimand from the court.
Frankfort seemed to him duller and more depressing
than ever; the memory of the vanished happiness of
Sesenheim, just as, four years before, that of Leipzig,
added to his discontent; and the disquieting ferment of
Herder's ideas was not conducive to an unperturbed
mental life. His brain was ringing with Alsatian
Volkslieder; his heart was with Homer, Ossian, and
Shakespeare; and on the last-mentioned's "name-
day"—that of William in the calendar—October 14th,
he held the exuberant oration from which a quotation
has already been made. So far, Goethe had but one
friend and confidante, his sister Cornelia; to her alone
he confessed the story of Sesenheim.

In November, 1771, Goethe lighted upon the
Lebensbeschreibung or autobiography of Gottfried von
Berlichingen, a robber-baron of the sixteenth century,
which had been printed at Nürnberg in 1731, by Franck
von Steigerwald. He at once saw in this naïvely
egotistic record of a stormy life of incessant feud a
mould into which he could pour his own irrepressible
Shakespeare enthusiasm. If the story which Crabb
Robinson relates is not apocryphal, he found the book
in a Frankfort library, and came home to his mother
in high spirits: "Oh, mother, I have found such a
book in the public library, and I will make a play of it!
What great eyes the philistines will make at the knight

of the Ironhand! That's glorious—the Ironhand!"
It is not, however, unlikely that Steigerwald was among
his father's books. In any case, having acquired a
copy, he set to work on his drama in feverish haste,
reading the scenes, as they were completed, to his
admiring sister. The origins of *Götz von Berlichingen*
go back, however, further than this; as a jurist he
had been interested in Strassburg in the legal system
of the Middle Ages, and had there studied Johann
Stephan Pütter's *Handbuch der deutschen Reichshistorie*
(Göttingen, 1762), and similar works; above all, he
had been fired by an article *Vom Faustrecht* which
Justus Möser had published in the *Osnabrückische
Intelligenzblatt* in 1771. His attention had been drawn
to it by Herder. Without any dramatic plan, or any
thought of producing a play that might be acted, he
plunged into the task of dramatizing the history of
this "noble German", and dashed it off in a few
weeks, entitling it *Geschichte Gottfriedens von Berlichingen
mit der eisernen Hand*.

Life began to grow more tolerable for Goethe in his
native town as new friends gathered round him.
Herder, or at least Herder in his critical and contra-
dictory mood, found a successor in Johann Heinrich
Merck, an army paymaster in Darmstadt. Although
restricted in his literary activities to journalism and
translation, Merck was a man of considerable intellectual and poetic gifts; and in company his geniality
and wit made him generally liked. He became to
Goethe now what Behrisch had been in Leipzig, the
Mephistopheles whom his Faust-like nature required
as a foil and supplement to itself; the new friends were
inseparable. And Merck's circle in Darmstadt, to
which he introduced Goethe in the beginning of 1772,
provided the young poet with a welcome resonance-
board. Its ladies, amongst whom were Herder's
betrothed, Caroline Flachsland, and a Fräulein von
Ziegler ("Lila"), who was sentimentality in person,

37

were the occasion of agreeable philandering. Amidst
these new distractions the Sesenheim memories receded
into the distance and lost their sting. Very soon after
his return he wrote his fine Pindaric ode *Wandrers
Sturmlied* :

> Wen du nicht verlässest, Genius,
> Nicht der Regen, nicht der Sturm
> Haucht ihm Schauer übers Herz.
> Wen du nicht verlässest, Genius,
> Wird dem Regengewölk,
> Wird dem Schlossensturm
> Entgegen singen,
> Wie die Lerche,
> Du da droben.

To the inspiration of these Frankfort years we owe,
too, *Adler und Taube*, the duologue *Der Wanderer*,
Pilgers Morgenlied and later, *Mahomets Gesang*.

From poetry Goethe had, however, turned to book-
reviewing ; he was a contributor to the *Frankfurter
Gelehrte Anzeigen*, the editorship of which had been
taken over by his friend Merck at the beginning of
1772. This journal, which had not much success,
appeared twice a week and contained only reviews of
books, Goethe's contribution being the most voluminous. His criticisms, mostly of indifferent and long-
forgotten works, are irresponsible and petulant, *jeux
d'esprit* rather than judicial estimates ; indeed, they
are, for the most part, most interesting to us now
when they are least relevant to the subject in hand.
In 1772 he wrote his glowing pæan in honour of
Erwin von Steinbach, the reputed architect of the
Strassburg Minster, *Von gotischer Baukunst*. It was
reprinted in the following year with the title signi-
ficantly altered to *Von deutscher Baukunst*, in Herder's
manifesto of the " Sturm und Drang ", *Von deutscher
Art und Kunst*. But the uncongenial routine of his
profession—which he could not bring himself to
regard as the real business of his life—and his father's

latent hostility to his literary interests and ambitions grew increasingly irksome; had it not been for his sister and the sympathy of his mother, who was always ready to mediate between him and his father when relations grew strained, life at home would have been quite intolerable.

It was consequently a relief to Goethe to fall in with the proposal that he should complete his professional training by spending some months at Wetzlar, the seat of the supreme courts of the Empire. The break with the newly-won Darmstadt friends was something of a wrench; but Wetzlar, as Leipzig and Strassburg before it, stood for freedom from the incubus of home. Goethe settled in this little town in May, 1772. We hear even less of Goethe's law studies here than we heard of them in Leipzig and Strassburg; and indeed it is difficult to see how he could have learned much in Wetzlar, where he had no duties of any kind, even had he had the will to do so. In this sleepy town the law had gone to sleep too; and so far was the legal business of the courts in arrears, that their decisions often did not concern the living at all. Just at this time, however, Joseph II had arranged a visitation by the various states interested, and the presence of their legations brought some life into the town. Goethe had lodgings in a dark and dingy house, which a great-aunt resident in Wetzlar had engaged for him. And he soon found himself at home in the lively circle of younger men which gathered, under the fantastic fiction of Knights of a Round Table—Goethe being immediately dubbed "Götz von Berlichingen"—in the Gasthof zum Kronprinzen. He found compensation, too, for the unpleasant, stuffy impression which the town and his rooms made upon him, in the beautiful environs, and revelled in the glories of the spring. Never, perhaps, in all his life was nature so intense an experience as now. A pocket Homer was his constant companion, to give place in sombrer moods to Ossian.

Goethe's Wetzlar love was Charlotte Buff, the nineteen-year-old daughter of the Amtmann of the Teutonic Order, whom he met at a ball on the 9th of June. The account which Charlotte's fiancé, Johann Christian Kestner, gives of the affair tallies in large measure with the fiction of Goethe's novel which Wetzlar inspired, *Werthers Leiden*. Kestner could only come late to the ball, and Lotte drove there in other company. In the carriage was Dr. Goethe.

> Lottchen [Kestner goes on] drew at once his whole attention upon her. She is still young, and although her beauty—I use the word here in the ordinary sense, and know very well that beauty has really no rules—is not of the regular type, her features are very attractive and engaging ; her glance is like a bright spring morning, as it especially was on that day, for she loves dancing ; she was quite artlessly dressed. He recognized in her a feeling for the beauty of nature and an unforced wit—humour rather than wit. He did not know that she was not free. I arrived a few hours later ; and it was never our custom to show more than friendship for each other in public places. He was on that day extravagantly merry—he often is so, and at other times melancholy—Lotte completely conquered him, the more so as she made no effort to do so, but gave herself entirely up to the pleasure of the evening. Next day he did not fail to call on Lotte and inquire for her after the ball. He had before seen her as a merry girl, fond of dancing and unmixed pleasure ; now he made her acquaintance from the side where her strength lay, the domestic side.

In Lotte Buff the spirit of Wetzlar, as Goethe saw it, took visible human form ; she stands for Wetzlar as Käthchen for Leipzig, and Friederike for Strassburg. Lotte with her Klopstockian sensitiveness to the beauties of the spring ; Lotte surrounded by her many brothers and sisters, mothering them—in the famous scene in *Werther* cutting their bread and butter—and capably managing her father's house, responded to Goethe's new mood, and dispossessed the fading muse of the Alsatian Volkslied. Goethe was again in love, and so whole-heartedly in love that he could in after years even speak of Lotte Buff as the greatest love of his life. But this is only one more testimony to the imagined element in all Goethe's passions; the "poetry" and "truth" became now, as always, inextricably mingled, and the Lotte Goethe loved was merged unwittingly in the Lotte for whom Werther took his life. It is significant, however, that of all the women Goethe loved, Lotte Buff is the only one who never inspired a single lyric.

The untenableness of this new passion was, more-over, almost immediately apparent. The young Leip-zig student had been long in undisturbed possession of Käthchen's love before her future husband appeared on the scene, and weeks of undiluted happiness had elapsed before Friederike broke the spell in Strassburg's streets. But now, before Goethe had time to grow intimate with Lotte at all, he learned that she was already engaged to Kestner, who was secretary to the Brunswick Legation, and a good friend of his own. As befitted her practical common sense and quite unpassionate nature, too, Lotte at once made it clear that she had no intention of breaking her engage-ment with Kestner. Kestner himself is something of an enigma. Goethe regarded his lack of jealousy as a sign of extraordinary magnanimity; but when one reads Kestner's almost callously objective diary of his friend's passion for his betrothed, one is inclined to use a less complimentary adjective. In any case, there was not passion enough in Kestner's attitude to Lotte to obscure his ardent admiration for Goethe, and the picture he has left us of him is the most vivid we possess from this period.

He has very many talents [he says], is a true genius and a man of character; he possesses extraordinary imaginative power and consequently expresses himself mostly in images and similes. . . . He is vehement in all his emotions, but often shows great self-control. His way of thinking is noble; being free from prejudices, he acts as occurs to him, without troubling himself whether it may please others, whether it is in the fashion, or consonant with good breeding. All constraint is hateful to him. He loves children and likes to busy himself with them. He is whimsical and there are many things in his demeanour and appearance which might make him distasteful. But with children, women and many men he stands, notwithstanding, in high favour. For the female sex he has a deep respect. In fundamental things he is not yet settled, and is still trying to find a definite system. He holds, for instance, a very high opinion of Rousseau, without being a blind worshipper of him. He is not what can be called orthodox; but not from pride or caprice or from a desire to make himself conspicuous. . . . He hates scepticism, strives after truth and definite formulæ in certain fundamental matters; he believes that he has arrived at such in the case of the most important; but as far as I see, this is not yet the case. He does not go to church, nor to communion, and rarely prays. " For ", he says, " I am not enough of a liar for that ! " . . . For the Christian religion he has respect, but not in the form in which our theologians present it. He believes in a future life, a better state to come. He strives for truth, but attaches more importance to the feeling for it than to its proof.

Whatever we may think of Goethe's love for Lotte Buff—and the more we know of it and the real Lotte, the greater appear the divergences between his own passion and the erotic obsession of Werther—it took strong enough hold of the poet's sensitive imagination. Suffer he certainly did, even if his sufferings did not bring him, like his hero, in any way near to a catastrophe. He sought safety from the approaching crisis—as always—in flight. Leaving Wetzlar by stealth on September 11th, he travelled home by way of the Rhine; and in the pleasant house at Ehrenbreitstein, of Sophie von La Roche, an old flame of Wieland's and by no means a negligible forerunner of the modern German novel, Goethe's elasticity of temperament asserted itself; the harrowing memories of Wetzlar became less acute. To this end Sophie von La Roche's black-eyed daughter, Maximiliane, then not quite seventeen, no doubt contributed; although to say that Goethe transferred his passion for Lotte to her would be to ascribe an incredible fickleness even to so mercurial a temperament as his. Later there might be some reason to regard Maximiliane as a counterbalance, but hardly yet, when the wound was still bleeding.

Goethe returned to Frankfort—and coming home was a less pleasant experience than ever to him—returned to the old round of occupations, and to the old conflicts with his father. Legal business was naturally slack after his long absence in Wetzlar; threads had to be picked up again, and Goethe was anything but eager to pick them up. Meanwhile, in spite of the precipitate flight from Lotte, Goethe's correspondence with her and her future husband continued; her silhouette hung above his bed and received his sentimental homage. As soon as the wedding took place—which it did on April 4th, 1773 —he was resolved to remove it out of sight. In November, 1772, he again paid a brief visit to Wetzlar. It was just before this visit that Goethe heard of the suicide, as the result of a love-disappointment, of one of his Wetzlar friends, Karl Wilhelm Jerusalem. Almost as disconcerting as the marriage of Lotte was the engagement of his sister, who had always been his closest friend, to J. G. Schlosser, followed by her ill-starred wedding in the following November. Early in January, 1774, Maximiliane von La Roche, the black-eyed antidote to Lotte in Ehrenbreitstein, whom Goethe's mother would perhaps have liked best to see as her son's wife, was married to an elderly widower of Italian origin, Peter Brentano, who had a large grocery business in Frankfort. Even in that age of apparently happy *mariages de convenance*, it would have been surprising if this ill-assorted pair had found happiness. The young wife was profoundly miserable, and Goethe's sympathy with her fanned the flame that had been gently kindled in the autumn of 1772. His attentions were sufficiently conspicuous to lead to a " scene " with Maximiliane's husband and his being forbidden the house.

These were shadows on Goethe's distracted and exciting life in 1773. Meanwhile, his literary activities showed no abatement. In the early months of the year his principal occupation was the revision of his historical drama for the press. It appeared as *Götz von Berlichingen mit der eisernen Hand, ein Schauspiel,* in summer and took the younger generation by storm : Goethe became suddenly the hero of the day. For the rest, we find him at one time interested in religious questions—his *Brief des Pastors zu *** an den neuen Pastor zu **** is visibly inspired by Rousseau's Savoy vicar— at another, giving vent to his wit and irony in satirical comedies. In the best of these, *Götter, Helden und Wieland,* the older poet comes under Goethe's lash for sentimentalizing, in his *Alceste,* the old Greek world in the manner of the French. In *Satyros, oder der vergötterte Waldteufel* Herder is satirized, and in *Das Jahrmarktsfest zu Plundersweilern* and *Ein Fastnachtsspiel vom Pater Brey* the excesses and absurdities of the " Sturm und Drang " apostles. These are, however, very minor productions and hardly readable to-day. Much more important is the unfinished drama of *Prometheus,* written in the latter part of the year, which showed that the Titan in Goethe was by no means dead. It did not get beyond two roughly sketched acts ; and among his *Gedichte* is to be found the magnificent soliloquy of Prometheus—whether it was intended to be ultimately incorporated in the play or not it is difficult to say—which must always

44

be included when the greatest of Goethe's shorter
poems are brought together :

Bedecke deinen Himmel, Zeus,
Mit Wolkendunst,
Und übe, dem Knaben gleich,
Der Disteln köpft,
An Eichen dich und Bergeshöhn ;
Musst mir meine Erde
Doch lassen stehn,
Und meine Hütte, die du nicht gebaut,
Und meinen Herd,
Um dessen Glut
Du mich beneidest. . . .

Ich dich ehren ? Wofür ?
Hast du die Schmerzen gelindert
Je des Beladenen ?
Hast du die Tränen gestillet
Je des Geängsteten ?
Hat nicht mich zum Manne geschmiedet
Die allmächtige Zeit
Und das ewige Schicksal,
Meine Herrn und deine ?

Wähntest du etwa,
Ich sollte das Leben hassen,
In Wüsten fliehen,
Weil nicht alle
Blütenträume reiften ?

Hier sitz' ich, forme Menschen
Nach meinem Bilde,
Ein Geschlecht, das mir gleich sei,
Zu leiden, zu weinen,
Zu geniessen und zu freuen sich,
Und dein nicht zu achten,
Wie ich !

CHAPTER IV

"GÖTZ VON BERLICHINGEN" AND "WERTHERS LEIDEN"

WITH the two works of his Frankfort years, the drama of *Götz von Berlichingen* and the novel *Werthers Leiden*, Goethe triumphantly entered the world of letters : the first inaugurated a great and virile movement in his own literature, the " Sturm und Drang ", of which he was at once acclaimed the leader ; with the second he initiated a widespread movement in the literature of Europe. Never again in the course of his long life did he enjoy such popularity ; and only *Faust* can vie with these works of his youth in the deep and lasting impress they left upon their time. Both, it is true, are essentially works of a definite age ; not in that often loosely-used phrase, works " for all time " ; they make for their appreciation considerable demands upon the historical sense of the reader of the twentieth century. He who reads as he runs will too readily dismiss the one as a type of a long effete " historical " drama, and the other as a still more effete and reprehensible example of morbid sentimentality. And yet in both cases an injustice will have been done ; for it would be difficult to point to many other works of the eighteenth century on which the stamp of high genius is more indelibly stamped.

From the biographer's point of view the first and cruder version of *Götz von Berlichingen* as Goethe wrote it in 1771 and 1772—it did not see the light until after his death—is more interesting than the *Götz von Berlichingen* which was published in 1773. Goethe

embarked upon his task of dramatization with more
enthusiasm than sober reflection on the difficulties of
his task. The picturesque sixteenth-century freebooter,
whose hand was against most men, and whose life was
one long round of feuds, fascinated him. But it is
difficult to see how, without Möser's guidance, the
" noble German " inspired by a disinterested cham-
pionship of the oppressed or lofty ideas of liberty
could be distilled out of Götz's account of himself.
Goethe, however, selects his materials from the biography with considerable skill. Leaving aside the first
thirty years of his hero's life, in which he was involved
in endless fighting, losing his right hand at the siege of
Landshut in 1504, Goethe sets in with Götz's quarrels
with Cologne and the Bishop of Bamberg between
1509 and 1511. He introduces in his second act his
hero's attack on ninety-five Nürnberg merchants, the
consequences of which had been that he was placed
under the ban by the Emperor Maximilian. In 1516
Götz assisted Franz von Sickingen and took an active
part in the Peasants' War. In 1519, when defending
Möckmühl, he was obliged to surrender owing to
lack of ammunition; assured of his freedom, he was
subsequently treacherously taken prisoner and conveyed
to Heilbronn where he languished in prison from 1519
to 1522. In the latter year he was set free by Sickingen
—an incident which provided Goethe with the admirable dramatic scene in his fourth act—but he was
obliged to pay a fine of two thousand gulden and enter
into obligations to keep the peace. He retired to
castle Hornberg on the Neckar, but he was soon again
engaged in endless frays, in 1525 leading for a time the
Odenwald peasants—Goethe utilizes this in his last act
—in their feud with Würzburg. Here Goethe winds
up his story, but the real Götz continued his adventurous fighting life for some thirty-seven years, his
death not occurring until 1562.

Goethe presents Götz as a blunt, " honest " mal-

content; but to make out a good case for the moral
justification of his client, who ruthlessly executes justice
according to his own ideas of right and wrong, and
casuistically reconciles his loyalty to his emperor with
disrespect for the emperor's laws, required all the
young advocate's professional skill. It could only
be done effectively by suppressing damaging evidence
of Götz's motives, and by blackening the opposing
party. And when his Götz dies with the cry for
freedom on his lips, one is tempted to ask : what
freedom ? Was this " noble " German anything more
than a disrupter of the peace, a rebel—it may be, a
rebel with a great heart, but still a rebel—who never
rises to the understanding which Schiller's Robber
Moor acquired, that " a fellow like him " would,
unchecked, soon bring the world about his ears.
Goethe had not proceeded very far with his dramatization when he felt instinctively that the chronicle of
Götz's life had not sufficient substance in it to make
a satisfactory play, free as were Goethe's " Shakespearean " ideas of what a play might be. He could
present his hero in effective episodes drawn from his feud
with the Swabian Bund and his share in the Peasants'
War; he could show us him besieged in his castle
of Jaxthausen or defying, Luther-like, the emperor's
councillors in the town hall of Heilbronn who had certainly more right on their side than he, ultimately to be
rescued by Franz von Sickingen. The period provided
picturesque costumes and colour; the spirit of the
Reformation could be touched in with a monk who
bears the name of the reformer; the exotic humanism
of the age in the person of Olearius, its romanticism
with the fascinatingly " creepy " episode of the " Holy
Vehmgericht ", which had an interesting reverberation
in our own literature. The sympathies of Goethe's
own sentimental age could be evoked by the introduction of the touching loyalty of the boy Georg and
" tender " scenes from Götz's family life, his wife,

48

sister and little son ; and the curtain could be ultimately
brought down on Götz dying for an unregenerate age
that was unable to appreciate his worth.   This might
have been enough to satisfy Goethe's contemporaries,
who interpreted Shakespeare's art as merely the artless
portraiture of great personalities ;   but Goethe felt
instinctively that it did not provide opportunities for
a real drama.   He felt, too, the need of a love-story,
and of some nexus with his own personal experience,
without which nothing he put his hand to thrived.
He thus superimposed a second plot for which the
autobiography of Götz offered no hint ;   and this invented plot has greater poetic virtue than the facts
drawn from Götz's chronicle.   He gives Götz an
old schoolfellow, Weislingen, who, in happier days, had
loved and been betrothed to Götz's sister Maria ;   but,
weak and vacillating, Weislingen had turned renegade
and entered the service of Götz's enemy, the Bishop of
Bamberg.   At the opening of the drama he falls into
Götz's hands, is generously treated, sees Maria again
and repents.   He returns to Bamberg to put his affairs
in order ;   but here he again succumbs ;   lured by a
court beauty, Adelheid von Walldorf, he marries her.
The " sentimental " plot of the drama is developed
tumultuously and melodramatically.   Götz becomes
Weislingen's prisoner ;   Maria implores him by his
old love for her to save her brother's life.   He does so
only to die, poisoned by his wife who is subsequently
condemned by the Holy Vehm and executed.   Out
of Weislingen Goethe has created a figure subtler and
more interesting than the heroic Götz ;   and in Weislingen's abandonment of Maria he relived the emotional
crisis of Sesenheim.   Not that there is much, or, indeed,
anything of Friederike in Maria ;   and Adelheid, a
monster of passion, is so crudely imagined—a young
man's erotic fancy decked out with feathers from
Shakespeare's Cleopatra—that it is safe to say she is
merely a foil, an exoneration, such as life itself failed

to provide, for the poet's own faithlessness. In Weislingen is thus meted out the retribution which the conscience-stricken lover of Friederike felt he had himself merited. He sent a copy of the play to Friederike, and to Salzmann he wrote: "Poor Friederike will to some degree find consolation in seeing the faithless lover poisoned." When Goethe revised his drama, he saw how little flesh and blood his Adelheid possessed, and he whittled down her rôle so ruthlessly that she became one of the minor characters of the play, and some scenes had to be reinstated in the acting version to make the rôle acceptable to the actress.

When Goethe showed his manuscript to Herder, the latter, enthusiastic as his appreciation was, put his finger on its chief weakness: he wrote to Goethe in his blunt way: "Shakespeare has completely spoiled you". This struck home and the young poet set to work to prune it of his "Shakespearean" excesses. The published drama of 1773 shows in technical respects a marked advance over the "Skizzo", but its lack of reasonable unity of action and its restless scene-shifting still make it an impracticable drama for the theatre. Goethe's justification was, of course, Shakespeare, but he had yet to learn wherein Shakespeare's form consists. And yet something of the great Shakespearean art of characterization has passed over into Goethe's drama; its people live in an immediate Shakespearean way; and its dialogue still leaves the impression, even in our day, of vitality and truth. *Götz von Berlichingen* has never meant for the world at large what it meant for Germany; but we in England cannot forget that it may have been the acorn from which sprang the spreading oak of our *Waverley Novels*. Scott translated it in 1798.

No work of Goethe's tempts more to the "autobiographic" kind of interpretation than *The Sufferings of Young Werther*, or, as we with our inveterate Anglo-Saxon sentimentality preferred to call it, *The Sorrows of*

Werther; it is much more closely bound up with Goethe's personal life and experience than anything he had yet written, or indeed, with anything else he ever wrote. To none seems applicable in a higher degree the poet's own dictum that " all my works are fragments of a great confession " than to this. And when the novel appeared and took the world by storm, it was accepted as a chapter of biography, a photographic reproduction of an episode in the poet's life in which, it was felt, he had dragged his friends Kestner and Kestner's wife into an unwarranted and cruel publicity. One still finds this view insisted upon by Goethe's biographers, who utilize the novel literally as an autobiographical document of his months in Wetzlar.

The reader, approaching the book in this spirit, finds himself, however, confronted with difficulties. It is true, Werther's first letter announcing his arrival in the unnamed town where the story plays, is dated May 10th and we know that Goethe went to Wetzlar in the month of May, 1772—not perhaps quite as early as the 10th, but at most only a few days later— although Goethe apparently introduces some mystification by pre-dating his hero's letters by a whole year. We know, further, from the account given by Kestner, that Goethe first set eyes on Lotte Buff on June 9th under conditions identical with those described in the novel; he accompanied her to a ball in the village of Volpertshausen some distance from Wetzlar; lastly, Goethe left Wetzlar on September 10th, the very day on which Werther departs at the end of the first part of the novel. Over and above this, the town and country which form the scene of the novel are clearly—in spite of Goethe's veiling them by the use of fictitious names—Wetzlar and its environs. Under these circumstances, it is obviously difficult to dismiss the conclusion that at least the first part of *Werther* is essentially a chapter of *Dichtung und Wahrheit*.

But a careful scrutiny of the correspondences between the fiction and the reality considerably weakens this claim. It is doubtful, indeed, whether we are justified, in spite of his introduction of actual dates and the name of the heroine of the novel, in saying that Goethe has done very much more here than what has been the privilege of imaginative writers in all ages, namely, utilize his personal experience and adapt it to the needs of a fiction that lay objectively outside that experience. We might, for instance, assume that Werther's letters to his friend Wilhelm are reproductions, or at least paraphrases of actual letters which Goethe wrote from Wetzlar to his friend Merck: but we have no proof at all of this assumption. Beyond two brief notes to Kestner and Lotte, not a single epistolary document of Goethe's has been preserved from the period of his life covered by the first part of his novel. Nor were any such letters likely to have been available to Goethe when he began to write *Werther*; in any case, Wilhelm, Werther's confidant, is obviously no Merck. Thus we may safely say that Werther's letters are invented. If they depict the course of Goethe's actual passion, it is that passion as the poet looked back upon it in memory after the lapse of many months, and as he adapted it to a hero whom he was far from regarding as himself.

When Goethe was in Wetzlar he had not the slightest intention of converting his emotional experience into a novel; nor did the incident with which the novel culminates, the suicide of young Jerusalem, which took place a few weeks after Goethe left Wetzlar, immediately suggest the composition of the novel. *Dichtung und Wahrheit*, which tells us that the suicide of his friend made the book possible " as water in a vessel which is on the point of freezing is suddenly converted to ice by the slightest shaking ", is misleading here as in much else that it tells us about *Werther*. In point of fact, some fifteen months elapsed between the death of Jerusalem and Goethe beginning to write the novel; it was then rapidly composed in little over a month in the spring of 1774, and was published in the autumn of that year.

Werthers Leiden was conceived with the clear intention that the hero was to take his own life; indeed, we might say that it was imagined backwards; the suicide was the starting-point. Thus if Goethe had any intention of portraiture, his model was Jerusalem, such as he conceived Jerusalem to be, not himself; Werther is not Goethe. The Goethe of Wetzlar, the active participant in the lively doings of the Knights of the Round Table, was no melancholy, solitude-loving sentimentalist. And his love for Lotte Buff was at no time an obsession that brought him to the verge of suicide. Commentators, it is true, have collected hints and suggestions to show that Goethe in those years was haunted by the thought of putting an end to his own life: but too much weight has surely been attached to impetuous phrases in letters, and some, no doubt, were but a backwash from the novel. Goethe had always too firm a hold upon life seriously to contemplate such an end.

To appreciate the objectivity of *Werther* it is worth while recalling the story in some detail. Werther's parents live on the market place of a small central German town; they are fairly well-to-do. The boy's childhood is happy. The first unpleasantness he remembers—and remembers with pain—is the daily imprisonment of school; but this is alleviated by the instruction at home of his grandmother who tells him fairy-tales. At an early age he finds pleasure and consolation in the beauties of nature. When he plays with his comrades by the river, the flowing stream awakens fantastic pictures in him of the lands through which it will flow: he loses himself in the contemplation of enormous distances. He loves best to wander out through the town gates, past the little garden house and into the open country. But his journeyings are limited by a linden tree a quarter of an hour outside the town; beyond this he may not go. Here he has his favourite seat where he dreams away the hours, letting his thoughts sweep far and wide beyond reality and the present. He longs to reach the mountains he sees on the horizon, and the great unknown world beyond. Other impressions follow these happy years of boyhood which develop the emotional side of his nature. His father dies and his mother moves to a larger town, the constraint of which he finds intolerable after the friendly country town of his birth. Here his mother, an energetic and matter-of-fact woman, takes his education in hand: she endeavours to counteract the brooding emotional indulgence of her son, and aims at making a " Gemeinderat " or an ambassador out of him: she induces him accordingly to study law. This leads to a certain friction and lack of confidence between mother and son; he sends her in the course of the story only the meagrest account of his doings through his friend Wilhelm: and when, at the critical point of his career, he resigns his post, he takes no consideration for her at all. Thus he turns to others for the sympathetic understanding which his senti-mental nature cries out for. Wilhelm understands him, and Wilhelm becomes his dearest friend. For a time they are inseparable; but the cooler and calmer temperament of his friend stands in the way of complete intimacy. This is compensated for by a girl friend who has a decisive influence on his life.

At the university he is inculcated with the Wolffian rationalism which runs counter to his own emotionalism and fills him with disgust. His whole soul turns to nature; he interests himself in drawing and music; and his antagonism to the prevailing philosophy becomes deeper. He hates all moralizing as a deadly sin. The social side of his education in these years is, however, not neglected; he learns to ride, becomes

54

a good dancer, pays compliments and carries on witty conversations; he even indulges in flirtations and gallant adventures. The main influence on his life at this time is, however, that of the girl friend. She is older than he: and, although endowed with healthy common sense, has patience with his impressionable nature. She gives him the sympathy which he failed to obtain from his friend Wilhelm; to her he can unbosom himself; her friendship provides a haven of refuge for him. Under her influence Werther's self-consciousness and understanding for his own nature develop. But then the tragedy happens: the girl friend dies. Werther's high mood sinks: he is again alone and friendless, unsatisfied, misunderstood; he becomes again indifferent to the claims of the present and lives only in the past. This morbid condition is aggravated by his experiences with a certain Leonora, for whose sister Werther had a passing fancy, Leonora herself being passionately in love with him.

Werther has no doubt certain capacities to be a useful servant of the State; but he himself distrusts these capacities; distrusts, too, the dictates of common sense; his actions are prompted by the heart, not by rational judgment. This vitiates his will-power: he becomes a slave to his moods; he is easily excited; rises to ecstasy to be subsequently depressed to despair. He gives himself up to bouts of dissipation. Thus, a thoroughly morbid nature, he turns in upon himself; disinclined for a practical life, disillusioned in all his hopes and dreams, he lives in an untrammelled world of longings which are more satisfying to him than reality. While in this mood an unexpected change takes place in his life. His mother again intervenes. She sends him to a distant town to regulate some business with an aunt who has retained more than her share of an inheritance. Werther is glad to get away from the complications of Leonora's passion. He finds his aunt not the shrew she had been depicted to him to be, but a cheerful, if rather hot-tempered woman with the best of hearts : he hopes soon to settle the legal affair with her. His mother is pleased with the practical way in which he has taken up his task : and indeed he does reform ; he solemnly vows to harp no more on the past.

He has, however, relapses. The town where he finds himself is unpleasant and not calculated to remove his depression, but this is compensated for by its extraordinarily beautiful surroundings ; and nature in all the glory of spring is balm to his lacerated heart. He takes long walks, revels in solitude, finds favourite spots where he enjoys the new paradise. Social intercourse, beyond the peasants with whom he readily makes friends on his wanderings, he does not need : nature is enough. And a wonderful serenity fills his heart ; he is happy.

It is needless to emphasise how materially these antecedents differ from Goethe's own. And in some of them we see dimly what Goethe may have known of his friend Jerusalem's earlier life. Jerusalem was born in Wolfenbüttel and brought up in Brunswick. After a legal education in Leipzig where Goethe and he had been fellow-students, and Göttingen, he had become a State official in Brunswick and in 1771 the Duke of Brunswick had sent him to Wetzlar as secretary of the legation. He is described to us as prone to morbid melancholy with a distaste for the mechanical tasks which were set him, and a love of poetry and philosophy. He spent much of his time in sketching and in solitary moonlight walks ; he was as much at home in Garbenheim—Werther's " Wahlheim "—as Goethe himself. He arrived in Wetzlar in the costume which the hero of the novel made famous, the blue coat and yellow breeches. His unsocial and solitary nature made it difficult for any of his colleagues to get into closer touch with him ; and he was only a passive member of the Round Table, although he was one of the

company who attended the ball at Volpertshausen when
Goethe met Lotte Buff. An unpleasant episode with
the president of the Kammergericht, Graf von Bassenheim, in which Jerusalem offended against etiquette,
and serious friction with his immediate chief, the
Brunswick ambassador, von Höfler, embittered his
stay and led to his dismissal. Meanwhile he had fallen
passionately in love with the beautiful young wife of
the private secretary of the Palatinate ambassador,
Frau von Herd. This led to his suicide, which caused
much stir in the little town, at the end of October, 1772.
Goethe learned the details of the story from an account
given him by Kestner. Jerusalem went to coffee to the
Herds' house, told Frau von Herd it was the last coffee
he would ever drink with them, and passionately
declared his love for her. He was repudiated, and,
borrowing Kestner's pistols, as the Werther of the novel
borrows Albert's, shot himself in the night. On his
table lay *Emilia Galotti*; no clergyman was present at
his funeral.

Turning back to the novel, it is clear that, however
much the first part may tally with the events, moods
and experiences which Goethe himself passed through,
his object was to reproduce in the form of fiction
Jerusalem's tragic fate. Probably Goethe knew little
enough about Frau Herd, and he supplemented his
defective knowledge with his own experience as the
lover of Lotte Buff. That the second part of the story
is definitely based on Jerusalem's life in Wetzlar has
always been recognized: " Graf C." is Graf von
Bassenheim; the ambassador, von Höfler; but Jerusalem's discomfiture took place in Wetzlar, not, as in
the novel, at a distant court. After this affair Werther
revisits his home, but is gradually drawn back to the
town of his woes like the moth by the candle. All
these things happen, according to the dates of the letters, between October, 1771, and May, 1772, his return
home being in the latter month. He is back in Wetzlar

in August, 1772, and the tragic close of *Werther*—where the author drops the epistolary form and takes, as it were, the pen into his own hand—follows closely the account he had received of the catastrophe.

In all estimates of *Werther* it is usual to insist on another subjective aspect of the story; Goethe, it is alleged, mixed the colours on his palette, and allowed his passion for Lotte Buff to combine with, if not to be displaced by, the love which, a few weeks after his departure from Wetzlar, began to supplant that for Lotte. The figure of Werther's Lotte, it is said, takes on colouring in the second part of the novel from Maximiliane von La Roche: and in the same way, Albert, originally a portrait of Kestner, shows traits of Maximiliane's elderly husband, and reflects the friction which arose when Brentano forbade Goethe his house in Frankfort. It is doubtful, however, whether there is as much ground for this inference as has hitherto been believed. The part which Albert plays in the closing scenes of the novel hardly justify us in discovering inconsistencies; and in any case, as has been pointed out, there is more of Frau von Herd's husband in him than of Kestner or Brentano. Similarly, the claims of a material change in the character of Lotte seem insufficiently founded.

Thus the tragedy of Werther, so far as it has a basis in fact, is primarily and intentionally the tragedy of Jerusalem: not a "confessional" reproduction of Goethe's love for Lotte Buff, with a tragic conclusion attached to it. Goethe himself put the case in a nutshell when he wrote on April 26th, 1774, to Lavater:

> You will feel much sympathy with the sufferings of the dear youth whom I describe. We were together for something like six years without coming nearer to each other, and now I have lent his story my own feelings, and it makes a wonderful whole.

In fame and popularity *Werthers Leiden* has been surpassed by no other book in the German tongue ; and
few books in any literature have made so immediate and
universal an appeal.   Goethe never again wrote a work
so completely " in the movement " as this.   Yet
unique as it is in form and contents, it is linked up
by innumerable ties with the literary tradition.   The
epistolary form had been firmly established since
Richardson had shown it best adapted to give the novel
that note of intimate personal revelation, which had
superseded the outward happenings of the old romance ;
Goethe only differed from his predecessors by the
fact that he reduced the complicated and unreal machin-
ery of the letter-novel to the utmost simplicity.   And
again, without *La Nouvelle Héloïse*, it is safe to say that
this passion, which is more enthralling than the gaudiest
pageant of adventure, could hardly have come within
the range of literary expression at all.   But to this,
his heritage, Goethe's genius brought the breath of life,
and not merely sentimental life.   For *Werther* is very
much more than a sentimental love story ; were it only
such, it would have passed with the sentimental vogue,
and the power it still possesses to stir our imagination
would be inexplicable.   If we read *Werther* aright, its
sentimental side is seen to be only part of a great whole ;
there are other thoughts, other motives in abundance—
these, in fact, were overlooked or resented by its first
sentimental readers.   The compelling, dynamic force
of the book lies, in the end, that it is a great human
document, the intimate study of a human soul in travail,
and that not merely in its relation to a loved woman,
but to its entire environment, to man, nature and God,
Above all, Goethe's Werther lives ; he is no mere
literary speaking-trumpet, as Rousseau's St. Preux—
also the victim of a great passion and great sufferings
—so frequently is.   Werther is a living being, writhing
under a fate that proves too heavy for him to bear ;
and Goethe's illuminating comparison in *Wilhelm*

Meister of Hamlet to an oak-tree in a costly jar might well be applied to his own Werther. This slim, dolorous figure in the blue coat, yellow waistcoat and breeches is more than the denizen of a particular age ; he is one of the immortal figures of imaginative literature.

Nowhere is Goethe more unjust to his past than when, in the thirteenth book of his *Dichtung und Wahrheit*, he came to speak of this triumph of his youth. He wrote of it then as if it were little more than a reprehensible justification of suicide ; and looking back upon it at the jubilee of its first publication in 1824 (*Trilogie der Leidenschaft*), he almost forgot that it had once been a living, quivering, piece of flesh cut from nearest his own heart.

For long years Goethe was to the world at large " the author of *Werther* ". It is questionable whether this is so great an injustice, so serious a slur upon his fame, as it is customary to think. So much at least is true : *Werthers Leiden* is the greatest work—the greatest completed work without question—that Goethe published before, in the noontide of life, he made his eventful journey to Italy.

Chapter V

THE LAST YEARS IN FRANKFORT

THE last years of Goethe's Frankfort life were extraordinarily full—full not merely of kaleidoscopic happenings, but also of productive energy; they form a splendid climax to his magnificent youth. It is, indeed, no exaggeration to say that now, between his twenty-fourth and twenty-sixth year, Goethe's genius attained its acme of spontaneity and intensity; no subsequent period of his life can vie with this in imaginative fertility. Great ideas crowded upon him faster than he could give them shape; and the poetry and prose into which these ideas took shape with so little apparent effort, possess a magnetic quality, which the more deliberate and reflective productions of his after-life never attained. Now, if ever, Goethe was the great " naïve " poet of Schiller's dream; he seemed to be swept along—his own volition the smaller part of the force behind him—by some mysterious power outside himself, call it what we will: genius, inspiration, " daimon ". In the lives of all men of genius there is always one period—rarely more than one, and a brief one at that—when they are, in the fullest sense, leaders of their time. In Goethe's life, this supreme moment came now, when he swayed all minds by the compelling power of his *Götz von Berlichingen* and *Werther*, and, as the leader of the Rousseau-inspired individualistic revolt, won, for the first time, the respect of Europe for his people's literature.

In a letter to Kestner of September 15th, we read :

I let my father now do quite what he likes; he tries to entangle me daily more in the official affairs of the town; and I acquiesce quietly. So long as I have the strength in me! One tug, and all the sevenfold ropes are broken! I am also much calmer, and see that human beings are to be found everywhere, everywhere great things and little things, beautiful and ugly. For the rest, I am going on working steadily and hope to further all kinds of things this winter. . . . One word more in confidence as an author. My ideals grow daily in beauty and magnitude, and if my energy does not desert me and my love, there will be much more for my dear ones, and the public will also have its share.

As we have seen, 1774 opened with the writing of *Werthers Leiden*. With the completion of the novel Goethe experienced to the full that relief which the objective unburdening of his conflicts and sufferings always brought with it. In the egotism of genius, however, he had strangely miscalculated its effect on the two dear friends who, with himself, were inevitably regarded by the outside world as the actual actors in the tragedy. Lotte and her husband resented deeply the publicity into which they were dragged; but this resentment soon passed, and the friendship continued unbroken.

In the month of May, 1774, and within a single week, Goethe gave his *Götz von Berlichingen* a not unworthy successor: *Clavigo*. To this year belong, too, *Erwin und Elmire* and *Claudine von Villa Bella* (finished in 1775) both " Schauspiele mit Gesang ", and of no great poetic value. Still less has the drama *Hanswursts Hochzeit* (1775). 1774 was, however, of peculiar significance for Goethe's spiritual development and the building-up of his life philosophy. For in this year he found the one thinker whom he, the most unmetaphysical of men, ever took completely to his heart, Spinoza. In the *Ethics* of Spinoza all the confused speculation, which, initiated by the warm, dissolving pietism of

Susanna von Klettenberg, led to so much religious doubt and vain puzzling over the problems of life, found guidance and direction. His religious thought and conception of God crystallized now in that confession of faith, with which Faust answers Gretchen's concern about her lover's religion :

Wer darf ihn nennen ?
Und wer bekennen :
Ich glaub' ihn ?
Wer empfinden
Und sich unterwinden
Zu sagen : Ich glaub' ihn nicht ?
Der Allumfasser,
Der Allerhalter,
Fasst und erhält er nicht
Dich, mich, sich selbst ?
Wölbt sich der Himmel nicht dadroben ?
Liegt die Erde nicht hierunten fest ?
Und steigen freundlich blickend
Ewige Sterne nicht herauf ?
Schau' ich nicht Aug' in Auge dir,
Und drängt nicht alles
Nach Haupt und Herzen dir,
Und webt in ewigem Geheimnis
Unsichtbar sichtbar neben dir ?
Erfüll' davon dein Herz, so gross es ist,
Und wenn du ganz in dem Gefühle selig bist,
Nenn' es dann wie du willst,
Nenn's Glück ! Herz ! Liebe ! Gott !
Ich habe keinen Namen
Dafür ! Gefühl ist alles ;
Name ist Schall und Rauch,
Umnebelnd Himmelsglut.

This spiritual side of Goethe's nature was deepened by the close ties that bound him in those years with Johann Caspar Lavater, a writer whom posterity, remembering only his *Physiognomische Fragmente*, to which Goethe made some contributions, has done less than justice. In June Lavater visited Frankfort and was received by the young poet with open arms ; and in July the two friends, together with Johann Bernhard

63

Basedow, that visionary enthusiast, who endeavoured to give practical effect to the educational doctrines of *Emile*, spent at Ems and on the Rhine a delightful and stimulating holiday which Goethe describes with very evident pleasure in his Autobiography. The charming little poem, *Diné zu Coblenz*, has preserved a memory from that time :

> Und, wie nach Emaus, weiter ging's
> Mit Geist- und Feuerschritten,
> Prophete rechts, Prophete links,
> Das Weltkind in der Mitten.

Such undiluted happiness he had not known since the first perfect days in Wetzlar ; the sufferings and conflicts of the intervening years were forgotten. In these happy weeks were written the dramatic fragments on the artist's calling *Künstlers Erdewallen* and *Künstlers Apotheose*, and an epic on the Wandering Jew (*Der ewige Jude*) was planned. Greatest of all, *Faust* was in preparation ; and in the background stood *Egmont* and possibly also *Wilhelm Meister*. In the autumn of 1774 Klopstock, who in Goethe's mind at this time was associated with the joys of skating rather than with the *Messias*, paid a visit to Frankfort, and the two poets met for the first time. The year closed with the most significant visit of all, a visit which was to turn the whole course of Goethe's life. On December 11th the two young princes of Weimar happened to pass through Frankfort. One of their tutors, Karl Ludwig von Knebel, who had been attracted by the fame of the poet, called upon Goethe and brought him for the first time into touch with the magic circle of Weimar. The elder brother, Karl August, was impressed and charmed by Goethe ; and, indeed, the liking was mutual.

It was reserved for the last year in Frankfort to provide the emotional element and the appropriate muse of this phase of Goethe's life. What Lotte Buff had been for Wetzlar, Lili was for Frankfort. On New

VIEW OF FRANKFORT ON THE MAIN IN THE 18th CENTURY
After C. G. Schütz

[*face p.* 64

Year's Day, 1775, he was invited to the house of a Frau Schönemann, the widow of a wealthy Frankfort banker; it was a world hitherto unknown to Goethe, this of the Frankfort plutocracy, and he felt no great desire to be drawn into it. But he was attracted by the seventeen-year-old daughter of the house, Anna Elisabeth, or, as she was familiarly called, Lili; and he slipped rapidly, and perhaps a little to his own surprise, into love. Lili sang his songs, and rode out with him. The love was not altogether without hindrances; not merely were the frivolous circles in which Lili moved little to Goethe's taste, but she, on her part, could have but little understanding for her lover's world. The families on both sides were difficult to convince that a union was desirable, a view to which posterity will not so readily subscribe; for the social butterfly of 1775 was to develop into a woman of singularly noble character, who bore up bravely in great adversity. It may be a little fanciful to say that Goethe erected a monument to her in his Dorothea; yet for none of his early loves did Goethe carry down with him to his grave so deep a respect and consideration as for Lili Schönemann. In spite of family opposition, and as a result of the intervention of a meddling match-making friend, Fräulein Helena Dorothea Delph, a formal betrothal was arranged. Goethe was once more in the toils of a very real passion, as may be seen from that best of proofs, the splendid lyrics she inspired. To her he wrote, " Herz, mein Herz, was soll das geben ? " and the poem *An Belinden* :

> Warum ziehst du mich unwiderstehlich,
> Ach! in jene Pracht ?
> War ich guter Junge nicht so selig
> In der öden Nacht ?
>
> Heimlich in mein Zimmerchen verschlossen,
> Lag im Mondenschein,
> Ganz von seinem Schauerlicht umflossen—
> Und ich dämmert' ein.

Träumte da von vollen goldnen Stunden
Ungemischter Lust !
Hatte schon dein liebes Bild empfunden
Tief in meiner Brust.

Bin ich's noch, den du bei so viel Lichtern
An dem Spieltisch hältst ?
Oft so unerträglichen Gesichtern
Gegenüber stellst ?

Reizender ist mir des Frühlings Blüte
Nun nicht auf der Flur ;
Wo du, Engel, bist, ist Lieb' und Güte,
Wo du bist, Natur.

Still, in his more objective moments Goethe could, as
it were, stand aside and wonder at the hold which Lili
in spite of her environment had upon him.   And there
was another disturbing thought : the fetters marriage
would lay upon him.   At no time of his life did his
genius, conscious of its growing strength, feel so much
the need of freedom as now.

Early in the year when Lili had just appeared on
Goethe's horizon, he was the recipient of enthusiastic
letters of admiration from the two young counts,
Friedrich and Christian zu Stolberg, two brothers, who
belied their aristocratic antecedents by their espousal,
in prose and poetry, of the rebellious doctrines of the
literary revolution.   Amongst the letters he received
from them, were some from their sister the Reichs-
gräfin Auguste zu Stolberg, which made a peculiarly
sympathetic appeal to the young poet ; and to this
unknown correspondent he was tempted to open and
unburden his heart.   Auguste, indeed, became—and
not merely now, but for years—a kind of confidante, to
whom Goethe opened his heart.   Some of the most
intimate letters of this time are addressed to her ; and
nearly forty years later, the old cordiality was renewed.
And yet Goethe and Auguste zu Stolberg never met
face to face !   Surely of all Goethe's friendships with
women this is the strangest !

In May the Stolbergs, contemplating a tour in Switzerland, arrived in Frankfort. They invited Goethe to accompany them, and he, vaguely uneasy under the binding tie to Lili, saw his opportunity: flight. He set out with his two companions through Baden; in Karlsruhe he not only met again the Duke of Weimar and Knebel, but also the duke's destined bride, Luise, daughter of the Landgraf of Hesse-Darmstadt, who made the pleasantest of impressions on him. "Luise is an angel," he wrote, and he picked up some flowers that had fallen from her breast and preserved them in his pocket-book. Thus were links for the future being forged. Strassburg, too, was revisited and old memories revived; but his way did not take him this time to Sesenheim. In Switzerland a long stay was made at Zürich, where his good friend, Lavater, for whom his feelings were still uncooled, introduced him to his circle, to Salomon Gessner, and to the old patriarchs of Swiss literature, Bodmer and Breitinger. In Zürich Goethe parted from the Stolbergs and, with another friend, made a tour which took him to the heights of the St. Gotthard Pass, almost within sight of Italy which, since his childhood, he had always hoped to visit. But even here, Lili could not be banished from his thoughts:

> Im holden Tal, auf schneebedeckten Höhen
> War stets dein Bild mir nah!
> Ich sah's um mich in lichten Wolken wehen;
> Im Herzen war mir's da.
> Empfinde hier, wie mit allmächt'gem Triebe
> Ein Herz das andre zieht,
> Und dass vergebens Liebe
> Vor Liebe flieht.

Thus the flight to Switzerland had failed in its main object; indeed, distance had only strengthened the magnetic force in Frankfort that held Goethe in its grip. Once home, he was again in the throes of the old conflict between his genius and his passion; and to this

67

were now added occasions for a jealousy that only fanned the flame.

The day of Goethe's release from Frankfort and the hemming fetters of his passion for Lili was, however, nearer than he thought. On October 12th, 1775, the young Duke of Weimar arrived with his newly-wed bride in Frankfort, and invited Goethe to accompany him on a visit to Weimar. Despite the opposition of his father, who saw in this dalliance with princes a serious dereliction of his son's professional duties and responsibilities, Goethe accepted the invitation. On the appointed day, however, the Duke's envoy, Kammerrat von Kalb, who was to fetch him, failed to appear. Days passed in which Goethe felt ashamed to face his friends from whom he had already taken leave ; he only ventured out under cover of night, and on one of these occasions—again, if *Dichtung und Wahrheit* is to be trusted—he found himself under Lili's window :

> She lived on the ground floor of a corner house, the green blinds were let down ; but I could see very well that the lights stood in their usual places. Soon I heard her singing at the piano ; it was the song " Warum ziehst du mich unwiderstehlich ? " which had been written to her not quite a year before. I could not but think that she sang it more expressively than ever ; I could hear it plainly word for word ; for I had pressed my ear as close to the window as the projecting lattice permitted. After she had finished singing, I saw by the shadow that fell on the blind that she had risen ; she walked backwards and forwards, but in vain I tried, through the thick material of the blind, to catch a glimpse of the outline of her sweet self. Only my firm resolution to depart, not to trouble her with my presence, really to renounce her; and the thought that my reappearance would make a strange impression, made me decide to leave a proximity that was so dear to me.

At last, convinced that the Duke of Weimar had forgotten his invitation, he agreed to his father's counter-plan, that he should visit Italy. Accordingly a post chaise was ordered, and he set out from Frankfort on October 30th. He had only, however, got as far as Heidelberg, where he was the guest of Fräulein Delph, who had been instrumental in bringing about his engagement with Lili. Here von Kalb overtook him; and in spite of the earnest pleadings of his hostess, who had other plans for him at the Karlsruhe court, his resolution was rapidly taken. For the second time the journey to Italy was abandoned.

> The chaise stood before the door packed; the postillion gave the usual signs of impatience; I tore myself away . . . passionately and enthusiastically repeating the words of Egmont: " Child, child, no further! The coursers of time, as if lashed by invisible spirits, hurry on the light car of our destiny, and all that we can do is, with calm courage, to hold the reins tight, and to guide the wheels, now to the left, now to the right, avoiding a stone here, or a precipice there. Who can tell whither he is being borne, seeing that he hardly remembers whence he came ? "

With these words *Dichtung und Wahrheit* closes. Well might Goethe see in this incident the finger of Providence, in which he never through the course of his long life of splendid opportunities and achievement, lost faith.

So ends what must always remain the most attractive and fascinating period of our poet's life: " der junge Goethe ". The youth of Goethe is the youth of genius incarnate. No arguments or pleadings are necessary to enlist the reader's sympathy for his wonderful personality ; and even if the brilliant series of his creations of these years may contain much that has faded from our interest now—and much that occupies but a modest niche in the treasure-house of German poetry—we accept them all with gratitude as illuminating documents on the growth of a great mind. In these years Goethe stood in the forefront of the intellectual movement of his time and country as its acknowledged leader; and indeed, this was the only time in the course of his long life that such unconditional leadership was granted to him. For he could not escape the lot of surpassing genius, that of outstripping the movement which it initiates, and losing touch with it. From now on he stands apart from his time; often out of sympathy with it and in antagonism to it; nor was he always—in respect of the developments which meant most for the future, notably those of the Romantic movement—in advance of it. But that he was the greatest of German men of letters could no longer be questioned.

Chapter VI

THE BEGINNINGS OF "FAUST"

OF the works and literary plans which occupied Goethe's mind in the years 1774 and 1775, the unfinished sketches are the more important. Amongst the dramas actually completed two demand, however, more than passing notice, *Clavigo* and *Stella*. The former of these, published in 1774, is usually damned with faint praise by modern critics. It is doubtful whether with justice. For in several important respects it shows an advance on its predecessor *Götz von Berlichingen*. It is much more firmly knit, a play much better adapted for stage presentation, as, indeed, it is perhaps the most playable of all Goethe's dramas. Goethe himself probably regarded it as an inconsiderable trifle ; for, if the story is to be credited, he wrote it as the consequence of a casual suggestion or wager thrown out by one of his female admirers : she expressed the wish that he should make a drama of the story, and he gallantly interpreted her wish as a command ; the drama was promised in eight days and completed in five. He found the story in the then just published *Mémoires* of Beaumarchais, the description of an episode in which Beaumarchais tells how his sister in Madrid was compromised by a young Spanish journalist Clavijo, who had loved her and promised her marriage, and how Beaumarchais had travelled to Madrid and called him to account. The French author was, of course, still alive when Goethe dramatized his story, and the real Clavijo did not die until 1806. It is even reported that he was well aware of the fact that he had been killed nightly on German stages ! The mere fact that Goethe wrote the play almost at a sitting is a great tribute to his effervescing genius in those days. The story seemed to shape itself under his pen : and although he often made literal use of the conversations retailed by Beaumarchais, the material—meagre enough—did require some fashioning to make it into an acceptable play, and also a play that would strike a responsive chord in its creator. But there was no time for those changes of plan which so frequently disturb the harmonious equilibrium of Goethe's works : no second thoughts cross and neutralize the first. Beaumarchais is not Goethe's hero, as he is the hero of his own story ; and the character of the vacillating Clavigo is handled with sympathy and fellow-feeling by the guilty lover of Friederike. Here he again executes the justice on his hero which he had himself escaped. Goethe himself described his Clavigo as an " indefinite figure, half great, half petty, a pendant to Weislingen : perhaps Weislingen himself in the full roundness of a chief character ". And this is true. To Clavigo he gave a friend and mentor who does not appear at all in Beaumarchais' *Mémoires* ; and in this Don Carlos, a kind of Merck, he created masterly contrast to his hero, a figure that often foreshadows the great antagonist of Faust. There is no more poignant, brilliant and clear-cut dialogue in the drama of the eighteenth century than in the wonderful scene of the fourth act where Don Carlos wins over Clavigo to abandon his sentimental attachment and realize the ambitions which beckon to him. *Clavigo* is frankly conceived on the lines of the conventional domestic drama of the day ; and the two women, Sophie Beaumarchais the elder sister, and the consumptive Marie, are visibly drawn from the milieu of that drama : but they, too, as even the subordinate characters of the piece, bear witness to the abundant life with which the Goethe of these years was able to endow his creations. The composition

shows many signs of haste, and the modern reader or
beholder has good ground to cavil at the melodramatic
climax where Clavigo finds himself confronted by the
funeral cortège of his abandoned mistress, and expiates
his fickleness in a duel with her brother over her body.
Goethe's friends, and especially Herder and Merck,
looked upon *Clavigo* as a sad backsliding ; what they
expected of the poet was another *Götz*. But even if
we regard it as a mere *jeu d'esprit*, tossed off in a few
hours, it bears for that very reason convincing testimony to the marvellous fertility of Goethe's genius in
these eventful years. Its merits have been unduly
overlooked.

Stella, written in the earlier part of 1775, has been
the target for much more captious criticism. In the
eyes of even the most indulgent biographers of the poet
it is usually represented as a mistake, a deplorable
aberration ; and with us in England it was more damaging to Goethe's reputation than any other of his
works. But here, too, something might be said in
defence, although the modern reader will have scant
enough sympathy for this " drama for lovers " with its
hero, a paler Weislingen and a still paler Clavigo,
enmeshed in a double passion. Again we have the
obsessing problem of the faithless lover of Friederike
with a new love tugging at his heartstrings ; but this
time Goethe has endeavoured to find a more conciliatory.
issue, and left his hero, when the curtain falls, as the
husband of both Stella and the formerly abandoned
Cäcilie—and to the apparent satisfaction of both ladies.
In later life he believed he could make the piece more
palatable and playable by a rough-and-ready conversion
of it into a tragedy : he represented Stella as taking
poison and Fernando shooting himself. But a comedy
cannot be changed by a hand's turn into a tragedy : the
alteration did not make it any more acceptable as a
stage-play. No doubt the better solution would have
been the tragic one, or, if not one of actual tragedy, at

least of renunciation; as it stands, indeed, the renunciatory motive is gently intoned and might well have
been developed. But the young rebel of 1775 was in
no mood yet to see life from this angle. The play had
literary antecedents, the chief of which may be read out
of its title: Swift's Stella and Vanessa provided the
idea, and this was reinforced by the German legend of
the Graf von Gleichen who likewise shared his affections with two wives. The play is difficult to defend,
although Goethe himself had always an affection for
it: but it is an interesting document of the poet's distraught eroticism, and it does open up unexpected
windows on the eighteenth-century soul in the era of
sentimentality. Its failure is due less to its theme—
for did not Goethe always maintain there was poetry
in all things if the poet knew how to discover it?—
but the way in which it is handled. It is deficient in
the larger dramatic life that inspires *Götz von Berlichingen*
and even *Clavigo*; its dialogue is often trivial, even
flat and fatuous: and its characters are conventionally
drawn and psychologically unconvincing.

But these completed works sink into insignificance
compared with the magnificent fragment of *Faust* as
Goethe conceived it in these Frankfort years. If the
testimony of *Dichtung und Wahrheit* is to be relied
upon, the origins of *Faust* date back to the momentous
winter of 1770–1 which the poet spent in Strassburg.
Describing his relations to Herder there, he says:

> Most carefully I concealed from him my interest in
> certain subjects which had taken root in me and which
> had gradually been assuming poetic form. They were
> Götz von Berlichingen and Faust. The significant
> puppet-play re-echoed and hummed in many tones in me.
> I, too, had roamed through all knowledge and had
> early enough been convinced of its vanity. I, too, had
> made experiments of all kinds with life, and had always
> returned more discontented and tormented. Now I
> carried these things and many others about with me, and

74

amused myself in lonely hours with them, without, however, writing anything down.

In Goethe's memory it would thus seem to have been
his experiences at the Academy of Strassburg and not
those earlier ones as a student in Leipzig that provided
the academic background for the first form of his
drama. At the same time, the figure of Faust was
necessarily familiar to him in the town of Auerbach's
Cellar. In fact, he does mention Faust in his Leipzig
comedy *Die Mitschuldigen* ; and the scene in *Faust*
between Mephistopheles and the young student, which
has always been recognized as one of the oldest constituents of the drama, seems to be rather a satire on
academic conditions in Leipzig than in Strassburg.
Between Goethe's return to his native town in August,
1771, and the end of 1774 we find frequent references
to *Faust* in his own records and in the letters of his
friends. Moreover, we have evidence of the poet's
preoccupation with the theme in similarities between
thoughts and scenes and other writings of the period,
notably with *Satyros* which, we have seen, was written
in the summer of 1773. Heinrich Christian Boie
visited him on October 14th, 1774, when Goethe read
to him his compositions ; and he adds to his account
of the visit : " His Dr. Faust is almost finished, and
seems to me the greatest and most characteristic of
all " ; and in a letter now lost he is reported to have
described the scene " Before the Gate " as Goethe had
then planned it. Of his visit to Goethe in December
Knebel, the tutor to the young Duke of Weimar, wrote :
" I have a bundle of fragments by him, among others,
of a *Doctor Faust* in which there are quite exceptionally
splendid scenes. He pulls his manuscripts out of
every corner of his room."

From the following year 1775 we have a considerable
body of records which indicate that the drama in its
first fragmentary form was practically complete as we

know it in the manuscript made by Luise von Göchhausen, a lady of the Weimar court, soon after Goethe
arrived there. The most noticeable of these records
are the coincidences between the tragedy of Gretchen
and a drama entitled *Die Kindermörderin* which Goethe's
friend Heinrich Leopold Wagner wrote in the winter
of 1775-6. Although Wagner is hardly to be accused
of very serious plagiarism, the correspondences between
the two tragedies—notably the utilization of the
motive of a fatal sleeping-draught—are too numerous
to be attributable to coincidence; Goethe himself
tells us in his autobiography that he had described
his play to Wagner and that the latter had thus abused
his confidence. This was likely to have happened
before Easter, 1775.

Faust in its earliest form contains, of course, neither
of the prologues which now open the drama. It opens
at once in the " Gothic Room "—Faust's study.
Faust's first soliloquy, his encounter with the Earth
Spirit, and the scene with Wagner are here essentially
as they stand in the completed poem. Faust does not,
however, resume his musings after Wagner's departure; there is no climax with his contemplated suicide
interrupted by the bells on Easter morning. In fact,
there is a very wide gap indeed. There is no scene
" Before the Gate ", no second scene in the study;
and we are left entirely in the dark as to how Faust
and Mephistopheles meet, or the terms of the pact to
which they agree. Scene II of the first *Faust* is that
little scene which has now its place at the close of the
second Study scene after Faust has signed his pact with
Mephistopheles. Here the latter, assuming the gown
and wig of a Leipzig professor, interviews the young
student who comes fresh to the university, a scene
subsequently abbreviated and otherwise modified.
The third scene is " Auerbach's Cellar in Leipzig ",
without, however, the dialogue between Faust and
Mephistopheles which leads up to it. Again this scene

underwent material changes before it took its place in the completed poem : Faust now stands aside, a disgusted onlooker at the proceedings, whereas originally he entered whole-heartedly into them, himself inviting the drinkers to choose their wine, boring the holes in the table, and leading the boisterous horse-play with which the scene culminates.

A very brief episode, subsequently omitted, of four lines follows : Faust and Mephistopheles are on the highway ; an old castle is visible upon a hill, a peasant's cottage is in the distance ; and by the wayside there is a cross.

> *Faust.* Was gibts, Mephisto, hast du Eil' ?
> Was schlägst vorm Kreuz die Augen nieder ?
> *Mephistopheles.* Ich weiss es wohl, es ist ein Vorurteil,
> Allein genug mir ists einmal zuwider.

There is no " Witches' Kitchen " in the oldest *Faust*, and we pass immediately to Gretchen. From now on the parallelism between the first version and the last is close : the whole series of scenes from that in the " Street " to that of Gretchen kneeling before the Mater dolorosa by the city wall is as in the completed poem with one exception : " Forest and Cavern " was interpolated at a later date. The " Mater dolorosa " scene is followed immediately by that in the Cathedral ; then comes the first soliloquy of Gretchen's brother Valentin—this is all we hear of him—followed by the beginning of the scene " Faust, Mephistopheles ", and lines describing Faust's despair which ultimately found their place at the end of the " Forest and Cavern " scene. There is no " Walpurgisnacht " ; and the three intensely tragic scenes entitled " Gloomy Day ", " Night ", " Prison ", bring the early fragment to a close. All three scenes are in prose, and the last briefer than when Goethe at a later date turned it into verse. This earliest *Faust* is, it is almost needless to say, unmitigated tragedy ; it ends with no " voice from above " proclaiming Gretchen saved. Still less had Goethe in those days of his " Sturm und Drang " any intention of allowing his hero to escape the doom demanded by the legend. There was no ambiguity then in Mephistopheles' words " Her zu mir ! "

Instructive as a comparison of the early *Faust* with the completed First Part, published in 1808, is, it by no means tells us all we should like to know concerning the genesis of the drama. The discovery of the manuscript in 1887 set at rest certain fundamental questions of chronology, and rendered invalid a great deal of earlier speculation—some of which proved to be right, and some, at least ingenious—but it has also opened up new problems. There is, for instance, the question how far the Göchhausen manuscript contains all that Goethe brought with him to Weimar. It is reasonable to think that Fräulein von Göchhausen only copied—or was permitted to copy—such scenes as were sufficiently complete to provide connected reading.

Indispensable links in the action, not included in the manuscript, must have already existed or, at least, have taken shape in Goethe's mind. He must have known how Faust and Mephistopheles were to be brought together. That, for instance, the devil is introduced in the guise of a dog certainly belonged to an early plan, as there is a definite reference to it in the scene " Gloomy Day " ; and, this being the case, some kind of setting similar to " Before the Gate " must also have been planned. That scene, moreover, contains hints which localize it in Frankfort. It is unlikely that the Goethe of the Weimar or Italian time should have deliberately gone back to Frankfort for inessential details of his scene ; and Boie, as we have seen, is reported to have described the scene as he was allowed to read it in 1774. There must further have been a pact of some kind, sealed with Faust's blood—probably on the lines indicated by the Volksbuch—a simple, straightforward agreement whereby Faust bartered his

78

soul for the satisfaction of his desires and aspirations. The fact that it is omitted from the oldest *Faust* might be accepted as a negative proof that, even thus early, the traditional pact was ill adapted to Goethe's intention and purpose ; and that he consequently hesitated to include it.   Towards the end of the drama Valentin, Gretchen's brother, is only introduced to deliver a soliloquy ; but this soliloquy involves the rôle which he has to play in the drama.   And from Mephistopheles' words to Faust in " Gloomy Day " we know that Faust was a fugitive with the crime of murder on his conscience.   It is possible, too, that Goethe had thoughts of letting his Faust be led by Mephistopheles through a series of temptations—not merely those of the wine-cellar and Gretchen—which might culminate in the wild orgy on the Brocken.

Other problems opened up by the early *Faust* concern the beginnings of the poem.   Was the initial step a drama planned more or less on the sixteenth-century tradition in which not Margarete but Helen of Troy was the heroine ?   It is difficult to think so, and this in spite of the fact that Goethe in his last years frequently spoke of Helen as a constituent of his plan from the beginning ; as far as our materials and evidence go, there was no room for Helen of Troy in Goethe's earliest *Faust* plan.   In fact, there is little justification for assuming that Goethe began by systematically planning a drama on the materials provided by the Volksbuch of *Dr. Faustus* at all.   The first draft of *Faust*, if we will judge it without bias, contains exceedingly little of the *Faust* legend.   Goethe makes no attempt to introduce serious historical colouring into his early drama, to reproduce—as he had done according to his lights in *Götz von Berlichingen*—the atmosphere of the sixteenth century.   His first *Faust* is, to all intents and purposes, a drama of Goethe's own day.   In common with the legend it has the names of its protagonists : Faust, Mephistopheles, and

Wagner; it has the location and some incidents of the scene in Auerbach's Cellar; and the general situation of the disillusioned and discontented adept and scholar who succumbs to the temptation of the Devil. But that is virtually all, and it is the merest framework.

Goethe's drama opens with Faust's soliloquy in his study; in so far he is faithful to the tradition initiated by Marlowe, and which had always been a feature of the popular German plays and marionette plays of *Dr. Faust.* But there is little enough in that soliloquy either of Marlowe or of the German popular plays; and the arguments recently put forward by an American scholar that Goethe in those early days was familiar with our English *Faust* drama are not very convincing. The Faust he presents to us might be no other than himself voicing his discontent with the dull learning and pedantry of the schools, and seeking to build up for himself a new faith in life, nature, God. Faust here is young as Goethe was young; he has only, as he tells us, been " leading his students by the nose " for some ten years, that is to say, he is in the early thirties. There is no question yet of an elderly greybeard who requires the rejuvenating draught of the Witches' Kitchen that he may play his rôle as Gretchen's lover. This Faust, convinced of the futility of his laboriously acquired learning, turns to his books of magic in the hope that they may help him to solve the riddle of the universe, just as Goethe himself, unsatisfied by the knowledge instilled into him at the university, had sought a deeper wisdom in old books of magic and the Swedish mystic Swedenborg, and had busied himself with alchemistic experiments. Faust, turning over his magic book, first lights on the sign of the Macrocosm, the spirit of the universe; but that spirit is too far removed from him, outside his sphere; with the vast universe he is not concerned. To the Spirit of the Earth—the planetary " archeus " of which Goethe had read in his mystic books—he feels more akin; and by his magic art he summons this spirit to his presence. From the Earth Spirit Faust hopes to obtain the key to his unanswered riddles, the satisfaction which learning had failed to give him. He aspires to identify himself with this active creative element in nature, only to be repudiated and crushed by the spirit's scathing retort: "Du gleichst dem Geist, den du begreifst, nicht mir!"

The Faust of the legend did not conjure up an Earth Spirit, but the Devil himself; and he, too, is baffled in his first attempt; like Goethe's hero he cannot endure the awe-inspiring experience. A second attempt is attended with more success, and Lucifer provides him with "Mephostophiles" as an attendant spirit. So, too, Goethe may have originally planned his *Faust*; the Earth Spirit may have been later substituted for Lucifer; and Faust's failure in his study have been the prelude to another and more fruitful meeting with the spirit in the open country to which he will flee.

So far, Goethe's earliest *Faust* drama brings us in what we like to call the *Faust* problem; and no further. This introductory scene leads nowhere. We have no hint that Goethe's first Mephistopheles—however and whenever Faust comes into his power—was to aid Faust in realizing his aspirations, as the Mephistopheles of the Volksbuch had done, or bring him into the contact for which he yearned with the unseen powers. Mephistopheles here merely provides a dulling narcotic, an antidote to Faust's high dreams by leading him into sensual temptations. As Goethe first conceived him, Mephistopheles is a robust, humorous incarnation of the popular tradition of the Devil; in fact, a very human devil of flesh and blood. For with the tradition Goethe combined, not so much the sixteenth century's grim interpretation of the adversary of God, as those ironical and satirical traits which he had observed in his particular friends Herder and Merck; Mephistopheles is, in fact, own brother to the masterly figure of Don Carlos in Goethe's *Clavigo*. His rôle in the early *Faust* is restricted to advising the young student about his studies, to bringing Faust to Auerbach's Cellar, and helping him to win and seduce Gretchen.

This *Faust* represents a fusion of two distinct elements; it is a satire on the pedantry of the university —the precipitate of Goethe's own experience at Leipzig and Strassburg—and it is a love tragedy. These two constituents Goethe grafted on the old Faust story, with which they have, of course, nothing at all in common; the legend is but the old bottle into which the new wine is poured. Such seems to have been the genesis of Goethe's great drama. He did not set out to dramatize the Volksbuch, as he had made a drama of the autobiography of Götz von Berlichingen, but to make use of it as a convenient vehicle for his own immediate and subjective experience.

The academic satire is conspicuous in the scenes between Faust and his *famulus* Wagner, and between Mephistopheles and the student. Wagner of course came from the tradition; he had been a feature of the popular plays of Dr. Faust; but he was also a type of pedant with whom young Goethe must have often enough rubbed shoulders. In the scene in the wine-cellar there is satire of another aspect of Goethe's Leipzig student days, and at a later date he had the idea of giving still greater scope to the academic drama by introducing an elaborate " Disputation " in which Mephistopheles in the guise of a wandering scholar was to have taken part. On the whole, it would seem as if this academic satire represents the oldest stratum in the *Faust* poem; and it allowed itself easily to be adapted to the Faust legend. But it would be unwise to dogmatize; for the love-tragedy in its language and style makes the impression of being equally old.

The provenance of this love tragedy is not so easily

explained. It lies, of course, just as much outside the legend as the academic constituent. In the later chap-books, it is true, we learn that Faust fell in love with " a beautiful but poor country girl " ; but it would be absurd to look to this statement—and it goes no further —for the genesis of the immortal Gretchen tragedy of Goethe's drama. In the legend there was no room for a Gretchen, Faust has, as our own Marlowe rightly felt, only one possible love, Helen of Troy. In their endeavours to account for Gretchen the commentators on *Faust* have thus fallen back upon subjective motives, on Goethe's own affairs of the heart. Goethe, as we have seen, had himself abetted them by lingering, in his Autobiography, on his own first love in Frankfort, but a connexion between this episode and the drama is surely improbable. Nor does Faust's Gretchen bear traits of any of Goethe's other loves—not certainly of Käthchen Schönkopf, Lotte Buff or Lili Schönemann. At most we might think of Friederike Brion ; but even here it is difficult to discover tangible resemblances. The emotional experience through which the poet passed in Sesenheim and Strassburg left its mark on *Faust*, but hardly Friederike herself. More might be said for the literary models afforded by the contempo-rary German " tragedy of common life " and the Percy-inspired ballad-poetry of the day. At most, however, Goethe only found direction here ; he had nothing to learn. And if he has borrowed from *Hamlet* in his final scene, it is merely the motive of a mind deranged and its mode of expression ; Gretchen has nothing of an Ophelia in her.

It is to be regretted that this early form of *Faust*, a handful of loosely connected scenes as it is, was not given to the world when it was written, instead of not until 1790, or indeed, 1887 when the Göchhausen manuscript was discovered. For it would assuredly have broadened enormously the fame of the author of *Werther*. It is a pity, too, that the sophisticated readers of our modern time cannot approach Goethe's master-work through this early portal, in all ignorance of the later transformation of this moving human tragedy into a philosophical drama. If English readers in-stinctively recall Marlowe when they take up Goethe's *Faust*, the parallel with Marlowe is most apparent in this ebullient creation of his youth. Faust is young ; and he rattles at the bars of the cage to which his zeal for knowledge has condemned him, as Goethe himself had rattled at his academic cage in Leipzig and Strassburg. The passionate disillusionment which Faust experiences, is the disillusionment of youth, not yet expanded into gnawing meditations over a long span of life lived unwisely ; the fairer world he seeks was still something which was within the power of the tempter to give him. We are not concerned here with hair-splitting speculations as to whether that tempter is an emissary of the Earth Spirit or not, or to what hierarchy he belongs in a world where evil is subservient to the furtherance of the good ; it is enough that for the young Goethe he is the arch-enemy, the Devil. And beside these two great dramatic figures stands Gretchen. Goethe has con-tributed no more living and sympathetic portrait to the gallery of his women than this simple burgher girl of the fragmentary first *Faust*. The naïver tone of the scenes in which she appears here, as compared with those of the completed poem, adds to the beauty and intensifies the pathos. No room is left for considera-tions of " tragic guilt " and dramatic theory ; Gretchen is merely involved in the meshes of the spirit of evil, and goes down in pitiful ruin. The harrowing pathos of her death in prison is one of the sublime things of dramatic literature. Did not George Eliot say these scenes were more moving than anything in Shakespeare himself ? There is no compromise here with the ruth-lessness of tragedy ; no " she is saved " at the close to mitigate our pity for Gretchen ; nor is there any

84

cheating of the devil out of his booty, to permit Faust to widen and enrich his experience in a larger earthly life. The relentless handling of the tragic problem in this early *Faust* was something that lay frankly beyond the power of the conciliatory Goethe of riper years. The completed *Faust* of 1808 contains loftier, more arresting and compelling thoughts ; but in respect of emotional poetry, the greatest in *Faust* is already here. It is what Goethe wrote now that has enshrined *Faust* in the hearts of the world, not the mature philosophy which was poured into it in his later years. With his *Faust* and *Werther*, to leave aside his lyrics and all else, this youth of twenty-five already stands among the great creators of literature.

PART II
THE MIDDLE YEARS
1775-1805

CHAPTER I

THE FIRST TEN YEARS IN WEIMAR

SO far, the biographer of Goethe has had the advantage of the leading strings provided by the poet himself in his Autobiography ; he has found the facts accumulated for him there, sifted, ordered. Sometimes he may have been tempted to cavil at the poet's own interpretation of himself ; but he has at least known what Goethe regarded as most desirable to be recorded. Now, however, a period is reached when Goethe's reconstructive labours cease, and when the architect of the poet's life is thrown upon his own resources ; he has to collect and fit in the stones of his edifice without more than hints of how the poet himself would have liked to see it built. Nor do we possess such reliable data now as in the Frankfort period ; there seem even to be fewer witnesses to testify to Goethe's life and thought ; we are left more in the dark—a dark which, it is true, recent years have helped to disperse—in respect of what Goethe actually planned and wrote in these years. But one fact emerges clearly : Goethe's power of bringing his work to completion, of wrestling with the poetic idea until it has rendered up its ultimate essence, visibly slackens ; to all appearance, a period of comparative sterility sets in. Thus Goethe's first ten years in Weimar are as difficult years to interpret satisfactorily as any in his long life.

The duchy of Saxe-Weimar with which Goethe was to be intimately associated for the remainder of his days, covered an area of only some 750 square miles, and its entire population was then little over 94,000.

The interests of this diminutive state and its sources of revenue were largely agricultural ; industries, even in the modest eighteenth-century sense of the word, hardly existed. Weimar, its capital, was little more than a small market-town of six thousand inhabitants. It lay, moreover, outside all arteries of traffic ; nothing passed through it ; and its own posts arrived irregularly. The one set-off to the poverty-stricken appearance of the town—its houses were mostly thatched—was the ducal castle ; and that had been destroyed by fire in the year before Goethe's arrival.

The ruling family had, however, some distinction over those of the other petty states among which the " Holy Roman Empire of the German Tongue " was parcelled out. Debarred by their poverty from following the example of the larger states of aping the splendours of Versailles, they showed an unusual and liberal encouragement of less material things. There was a genuine desire in Weimar to make poetry and the arts something more than an amusement for idle courtiers, an antidote to the tedium of a dull provincial town : here was, in fact, a court which prided itself on bidding the muses welcome. This was largely to the credit of Duke Karl August's mother, the dowager Duchess Anna Amalia, a Brunswick princess and niece of Frederick the Great. Left a widow before she was out of her teens, she had on her shoulders the responsibility of the regency and the education of her two sons, Karl August and Konstantin. When Goethe came to Weimar she was still only thirty-six. A woman of considerable intellectual distinction, she cherished a serious ambition to improve the conditions of her little state : and that not merely materially. She imbued her court with her own tastes for literature, music and the theatre and interested herself in the welfare of the university of Jena. And when it was a question of finding tutors for her sons, her choice of the chief of these fell on the poet Wieland, whose books she especially admired :

his didactic *Goldener Spiegel*, in which were set forth his views on the education of princes, particularly recommended him. Thus, since 1772, Wieland had been attached to the Weimar court.

The young duke, Karl August, had talent and in-herited his mother's tastes ; but his upbringing, Wie-land's theories and a certain amenableness to guidance notwithstanding, had been none of the best. Way-ward, passionate, self-indulgent, he had been too much given his own way ; and he early assumed the privi-leges of an absolute ruler to give rein to his whims and passions, these being fostered by the general unrest of the age of Rousseau and the German " Sturm und Drang ". The better side of his nature was to be seen in his generous impulses, a sensitiveness to artistic impressions and a love of nature. He disliked the stiffness of court etiquette, and was always happiest when freed from it ; at the same time, he was not averse from ostentatious display, especially with his tiny army when at home. Seen through Goethe's eyes, the duke has appeared to later generations in a perhaps unduly generous light : for his intellectual interests did not in reality go very far. His extravagance, which was out of all proportion to the means of his state, his looseness of life and lapses from ordinary moral con-duct, hardly entitle him to be extolled above the other petty rulers of the pre-Revolutionary era : and it is doubtful whether even those claims which have been made for his political wisdom when he came to staider years, are justified.

Two months before Goethe's arrival Karl August had come of age, that is to say, attained his eighteenth year ; and the reins of government had been handed over to him by his mother. Steps had already been taken to provide him with a consort, the choice falling, as we have seen, on the daughter of the Landgraf of Hesse-Darmstadt ; and his visit to his future bride, then at Karlsruhe, was the occasion when he first came

into personal contact with Goethe. It was a loveless
and indeed quite unhappy marriage. The young
duchess never became reconciled to Weimar, and she
languished under her husband's callous neglect of her
and his promiscuous love-affairs. She was a woman for
whom everybody had respect and admiration, and
deserved a better fate : her brave stand when Weimar
was threatened by Napoleon in 1806 has preserved for
her a particularly bright memory.

Such was the court to which Goethe had accepted
an invitation. He arrived on November 7th, 1775, at
five o'clock in the morning. The first Rubicon of his
life—and the deepest—was crossed. The past was
past : the break with the old friends and the disturbing
passion for Lili Schönemann was complete ; a new
chapter had begun. Here Goethe had to make a fresh
start, in a totally different *milieu*, and under conditions
which were worlds apart from those under which he
had grown up. It was arranged that he was at first
to stay in the house of Kammerrat von Kalb in whose
chaise he had travelled ; and his welcome could not
have been more cordial. A dinner was given that
same day in his honour, and here he met Wieland.
The latter, in his delight at making the acquaintance of
the author of *Werther*, magnanimously forgave and
forgot the offence of which the author of *Götter, Helden
und Wieland* was guilty—as indeed he had already done
in his generous review of the farce published in his
Teutscher Merkur. The relations between the two men
became, in fact, exceedingly cordial.

Goethe could hardly have been favourably impressed
by the town, but the conditions under which he came
were peculiarly flattering ; he was not only the guest
of the duke, but he had been pressed to accept the
invitation after, to all appearance, he had sought to
evade it. It is pleasant to think that this invitation
was due to discriminating appreciation of Goethe's
genius. But, looked at without bias, it is difficult to

attribute to the duke, then only a youth of twenty-two, very lofty motives. He had taken a personal liking to Goethe; he saw in him a man who would be an attractive associate; and in the early months the poet no doubt came up to his host's expectations. He was only too willing to be boon companion of the young ruler in his quest for amusements that were often neither respectable nor decorous. This was what the duke looked for in Goethe, not poetic genius—the sentimentalities of *Werther* were little to his taste—and Goethe did not disappoint him. The unvarnished story of these days—the wild hunts and drinking bouts, the discreditable amours and rough horse-play which appealed to the duke's tastes—does not make pleasant reading. No wonder that Goethe fell into bad odour in the better circles of Weimar, was accused of leading the duke astray; and the situation was not improved when Goethe's literary friends—Lenz and Klinger, neither of them very respectable—visited him. Even Klopstock, whose ears no doubt exaggerated gossip had reached, felt it incumbent upon himself to write Goethe a serious letter about his doings—a letter which marked the end of Goethe's friendly relations with the older poet. This was certainly not a good beginning.

To the duke Goethe proved so acceptable a companion that he was determined not to let him go; he took steps to make his residence permanent. Goethe's father, who bitterly resented his son's abandonment of his legal career in Frankfort, did what he could to prevent the realization of these plans by refusing to supply him with money; Goethe had to fall back on his old friend Merck for a loan. But the duke was not to be baulked; he insisted on 'drawing Goethe into the government of the duchy; he bestowed on him the title of " Geheimer Legationsrat ", gave him a salaried position in the Cabinet and delighted his heart with a garden house on the river. These favours could not but give grave offence to the bureaucrats who had

93

grown grey in the service of the state; and the chief
minister of the duchy, Jakob Friedrich von Fritsch,
tendered his resignation. He could not, he said, continue to sit in the same council with this young doctor
from Frankfort who had not gone through the routine
training of government officials, and was being pro-
moted over the heads of men who had. The duke,
however, insisted and defended his action in an admirable letter to his minister:

> Were Dr. Goethe [he wrote] a man of ambiguous
> character, everyone would approve your decision; but
> he is upright, and has an extraordinarily good and feeling
> heart. Not only do I congratulate myself, but men of
> insight congratulate me on possessing him. His mind
> and genius are well known. You will yourself see that
> a man like this would not endure the tedious and
> mechanical labour of state service from the beginning
> upwards. Not to use a genius in the place where his
> extraordinary talents can be used is to misuse him.

Thanks to the mediation of the dowager duchess, the
quarrel ultimately blew over, and Fritsch withdrew his
resignation.

To Goethe's credit it must be said that he did not
acquiesce without some struggle; it was February,
1776, before he yielded wholly to the duke's temptations. Again we are asked to applaud the insight of
this young ruler who perceived possibilities in Goethe
for the welfare of his state to which others were blind.
But was his action other than that of any eighteenth-
century prince who raised a friend or a favourite to
power? Nor did Goethe at first assume his rôle of
statesman very seriously, a rôle for which, in any case,
his training in Strassburg and Wetzlar had been an
inadequate enough preparation. His diaries for several
years reveal a record of inane and frivolous diversions
which is difficult to reconcile with seriousness of any
kind. Once, however, he had taken to heart the well-
grounded complaints about his behaviour; once, too,

he felt sure of his position, he did exercise a salutary
influence on his patron, helping to mould his intract-
able character and educating him into a wise ruler of
his little state. No favourite in the end justified the
responsibility with which he was entrusted better than
Goethe did. And as the years went on, his energy
became enormous, and concerned itself with every side
of the country's resources and activities. He interested himself in agriculture, forestry and mining. As
a member of the building commission, he was concerned
with the reconstruction of the ducal residence ; and he
reorganized the roads of the duchy. As director of the
War Commission, he reduced the country's little army
of six hundred men to three hundred, and successfully
circumvented the claim of Prussia—a delicate matter
happily ended by the cessation of its necessity—to
enlist men on Weimar territory.

The most onerous of Goethe's duties was the presi-
dency of the Kammer or Treasury which the duke
induced him to take over in 1782. Here he showed a
firm hand, curbing the extravagance of his master,
rebuking the slackness of the officials and dismissing
dishonest ones ; and although he did not entirely suc-
ceed in making ends meet, he went a long way in that
direction. Nor was the spiritual welfare of the state
neglected. One of Goethe's first acts was to induce
the duke to invite Herder to be court preacher and
general superintendent of the Church in the duchy.
This was a real gain to the intellectual life of the little
capital, although hardly a wise step in the interests of
the Church, for the Weimar clergy were strongly
opposed to Herder's appointment. As " Intendant "
for the redoutes and theatrical entertainments of the
court, he took the leading part in those amateur performances which, until Weimar, from 1784 on, maintained a more or less permanent professional company,
provided a surrogate for a court theatre. Lastly, on
the more human side, he often helped to smooth over

the frictions between the duke and his spouse, and to extricate his ne'er-do-well brother Prince Konstantin from his amatory delinquencies. Obstacles there were, of course, in plenty to this assumption of power by an outsider; but Goethe's magnetic personality of itself cleared them away. " Goethe ", said Merck, " exerts authority and directs everything ; and everybody is content with him, because he serves many and injures no one. Who can resist the disinterestedness of the man ? "

There can be no doubt of it : Goethe carried out all these manifold activities supremely well ; he was the soul of the government and the duke's right-hand man ; he developed into a minister of state as to the manner born. But there was surely another side, and a grave side to it all : as the years moved on, Goethe's life was more and more swallowed up in these duties. Was it not tragic that this, the first poetic mind of his age, should have expended his splendid energies, playing at statesmanship in this duodecimo state ? Such things might well have been left to the men of official routine. It fills one with resentment to think of Goethe when composing his *Iphigenie auf Tauris*, having to interrupt his work to enlist recruits—and the Goethe, moreover, whose Götz and Egmont had died for freedom, nay, who only a few years before had wrecked his own happiness to attain that very freedom which he now so readily renounced. The magnificent young rebel of Frankfort had, thus early, accepted as a rule of conduct the obsequious words which, years later, he placed upon the lips of his Tasso :

> Doch glaube nicht, dass mir
> Der Freiheit wilder Trieb den Busen blähe.
> Der Mensch ist nicht geboren, frei zu sein,
> Und für den Edlen ist kein schöner Glück,
> Als einem Fürsten, den er ehrt, zu dienen.

It has been admitted that Goethe's creative energy as a poet suffered when he became what Schiller would

GOETHE IN 1779
From a Portrait by G. O. May

have contemptuously called a " Fürstendiener " ; but it has equally been urged that the experience which Goethe gained in the government of a state stood him in good stead by widening the basis of his life ; and that his preoccupation with mineralogy and botany, his official contact with the university of Jena, turned his thoughts to natural science and made him a pathfinder here. All this is true ; but a doubt must enter into many minds, whether Goethe's scientific interests were not as real a crime against the majesty of his poetic genius as his immersion in the routine of state government. But of Goethe as a scientist it will be fitter to speak at a later stage. As the years moved on, he himself began to see what a waste of life the favours he enjoyed at the Duke of Weimar's hands entailed ; perceived even that Weimar was another of these hostile forces that prevented the tree from growing into the sky. Perhaps, after all, Goethe's father was right when he so stubbornly opposed his son's acceptance of the Weimar invitation.

Goethe's first period in Weimar was punctuated by many journeys, usually in the company of his duke ; and his official duties required him to familiarize himself with every corner of the duchy. In 1776 he visited Dessau and Leipzig where he saw again Käthchen Schönkopf, now Frau Doctor Kanne ; and in November of the following year he made a journey—this time alone—to the Harz. His object was to obtain a practical knowledge of the mining centres there with a view to reinstating the silver and copper mines at Ilmenau, an unfortunate enterprise which swallowed up large sums of money and could not be made to pay. On this occasion he made the ascent of the Brocken—then an unheard-of undertaking in midwinter—and was rewarded by a magnificent view above the clouds. The journey left its precipitate in his vivid letters to Charlotte von Stein and the fine poem *Harzreise im Winter* ; it also inspired the first of

Goethe's published contributions to science—poetic, it is true, rather than scientific—his essay *Über den Granit*. In 1778 he was in Berlin—for the first and only time—a city for which he had a real dislike; he returned more satisfied than ever that his lot had been cast in little Weimar.

On September 12th, 1779, Goethe and the duke set out on the most ambitious and interesting of all their journeys of these years, that to Switzerland. Their route took them first to Cassel and Frankfort, where Goethe had the pleasure of entertaining the duke under his father's roof. It is true, the old councillor was still sullenly unreconciled to his son's false step; but his mother could not conceal her delight. Speier was then visited, from which the travellers turned southwards to Strassburg. For Goethe it was a journey into the past; he visited Sesenheim, where he saw Friederike again. Motives have been suggested for this visit connected with Lenz's efforts to take Goethe's place in Friederike's affections, but it is pleasanter to accept it as Goethe described it to Charlotte von Stein, as a visit of reconciliation :

> I found there together a family as I had left it eight years before, and was received in a friendly and kindly way. As I now feel so pure and calm, the breath of good people is very welcome to me. The second daughter of the house had formerly loved me more beautifully than I deserved and more than others on whom I have expended much passion and faithfulness. I had to leave her in a moment when it almost cost her her life. She passed lightly over it.

Nothing of the old feeling was revived; they talked of old times in the garden arbour; and the past was as vivid as if it had happened only six months before. Friederike Brion died unmarried in 1813.

In Strassburg Goethe found Lili, now the wife of a banker there, Bernard Friedrich von Türckheim, and happy with a child of seven weeks upon her knee.

The travellers now re-crossed the Rhine, and in Emmendingen Goethe paid his respects to the grave of his unfortunate sister Cornelia Schlosser, who had died in childbirth in the summer of 1777. The journey was thus for him a kind of final winding-up of the accounts of his youth, a rounding-off of his early life. In October the duke and Goethe reached Basel, and in exceptionally fine weather for the late season of the year, visited Bern and the Bernese Oberland. And watching the Staubbach waterfall at Lauterbrunnen on October 9th, Goethe wrote that wonderful poem, *Gesang der Geister über den Wassern (Song of the Spirits over the Waters)*, in which we seem to catch a first glimpse of the wise, contemplative Goethe of later years :

> Des Menschen Seele
> Gleicht dem Wasser :
> Vom Himmel kommt es,
> Zum Himmel steigt es,
> Und wieder nieder
> Zur Erde muss es,
> Ewig wechselnd.

They then proceeded by way of Lausanne and Geneva where the author of *Werther* was much fêted, to the Valais, ascended to Chamounix and, undeterred by possible dangers so late in the year, crossed the glacier to the Furka and St. Gotthard passes. Again Goethe looked down towards Italy.

> For the second time [he wrote] I am in this room on the summit ; what my thoughts are I do not say. Nor does Italy attract me this time. Such a journey would not benefit the duke now ; it would not be well to stay longer away from home. This—and the prospect of seeing you all again—turn away my eyes for the second time from the Promised Land, which I hope I shall not die without beholding.

On the return journey some time was spent at Zürich, where Goethe had pleasure in meeting Lavater again. Visits were also paid to the courts at Stuttgart and Karlsruhe, and in the former town the duke and Goethe were present at a distribution of prizes in the Military Academy, where Schiller, then a lanky youth at the Academy, first set eyes on the greatest of his contemporaries. The travellers were home again in Weimar in the middle of January, 1780, after an absence of four months. Goethe subsequently put together his letters to Frau von Stein, as *Briefe aus der Schweiz*, which were published as an appendix to *Werther* (" Aus Werthers Papieren ") in the edition of his works of 1808. The reader smiles over Goethe's suggestion in his preface to these letters that they might have been written by Werther before he met Lotte ; for there could be hardly a greater contrast than that between the dithyrambic homage to nature of 1774 and the contemplative note of 1779.

This Swiss journey was a turning-point in Goethe's life and his relations to Weimar. The four months of comradeship with the duke had converted his friendship into intimacy ; and in 1782 his position at the court was established on a footing of permanency. A patent of nobility was conferred upon him which removed all the disabilities hitherto imposed upon him by court etiquette ; and he acquired the spacious house on the Frauenplan—Goethe's increasing responsibilities made it desirable that he should be nearer at hand than at his garden house—which was to remain his home for the rest of his life. In 1782, too, his father died.

Weimar would have been less tolerable to Goethe than it was, had it not been for a new *liaison* which he formed there, the most lasting he ever knew except that with Christiane Vulpius. Charlotte von Stein, and Charlotte alone, made it possible for Goethe to remain fairly content in Weimar through nine long years ; she kept the vital spark of poetry alive in him ; his relations to her provide the background for his spiritual development. She was the wife of the duke's master of the horse, Freiherr Friedrich Karl von Stein ; but the couple had nothing in common and virtually lived separate lives. She had borne seven children, which left her prematurely aged and in delicate health ; she was thirty-three when Goethe met her, seven years his senior. As befitted the rôle she had to play as the poet's Weimar muse, she was a lady of the court, and, moreover, a " schöne Seele ", and admirer of Rousseau. She had literary tastes such as Goethe would not have dreamt of looking for in Lotte Buff or Lili. But her own incursions into poetry, notably an amateurish tragedy, *Dido*, in which in later years she avenged herself on Goethe when he turned faithless to her, do not give us, if we discount the poet's glorifying halo, much confidence that she could have proved an inspiring companion in this capacity. When their relation came to an end, she demanded back and destroyed all her letters to Goethe. It is thus difficult to get at the truth of the *liaison* ; for what we can discern through Goethe's eyes is naturally untrustworthy. More than sixteen hundred letters from Goethe to Charlotte von Stein, beginning in 1776, have been preserved, and no doubt there were still more : Charlotte, who laid store by respectability, could not but have exercised some discretion in destroying what she regarded as too compromising. A large number of these are, however, the merest notes, there being no occasion for real letters unless when either Goethe or Charlotte was absent from Weimar. Like all love-letters, they are monotonous reading in the mass ; nor do they make the course of the passion very clear. From inferences and outside hints, however, we are able to distinguish three stages in his relation to her. The first covered the five years to 1780. Here the love was, if not platonic, at least kept within the bounds of social propriety as it was understood at an eighteenth-century German court. Although not of a particularly passionate nature, Charlotte found in her devoted cavalier an outlet for a suppressed emotionalism, to which a loveless marriage to an uncongenial partner had condemned her. But it is clear from the offences taken and forgiven on the lady's part, the petty quarrels and reconciliations, that the love was not exclusively on his side. While jealously appropriating Goethe, she damped his ardour and kept him at his distance; she taught him—at least, so he interpreted it—to prize in her, not emotional return for emotion, but a certain protective motherliness; he felt that he found in her a refuge from his previous erotically storm-tossed life. The poem *Warum gabst du uns die tiefen Blicke*, written in April, 1776, sums up in a few lines what she meant for him :

> Kanntest jeden Zug in meinem Wesen,
> Spähtest, wie die reinste Nerve klingt,
> Konntest mich mit einem Blicke lesen,
> Den so schwer ein sterblich Aug' durchdringt :
> Tropftest Mässigung dem heissen Blute,
> Richtetest den wilden, irren Lauf,
> Und in deinen Engelsarmen ruhte
> Die zerstörte Brust sich wieder auf.

This was something new in Goethe's relations to women, or, at least, new in its combination with the erotic element; and it never recurred. Charlotte was the first woman who understood Goethe—all sides of him; she even shared his scientific interests; and his love for her was invested, in his own mind, with a halo of sanctity.

In the end of 1780, or the beginning of 1781, however, this love underwent a change which can only be explained in one way : the relationship passed over into an actual *liaison*. Possibly jealousy played a part. Goethe had induced the duke to invite from Leipzig the actress and singer Corona Schröter to take part in the theatrical and musical diversions of the court; and Goethe's admiration for this, the first impersonator of his Iphigenie, was by no means platonic. Charlotte may have felt the need of tightening her hold upon Goethe in face of such threatening alienation. In any case, for the next four or five years from 1781 onwards, Goethe in his relations with Charlotte was entirely happy and contented. This phase is rung in by his letter of March 12th, 1781 :

> My soul is firmly grown into yours ; I cannot make words about it ; you know that I am inseparable from you, and nothing high or deep can divide me from you. I would that there were some vow or sacrament that might make me yours visibly and legally ; how precious it would be to me ! And my noviciate has indeed been long enough for reflexion.

About 1785 begins a third stage in Goethe's love for Charlotte. That disillusionment which, sooner or later, undermined all Goethe's passions, gradually— at first almost imperceptibly—crept over his relations to her. But it was not until Goethe had been many months in Italy that he became conscious that the end was approaching.

The early eighties form one of the most crucial periods—perhaps, indeed, the most crucial—in the poet's whole development. A spiritual change, no doubt subtly influenced by these relations to Charlotte von Stein, came over him, which profoundly influenced the character of his imaginative work. For the first time, freed from his earlier obsessions, he could look back on himself objectively—look backward and forward—plan and build for the future. A more serious note comes into his diary, and in September, 1780, he wrote the often quoted letter to Lavater :

> The daily work which has been meted out to me, and which every day becomes easier and harder to me, demands my presence, awake or dreaming. This duty becomes continually dearer to me, and in fulfilling it, I wish to be the equal of the greatest men, and in nothing greater.

This desire to raise the apex of the pyramid of my existence, the basis of which has been given and laid for me, as
high as possible into the air, surpasses all else, and can
hardly for a moment be forgotten. I must lose no time.
I am already on in years, and fate may perhaps break me
in the middle and the Babel tower be left blunt and
uncompleted. At least it shall be said : it was boldly
planned ; and if I live, my powers, with God's favour,
will hold out until I reach the top. And very powerful
is the talisman of a beautiful love, such as that with which
Charlotte von Stein seasons life for me. She has by
degrees succeeded to my mother, my sister, and my
former loves, and a bond has formed between us as
strong as are the bonds of nature.

Clearly Goethe is beginning here to emerge as the
self-conscious artist of life—of his own life. In lack of
balance, " Schwärmerei ", Goethe saw the enemy of all
well-being ; and from now on it is his constant endeavour to divest himself of this " Schwärmerei ",
to give his life stability, order and purpose, to envisage
it as a gift entrusted to him by the Creator. Thus
early the problem, which was ultimately to become that
of *Wilhelm Meisters Lehrjahre,* had begun to engross
him, even if he had to wait until his journey to Italy
to obtain complete understanding of it. And with the
strengthening of this new positive and constructive
attitude to life a change comes over his writings. His
dualism—the " two souls within his breast "—assumes
a new form. In his " Storm and Stress " days there
was still no conscious gap between the experience and
its imaginative precipitate : life and poetry were then,
as it were, one. He had felt no need to subject the
emotions of *Werther* to a refining, sublimating process,
or to generalize and idealize the figures of *Götz von Berlichingen* and *Clavigo,* or of the first sketch of *Faust* :
they were transferred glowing or bleeding to the printed
page. But now, in these later Weimar years, his
" Storm and Stress " passed ; his originally unreflective

genius became reflective ; his attitude to himself and to his art became henceforth an objective one. Life and poetry are no longer co-extensive ; poetry has become the literary interpretation of life, an " abstract " of reality.

It is a debatable question whether this substitution of objectivity for subjectivity in Goethe's art was to his advantage as a poet. In the end, Schiller was perhaps right : Goethe was essentially a great " naïve " poet, not a " sentimental " one. When he renounced the " naïve " for the reflective, the high lights of his genius went out. From now on he grew mightily in wisdom ; but with the passing of the spontaneity to which we owe the great creations of his youth, he lost something which his long and rich intellectual life was never able to compensate for. Our lack of documents makes it difficult for us to arrive at any more precise date than the early eighties for this momentous change in Goethe's genius ; in any case, it was necessarily a gradual change. One thing, however, is clear : just as Goethe's " Sturm und Drang " did not come to an end, as used to be assumed, upon Goethe's arrival in Weimar, so the conversion into the classic and reflective poet was equally not the consequence of his journey to Italy ; rather did Italy bring the consummation of a process of development that had begun long before.

The literary harvest of these years when Goethe's life was filled by his great passion, and his time divided between his state duties and the diversions of the court, was barren enough. The plays he wrote—apart from *Iphigenie auf Tauris*, which was completed in its first form in 1779—were entirely unworthy of the author of *Götz von Berlichingen* and even *Clavigo. Die Geschwister*, a one-act piece dashed off in three days in 1776, the theme of which, perhaps for Charlotte von Stein's benefit, is the inadequacy of sisterly affection, points back to the sentimentalities of *Stella*; *Lila* (1777), *Der Triumph der Empfindsamkeit* (1777-8), *Jery und*

Bätely (1780), written in Switzerland and superficially
Swiss in its colouring, an adaptation of *The Birds* of
Aristophanes (1781), *Die Fischerin* (1782), and *Scherz,
List und Rache* (1785) are either satirical or merely
trivial. In the short poems of these years alone
Goethe is still the master; indeed, under the tran-
quillizing influence of Charlotte, Goethe touched now
perhaps the highest point it was ever given to him to
attain as a lyric poet. He has written nothing more
beautiful than the matchless verses *An den Mond* (" Fül-
lest wieder Busch und Tal ", 1778), or that most perfect expression of man's oneness with nature, the lines
he inscribed on the wall of a little hut on the Kickelhahn
at Ilmenau :

> Über allen Gipfeln
> Ist Ruh,
> In allen Wipfeln
> Spürest du
> Kaum einen Hauch ;
> Die Vögelein schweigen im Walde.
> Warte nur, balde
> Ruhest du auch.

Or once again, the *Zueignung* (1784)—originally part
of a larger plan, an epic with the title *Die Geheimnisse*
—which now stands at the head of Goethe's collected
poems ; *Meine Göttin* (1780), and, perhaps most inspired
of all, *Das Göttliche* (1783) :

> Edel sei der Mensch,
> Hilfreich und gut !
> Denn das allein
> Unterscheidet ihn
> Von allen Wesen,
> Die wir kennen.

Nor must be forgotten the two longer poems *Auf
Miedings Tod* (1782) and *Ilmenau* (1783), and, standing
on a more objective plane, the magnificent ballad of
Der Erlkönig (1782). In all this verse we have eloquent
testimony to the calming and purifying influence of
Charlotte von Stein on the poet.

CHAPTER II

"EGMONT" AND "IPHIGENIE AUF TAURIS"

THERE is no denying that the young poet, for whom Strassburg, Frankfort and Wetzlar marked a steady crescendo of irresistible genius unfolding itself—each year richer in imaginative creation than its predecessor—had in Weimar received a serious set-back: he reconciled himself, to all appearance, to the modest rôle of an amateur in the amateurish atmosphere of a provincial court which, having no larger political interests, had time and to spare to cultivate its literary tastes. The Goethe who had given the world a *Götz* and a *Werther*, who had consorted with Prometheus and Faust, with Cæsar and Ahasuerus, found his occupation and inspiration gone, stifled in an atmosphere of triviality. This genius incarnate—and no poet entered upon his career with the brand of genius stamped so indelibly on his forehead as he—became what in the after-time he so often castigated, a dilettante. He read his poems and sketches of plays which he had brought with him from Frankfort, to admiring court ladies; he wrote plays and masques for the court, and he took the leading part in acting them. He sank back, a new Rinaldo, complacently into the arms of his Armida, Charlotte von Stein. Only a few years before, we are reminded, he had heroically sought release from the snares laid by the fates for his genius with the gay witchery of Lili Schönemann in flight to Switzerland; but there was no flight—not at least for ten long years—from Charlotte von Stein.

But this impression of dilettantism which the literary

output of the Weimar years creates, is, as we now know better than the early biographers of Goethe, not justified. What has to be deplored is not the infertility of his genius, but the lack of ability or time to bring to completion what he put his hand to. To the credit of these years, as we have seen, has to be placed *Iphigenie auf Tauris* ; *Egmont*, which Goethe brought with him from Frankfort, also received the form we know in these years, even if some scenes and the finishing revision were not to be given to it until the poet was in Italy. He planned and made considerable progress with his drama of *Torquato Tasso* ; and a new classical theme engrossed him for a time in *Elpenor*. Above all, the major part of Goethe's greatest novel, *Wilhelm Meisters Lehrjahre*, was written now in the form of *Wilhelm Meisters Theatralische Sendung*.

Egmont is Goethe's second incursion into the field of the historical drama ; but in the case of none of Goethe's greater works are we so ill-informed of the stages of its composition. It is largely a matter of inference and conjecture, how much was conceived and written in Frankfort, how much in Weimar, and what precisely were the finishing touches put to it in Italy. One thing, however, seems clear : it was originally planned in Goethe's " Sturm und Drang " period as a drama of a type similar to *Götz von Berlichingen*, that is to say, it was to be a dramatic portrait of a hero. This is the only dramatic " unity " to which both dramas aspire. It is noticeable, however, that the poet has freed himself from certain excrescences of his misunderstood Shakespearean form ; he has not allowed himself the liberty of restless scene-changing which makes *Götz* so difficult a drama for the theatre. There is in *Egmont* a stringency of dramatic form which was all to the good, although he was very far—and this no doubt presented difficulties in the final revision of the play by the classic Goethe in Italy—from submitting himself to the yoke of regular form. In many ways, however, *Egmont* is less defensible than its predecessor; it has much less of a plot; there is little dramatic movement, whereas the portrait of Götz was at least accompanied by progressive and involved dramatic action.

Goethe set to work in the same conscientious and methodical way in which he had prepared himself for his *Götz von Berlichingen* : he read systematically in the historical literature of his period.

> Among the single parts of the world's history [he tells us in *Dichtung und Wahrheit*], which I had studied with more particular care, were the events which made the afterwards united Netherlands so famous. I had diligently examined the original sources, and had endeavoured, as far as possible, to get my facts at first hand and to bring the whole period vividly before me. The situations appeared to me in the highest degree dramatic ; and it occurred to me that the principal figure, round whom the others might be grouped with the happiest effect, was Count Egmont, whose greatness as a man and a hero appealed to me most strongly.

His principal source was the *De Bello gallico* of the Jesuit Famianus Strada (Rome, 1632), or more probably, the French translation of that work published at Amsterdam in 1729. Here he found an attractive and on the whole sympathetic portrait of his hero, from which he distilled the elements he could use in his drama. He took, however, very considerable liberties with history. The Egmont whom Strada depicts is no longer a young man; he is married and the father of a family. Goethe, to whom it was a necessity to project himself into his hero, frees him from hampering domestic restrictions, and decks him out with qualities which awakened a responsive chord in his own temperament. Similarly he has no compunction in altering the characters of the other historical figures of his play, not to speak of creating a number of new characters for whom Strada does not give him the slightest handle. Perhaps the most historical aspect of the play is its background, its depiction of the events and *milieu* through which Egmont's fate carries him.

It would thus seem that Goethe set out with the purpose, not of writing a regular drama, but of presenting a series of dramatic pictures which should throw light from different sides on the character and personality of his hero. We see Egmont adored by the populace of Brussels, Egmont in his relations to the wise and moderate regent, Margarete von Parma ; we see him vividly contrasted—and it might well be that this scene was the kernel of the whole drama—with the wise realist Oranien ; again, we see him in love with the adorable Klärchen, the victim of the Spanish oppressors, and finally marching in defiant elation to the scaffold. Egmont throws caution to the winds : remains in Brussels when flight would have been the most ordinary prudence ; he falls into the snare Alba has prepared for him, is thrown into prison and executed. That is the whole " story ". All these episodic scenes are but loosely strung together ; they do not form a satisfying drama. With almost culpable indifference to the requirements of dramatic technique, Goethe introduces motive after motive, which with skilful handling might well have provided an adequate dramatic weft ; but he lets them slip unused ; the play is full of broken ends. Even the great Oranien, who, after all, was the real hero of the Netherlands, only appears in a single scene. *Egmont* has in it the material for a great political drama—a depiction of the revolt against Philip of Spain ; and this might well have been the binding medium ; instead, Goethe makes its theme the personal fate of Egmont himself. Schiller put his finger on some of these defects in the not very sympathetic criticism of the play which he published in 1788, before the two poets had become friends ; but the last thing Goethe could have done was to write a political drama of the kind the poet of *Wallenstein* could approve.

It is difficult to decide how much of all this was already in the Frankfort sketch of the play. But it is suggested that he had then written in some form the first three acts, and, no doubt, also the scene between Egmont and Alba in Act IV. Goethe took up the play again in Weimar in 1778, and we find frequent references to his work on it in diaries and letters throughout 1779 and 1780. In December, 1781, he says : " My *Egmont* will soon be finished, and if it were not for the miserable fourth act, which I hate and shall have to revise, I should complete this year a piece on which I have wasted so much of my time." During the spring of 1782 he was closely engaged upon it, and by the beginning of May it seems to have been " finished ".

We may infer that the main difficulty which confronted him in Weimar lay in the political standpoint of the hero in the Frankfort sketch ; Goethe the irresponsible rebel had become Goethe the chief minister of the Weimar state, and could hardly be expected to countenance the radicalism of his Egmont of 1775. He must have felt that a better balanced political point of view must be maintained in the play. Thus much political " Sturm und Drang " in the original was softened, and the views on statecraft which are expressed in Egmont : scene with the Regent inserted ; also to this time belong probably the fine scene between Egmont and Oranien in Act II, and that with the Duke of Alba's natural son Ferdinand in Act V, as well as Alba's talk with his son and Egmont's scene with his secretary. It has further been suggested that the marked tendency to fall into iambic verse of some scenes was alien to the Frankfort years, and justify us in claiming such passages for Weimar. In any case, not much, except stylistic revision, and at most the closing scenes remained to be added to the play when Goethe finally revised it for publication in Italy. The date of the actual completion was September 5th, 1787, and it appeared in the following year in the new edition of the poet's works.

The French romantic critic Ampère regarded *Egmont* as one of the brightest jewels in Goethe's crown. This is hardly a view which will find general endorsement with modern readers; but it is surprising that the play found so little favour with Goethe's own friends on its appearance. They all had faults to find with it, and cavilled at things which by no means seem to us defects to-day. Notably they looked upon Klärchen and her share in the play as an excrescence and a mistake; even Schiller thought so. No doubt from the Voltairean standpoint that affairs of the heart are out of place in plays dealing with great historical happenings, she is; but it is difficult to see what would have been made theatrically of *Egmont* without Klärchen. Finally, the first performance of the drama in Weimar in 1791 was little short of a failure.

As a drama, *Egmont* is, of course, defective; perhaps, indeed, the most defective of all Goethe's greater achievements in this field. Its freedom from the shackles of traditional technique is not—as such freedom was to be in a work like *Torquato Tasso*—a welcome enfranchisement and a foreshadowing of the modern psychological drama; it is merely a helpless neglect of indispensable essentials; a wilful elimination of a " plot ". The close of the play—effective enough as a stage spectacle—has been generally condemned; it has been called operatic and romantic when to Egmont in prison awaiting his execution the goddess of liberty appears in Klärchen's form and bestows on him the wreath of victory. Whether any such close was contemplated in the first version is doubtful; it bears traces rather of that desire which grew on Goethe with the years to sugar the pill of tragedy and expunge the bitterness of suffering and tragic disharmony. But, looked at fairly, *Egmont* has very conspicuous merits. The poet's handling of the " crowd " scenes is admirable, each figure being delineated with Shakespearean sharpness; and all the characters of the drama, even. those who appear episodically and have little to do or say, are clear-cut; Klärchen's lover Brackenburg is even subtly conceived. The dialogue, realistically arresting and brilliant—qualities of which we had already a foretaste in the best scenes of *Clavigo*—is in the truest sense dramatic.

Conspicuous above all is Egmont himself, the most rounded and complete dramatic figure Goethe had yet created, and still the most attractive of all Goethe's heroes. Whatever may be the situation in which he is placed, he never forfeits our sympathy; impatient of the dead hand of authority, joyous, pleasure-loving, self-reliant and full of optimistic faith in the destiny Providence has marked out for him, he is the embodiment of the magnetic power—Goethe calls it " daimonisch "—of bending other mortals under his personal spell. Goethe himself possessed this quality in a high degree, and, as he tells us, he had observed many and diverse examples of it in others. A similar winning charm is to be seen in Klärchen; indeed, it would be difficult to point anywhere in dramatic literature to a figure depicted with such economy of words—she appears only in four episodic scenes—who is able to win over so completely a theatre audience. Hardly less living a creation than Faust's Gretchen, she stands beside her—as, indeed, Egmont stands beside Faust—as the personification of a lighter side of life. Where the modern reader is apt to be disappointed is the visible gap between the delightful naïve scenes of the early acts and the change to a tragedy-queen of the last act, when words and sentiments are put on her lips which are difficult to reconcile with the child of the people as we first know her. The change—and of course it had to come—is not convincingly managed. Here the difference between the style of the Frankfort Goethe—the style that has made Gretchen immortal —and the somewhat heavy-handed " literary " style of the Weimarian Goethe is distinctly disturbing. But when all is said, *Egmont* remains a drama of living people, not stage-puppets ; and that is the supreme criterion of an historical drama, not its historical accuracy or the soundness of its political philosophy. Perhaps of all Goethe's works in dramatic form, it is the one which still has for us of the twentieth century, even from the stage, the greatest fascination. With *Egmont* Goethe found himself at the parting of the ways ; it marks the beginning of a more conciliatory and objective attitude to life than he had known in his Frankfort days ; and it testifies to the change that was coming over his poetic art. *Egmont* is the transition work which leads from his " Sturm und Drang " to the sedater middle years.

The conditions under which *Iphigenie auf Tauris* was composed in 1779 were none of the best : it was written in a hurry in February and March, as we have seen, amidst uncongenial distractions ; its purpose was merely to provide a suitable piece for the amateur performances of the court and give Corona Schröter a rôle worthy of her talent. In this, its first prose form, it was played on April 6th, 1779, Goethe himself impersonating Orestes. Subsequently, it went through several metamorphoses, was turned into verse and back into prose, before it was in Italy clothed in the liquid iambics in which it appears in Goethe's works. But in all these changes the drama remained essentially the same. In respect of its theme, there is little besides the debt of it to Greek antiquity, to divide it from the " Sturm und Drang " works of Goethe's Frankfort time. Orestes with the unforgivable crime of matricide on his conscience, and the avenging Furies at his heels, was a hero after the heart of the rebels of the

seventies. The theme, too, had for Goethe its subjective aspects ; for was not he himself an Orestes
tortured by remorse for his abandonment of Friederike
and Lili ; and Charlotte von Stein an Iphigenia at whose
feet he had found, if not absolution, at least peace ?
But it would be to ignore the growing objectivity of
Goethe's art to look to the work for the same kind of
immediate " confession " that *Werther* had been. There
is obviously much less of Goethe himself in Orestes
than in the heroes of the earlier time ; and if Charlotte
stands in some degree behind the Greek priestess, an
idealization and transformation have taken place which
are not to be found in Goethe's earlier art.

Goethe's choice of the subject was, no doubt, largely
influenced by the revival of an interest in the antique
which had set in in the late sixties. Gotter's dramas on
classic themes and Wieland's *Alceste*, which Goethe
had held up to ridicule, prepared the way ; so, too, had
Gluck's epoch-making reform of the opera. There
were difficulties, however, in the way of modernizing
Euripides' tragedy. The northern imagination and
modern ethics were not so easily pressed into the
mould created by the Greek poet ; once Iphigenia and
Orestes were given modern souls, they comported
themselves with difficulty in the world in which they
were placed. The Greek Iphigenia achieves her end
by the exercise of what to the Greeks was an estimable
virtue, the Odyssean virtue of cunning : she outwits
the barbarian king. A modern heroine could not thus
build up her life upon a lie ; if she is to retain our
sympathies, she must take her stand by the truth. In
the same way, a modern Orestes could not obtain
absolution by the mere decree of a god clothed in the
authority of moral dictatorship. The knot must be
untied by some other means.

Goethe has received perhaps more credit than he
deserves for the way he chose. Other poets of the
eighteenth century had taken steps to rehabilitate

Iphigenia in accordance with Christian ethical tenets
—one can even trace a foreshadowing in the *Orest und
Pylades* of Lessing's predecessor Elias Schlegel—but
the immediate predecessor of Goethe, and one whose
drama Goethe could not but have known, was the
French poet Guimond de la Touche. That writer's
Iphigénie en Tauride was produced in Paris in 1757 and
created a veritable furore, an echo of which soon
reached Germany. De la Touche is the virtual creator
of the "humane" heroine with whom a modern
audience can whole-heartedly sympathize; his play
was the most popular Iphigenia drama of the eighteenth
century. If we compare Goethe's play with the
French one, his debt seems beyond dispute; and
incidentally, it explains those similarities which have
always been noticed between the German drama and
Gluck's opera on the same theme, for Gluck's librettist
had also drawn upon De la Touche.

Goethe's first act, with the exception of the wooing
by Thoas—which, by the way, is to be found in another
French drama, the *Oreste et Pilade* of Lagrange Chancel
—is the first act of De la Touche's play. Here is the
noble Iphigenia with the "grand cœur", the home-sick
exile, who recoils in horror from the human sacrifices
she is obliged to carry out. And to her comes
Eumène, as Arkas in Goethe's play, to announce his
master's demand that these sacrifices be renewed with
all vigour. Act II opens as in Goethe with a scene
between Orestes and Pylades. Orestes is pursued by
the pitiless Furies; and, terrified by visions of his
murdered mother and Aegisthus, he falls unconscious
in his friend's arms as Goethe's Orestes at his sister's
feet. Significant above all for the relations of the
two dramas is the calming, purifying influence which
goes out to Orestes from the priestess:

> Quelle femme vers nous avec effort s'avance?
> Je sens que ma fureur se calme en sa présence.

And again :

> Quelle est cette prêtresse,
> Dont le sensible cœur, digne de sa beauté,
> Sait dans les malheureux chérir l'humanité . . .
> D'où vient qu'à son aspect s'éclaircissoit la nuit
> Qu'autour de moi répand le malheur qui me suit ?
> Par quel charme inconnu la terreur qui me glace,
> Quels sont les sentiments dont j'éprouvois l'attrait ?
> Enfin, de mes remords qui peut m'avoir distrait ?

In a dramatic scene Orestes tells Iphigenia of his terrible crime. The recognition in the French play is longer in coming than in Goethe's, and Iphigenia has more time to bewail the brother she believes to be dead ; the close, too, is more crudely theatrical. But here, too, it is the majestic personality of the priestess that cuts the knot, and helps to secure the safe departure of the friends. In the French play, as in Goethe's, the pivot is the purification of Orestes :

> J'en sens déjà l'effet ; quel changement j'éprouve !
> Dans quel calme profond soudain je me retrouve !
> Je sens tous mes forfaits dans mon cœur expiés ;
> L'abîme dévorant se ferme sous mes pieds.
> L'horreur me fuit ; tout semble autour de moi renaître ;
> Dans un monde nouveau je prends un nouvel être.

And there is no deception on the part of Iphigenia and Orestes at the close : both are open and frank with Thoas.

There is no " problem " in the *Iphigenie auf Tauris* of Goethe which has more persistently engaged the minds of the elucidators of this play in recent years than the " healing "—the purification of Orestes. How are we to understand, is this central περιπέτεια of the drama effected ? And, more particularly, what is the rôle of Iphigenie herself in bringing it about ? Some confusion has been introduced into the problem by the use—a use for which the Goethe of a later time is partly responsible—of the word " Entsühnung " or expiation ; and it would be well to avoid it. It is not expiation that either the Greek Orestes or Goethe's seeks and finds. Grave as his crime had been—and

117

none could be graver than the murder of his own
mother—he had not, he felt, committed it as a free
agent, but as an instrument of the gods.   So, too, does
Iphigenie regard it.   And indeed, this conviction of
irresponsibility is brought home to him by the gods
themselves, by the fact that they point out the way to him
—not the way of contrition—by which he may obtain
relief.   Again, if Iphigenie is the agent of her brother's
cure, in what capacity does she effect it ?   As sister, as
priestess, or merely as a pure and high-souled woman ?
And finally, what is the critical turning-point whereby
Orestes is restored to sanity ?   Is it when he unburdens himself to his sister, or when he believes himself to be in the underworld, or when he finds himself
once more among the living ?

The view which used to be in favour was the religious interpretation ; that Iphigenie as priestess brings
about her brother's expiation, that expiation taking the
essentially Christian course of confession and remorse
followed by absolution.   It was pointed out in defence
of this interpretation that Goethe himself, especially
in his first act, emphasizes the priestess in his heroine
rather than the woman ; and Lewes, long ago, finding
it unnatural that Iphigenie should remain so stolidly
indifferent when she hears of the terrible fate of her
family, sought exoneration for her in her priesthood.
It may be that Goethe did set out with the purpose
in his mind of presenting Iphigenie as, before all
things, the priestess ; but he certainly did not maintain
it consistently.   We are not asked to believe that her
prayer in the third act has any part in her brother's
healing ; and indeed, so unconscious is Iphigenie of
her priestess-rôle that in the fourth act she is still
ignorant that her brother has surmounted the crisis.
It is difficult, too, to be convinced that this religious
interpretation would have appealed to Goethe's mind,
or indeed, have been anything but repugnant to him.
It was never his way to untie a spiritual or emotional

knot by recourse to a religious miracle. In the great crises of his own life, in his own crimes of conscience, Goethe never fell back on repentance and confession. The unhappy past, he held, must be lived down, neutralized, eliminated, not by thoughts and words, however contrite, but by new redeeming deeds ; the sinner must not look backward in vain regrets, but forward to a new life. When Orestes lays his guilt before his sister, he is merely narrating the facts— narrating them in accordance with the traditional technique of the theatre, for the enlightenment of the audience—not confessing in any religious sense. And if this is so, what share has Iphigenie in it ? Can we say more than that the emotional upheaval in Orestes, when he discovers that she is his sister, facilitates his healing in so far as it strengthens him to face life with fresh zest and courage ?

Thus, psychologically, the healing of Orestes is not dissimilar to that effected by the curative process of psycho-analysis, where the patient unburdens himself of his complexes and thereby regains sanity and balance. The task of Iphigenie is not that of priestess, but rather of analyst, in which she is assisted by Pylades ; she provides the opportunity for Orestes to taste in spirit the pangs of death, and to forget his past in a new life. And in this healing the all-essential factor is Orestes' belief that his earthly life is over, and that he has descended to the underworld. This scene, especially as it now stands in the matchless beauty of its final form, is perhaps the noblest poetic conception that ever came from Goethe's brain ; and the great thought that all earthly hates and evils disappear in the life beyond the grave is one of the most inspiring fruits of the poet's optimism :

> Welch ein Gelispel hör' ich in den Zweigen,
> Welch ein Geräusch aus jener Dämmrung säuseln ?—
> Sie kommen schon, den neuen Gast zu sehn !
> Wer ist die Schar, die herrlich miteinander

Wie ein versammelt Fürstenhaus sich freut?
Sie gehn friedlich, Alt' und Junge, Männer
Mit Weibern; göttergleich und ähnlich scheinen
Die wandelnden Gestalten. Ja, sie sind's,
Die Ahnherrn meines Hauses!—Mit Thyesten
Geht Atreus in vertraulichen Gesprächen;
Die Knaben schlüpfen scherzend um sie her.
Ist keine Leidenschaft hier mehr unter euch?
Verlosch die Rache wie das Licht der Sonne?
So bin auch ich willkommen, und ich darf
In euern feierlichen Zug mich mischen.

And then Orestes' jubilant pæan of hope when he grasps
that he is still among the living:

O lasst mich auch in meiner Schwester Armen,
An meines Freundes Brust, was ihr mir gönnt,
Mit vollem Dank geniessen und behalten!
Es löset sich der Fluch, mir sagt's das Herz.
Die Eumeniden ziehn, ich höre sie,
Zum Tartarus und schlagen hinter sich
Die ehrnen Tore fernabdonnernd zu.
Die Erde dampft erquickenden Geruch
Und ladet mich auf ihren Flächen ein,
Nach Lebensfreud' und grosser Tat zu jagen.

Goethe himself, no doubt, believed that in some
mysterious way, his Iphigenie effected the cure of her
brother by means of her sanctity and noble woman-
hood; in fact, this is a direct development from the
French *Iphigénie* of De la Touche where she does effect a
" purification "; but the logic of psychological facts
and the intuition of creative genius were greater than all
" graue Theorie "; and Orestes—even if Goethe himself did not recognize it—finds his salvation otherwise.
When Goethe conceived his drama he was still in the
naïve period of his poetic activity when intuition and
inspiration meant more for him than ratiocination; and
it is questionable whether he troubled himself with such
theoretical considerations at all. It was not until
forty years after *Iphigenie auf Tauris* had been published
that he offered a clue to his view of the psychological
process of his drama. In 1827 he presented a copy

of it to an actor friend in which he wrote a short dedi-
catory poem. Here occur the lines:

> So im Handeln, so im Sprechen
> Liebevoll verkünd' es weit:
> Alle menschliche Gebrechen
> Sühnet reine Menschlichkeit.

But how can one possibly say that Orestes is healed
by Iphigenie's "reine Menschlichkeit"? "Reine
Menschlichkeit" may effect much in human relations,
but there are abysses of crime such as those which
stained the accursed race of Tantalus, or the relentless
hatred of the gods which no humanity, however pure,
or even no faith in and reliance on the gods themselves,
can purify. The Goethe of 1779 or of 1787 did not
assuredly believe that his Orestes was expiated by
"reine Menschlichkeit". Too much weight has been
ascribed to this afterthought—for afterthought it is—
of Goethe's; he was here imposing on his drama a conception of the redeeming power of "reine Menschlichkeit" similar to that which effects the salvation of
Faust. But the idea was foreign to *Iphigenie auf Tauris*.

It is a commonplace to say that fatalism is the essential background of Greek tragedy. There is fatalism
in Goethe's drama, too; but it is very far from being
the controlling factor. The crisis of the action, as
Goethe conceives it, depends not on the decree of the
gods, but on a decision of human will; or, to put it
in another way, the purpose of the gods is made
effective by the exercise of what we like to believe is
free will. This is a complication of the situation which
may be in accordance with the spirit of philosophic
compromise of Goethe's own century, but it is irreconcilable with the simplicity and directness of Greek
religious thought. Goethe's *Iphigenie* is not a fate
tragedy in the Greek sense; or rather, it compromises
between the motive of fate and man's power to sway
the course of events by the exercise of his will.

The decisive act by which Goethe's dramatic knot is untied is surely Iphigenie's decision—a decision on which hangs the life of Orestes, of Pylades, of herself —to destroy the tissue of lies and deceit with which, for a brief space, she had hoped to achieve her end. There are various aspects of this crucial decision. First, it is a tremendous risk, for she cannot foresee how the king will receive her confession. In fact, were Goethe's Thoas a real barbarian king, and not an enlightened eighteenth-century potentate, the consequence would inevitably have been disastrous. Still, granted the conditions which the poet lays down, the risk was perhaps worth taking ; but in the event of failure would a hazard of this kind have been an adequate basis for a great tragic action ? Secondly, Iphigenie's appeal to the truth might be regarded as a noble moral act. Here we have certainly a worthy theme of tragedy, and one that is, moreover, simple and straightforward ; with a tragic close—but only with such a close—it is a motive calculated to purge the modern soul by pity and fear. It is the kind of motive which would have appealed to Schiller, and would probably have been an important ingredient in that last tragedy which it was not given to him to complete, *Demetrius*. But it is not the issue round which Goethe's plot turns. He chooses a much more subtle one : Iphigenie's deliberate decision to make her appeal to the truth a test of the gods themselves :

> Allein euch leg' ich's auf die Kniee ! Wenn
> Ihr wahrhaft seid, wie ihr gepriesen werdet ;
> So zeigt's durch euren Beistand und verherrlicht
> Durch mich die Wahrheit !

Iphigenie is convinced that the gods have played Orestes into her hands ; she believes that it is their purpose to pave the way for her back to her father's house ; to absolve Orestes from his crime and destroy the malignant power that overhangs him. But at the same time, she is shrewd enough to suspect that the gods may be laying a trap for her. She beseeches them in a tone that reveals this distrust :

> Rettet mich,
> Und rettet euer Bild in meiner Seele!

In other words, she implores them to vindicate her faith in themselves. "If ye gods do not stand by me now in my hour of need, my faith in you will be destroyed, and with it my whole confidence in a providential guidance of human affairs from on high. Take your choice : accede to my prayer, and I will continue to believe in you ; disappoint me, and I repudiate you!"

Is this not arrogance in its most desperate form—that ὕβρις which the gods of Greece would not tolerate for a moment in any mortal ? Had the Greek Iphigenia dared so impious a thought, she would have been inevitably shattered by Zeus's thunderbolt. But no thunderbolt falls ; the gods meekly justify this mortal's faith, and all ends happily. Such a situation is in crying antagonism to the profound fatalism of Greek tragedy ; perhaps of all tragedy, and even of life itself.

It may be argued, however, that the conciliatory close was already provided by Euripides ; and that Goethe had no intention of writing a tragedy, but merely of providing a psychological and religious justification of Euripides' plan, such as a modern audience could accept. In doing so, Goethe, however, raises issues which the Greek poet had avoided, if indeed he thought of them at all ; and these deeper issues cry out for a tragic close, and a tragic close only. The gods must inevitably leave the mortal in the lurch —it is the very essence of the conception of deity in all religions—who arrogantly challenges them as Iphigenie does ; who dares presumptuously what she dares. Her act necessarily involves tragic consequences ; but Goethe will have none of them. The conciliatory close of his drama is not effected, as in Euripides, by the exercise of purely human wits; it is due to a happy chance; we must deem his heroine lucky in for once finding the gods of Greece in good humour and willing to close an eye. Whatever we may urge in Goethe's defence, the fact remains that the great dramas of the world are not built up on such exceptional accidents.

And this leads to a wider thought. The fact that Goethe deliberately should have chosen this issue of the three that have been suggested, is but one more proof of the deep-seated antagonism in his mind to tragedy of any kind. And might we not say that in this drama, as in other works by Goethe, his shirking of tragic discord, his conciliatory optimism, defeats itself? If we think seriously about the close of *Iphigenie*, is it quite so happy and serene and conclusive as Goethe would have us believe? Are we so sure that Iphigenie, Orestes and Pylades, having escaped unscathed from Tauris, will "live happily ever afterwards"? If we try to visualize the future of these mortals after the curtain has been rung down on the king's friendly parting words: "Lebt wohl!" can we believe—however committed we may be to Goethe's optimistic faith—that moments will not come in the lives of brother and sister when the black past will rise up again, when the Furies will once more raise their ugly heads and be at Orestes' heels? It is not human that these two can ever forget the dire fate in which they and their curse-laden race have been ensnared. And can we believe that the Iphigenie who, in her darkest hour, had intoned her grim song of the Parcæ:

> Es fürchte die Götter
> Das Menschengeschlecht!
> Sie halten die Herrschaft
> In ewigen Händen,
> Und können sie brauchen,
> Wie's ihnen gefällt—

that this Iphigenie will never again be haunted by doubts
of the divine governance of the world, merely because
the gods have for once relented and granted her
prayer ?

As we read this great drama to-day, however, these
inconsequences disturb us little ; it is not in the solution or lack of solution of these problems that its
greatness lies. The ultimate spiritual thought lying
behind its outward conflicts is that which points the
way to spiritual regeneration, the " rising on our dead
selves to higher things " which lies behind so much
of Goethe's poetic creation and still more emphatically
dominates the tragedies of Schiller. This inspiring
ethical idea is the most precious legacy to us of German
classical poetry ; the most vital of all the great thinking which that poetry sublimated from the noble
humanism of the eighteenth century. In *Iphigenie auf
Tauris* this process of regeneration is most obviously
set forth in the figure of Orestes ; but it is none the
less exemplified by the deep spiritual crisis by which
Iphigenie towards the close of the drama rises superior
to deceit, and becomes a testifier to the majesty of
the truth—and more : to the great positive values of
life which she had hitherto doubted. Through darkness
to light ; from despair to hope and faith ; to trust in
God's guidance of human affairs. It may be urged that
to place this thought in the forefront of the drama's
message relegates Iphigenie to a part entirely subordinate to that of Orestes. But is not the spiritual
development of Iphigenie a far more subtle factor
than that of Orestes ? For it directs the action of the
whole play, and controls the fortunes of all its personages. But how far, how infinitely far, removed is
this conception of a happy and triumphant rising to a
higher life from that grim iron necessity, which
is the foundation of Greek tragedy ! What Goethe
will visualize for us in his *Iphigenie* is, as Professor
Christoph Schrempf—to whom much of the preceding

argument is indebted—concludes, that we stand in the protection of loving gods who care for us better than we can care for ourselves. His drama embodies that buoyant optimistic faith which never deserted him; his doctrine that impatient and violent revolt are never wise; and that all things come in the fullness of time to him who waits in patient confidence.

CHAPTER III

THE ITALIAN JOURNEY

ITALY has always played a decisive rôle in the intellectual and spiritual life of the German people; she
has had a share in most of those rebirths and recon-
structions which punctuate the chequered development
of the North. The ties go back, if we will, to the
shadowy historical past when the northern hordes
sapped the declining strength of the old Roman empire
and destroyed its unity and world domination. These
ties were knit anew by the Mother Church which for
centuries held the Germanic world in its embrace;
and in the spacious days when the Holy Roman Empire
was still a great reality, Italy had stood for the complement of the northern soul. She provided—from
Bari to Ravenna—a background of exotic sunshine to
the German imagination of the Middle Ages. With
the coming of the Renaissance a new spiritual allegiance of the North to the South was established. From
Italy emanated the light of humanism which stimulated
the dormant intellectual life of the Germans to new
activities; and in the train of the humanists came a
new German literature. Even in the revolt of the
North against the spiritual bondage to Rome in the
sixteenth century Italy still played a dominant, even
if, this time, necessarily a negative, rôle. Still later,
in the seventeenth, the German mind seized with
avidity on the romantic revolt in Italy against the
sobriety of the classic ideal which we know as the
baroque; and in the Janus-headed eighteenth century
the classic face of that century turned southwards

and sought in the Italian tradition an antidote to the unclassic stirrings which were ultimately to dominate the North as Romanticism; the great Winckelmann found in Italy a new key to unlock the heart of Greece. Indeed, without Italy there might have been no classicism at all in the supreme age of Weimar's achievement; and even the young Romantic poets sought the blue flower of their longing less in the gloomy forests of their own land than in the sunny serenity of the South. All the great German poets and writers found their way to Italy. From Lessing, Goethe and Herder to Grillparzer, Heine and Hebbel—variously as they reacted to it—all sought in Italy the complement to their national inheritance. Thus in every age when the northern mind felt conscious of its shortcomings, the light of Italy threw gigantic shadows on the wall.

To none of Germany's great minds did Italy mean more than to Goethe. His Italian journey was the greatest event of his life. Nothing that ever happened to him involved such many-sided and far-reaching issues both for his personality and his imaginative work. Thus all writers upon him dwell with peculiar emphasis upon this chapter of his life; and, indeed, it supports with remarkable fitness that mystic interpretation of his life-mission which the poet at heart always cherished, an activity in accordance with a predestined plan. There were, however, unmystic enough reasons for Goethe's yearning for the South. They went back to his earliest childhood, when the pictures on the walls of his father's house fired his imagination. Through the busy Frankfort years of his early manhood Italy was never far from his thoughts; twice he had extended his visits to Switzerland far enough to look down into the Promised Land from the heights of the St. Gotthard Pass; and again in that great crisis of his life when his " daimon " seemed to be shaping his destiny towards Weimar, he had been on his way to Italy.

But, as we have just seen, there were also other

Rischgitz Photo

GOETHE IN ITALY

From a Picture by J. H. W. Tischbein

[face p. 128

reasons which with cumulative force urged his decision to visit Italy in September, 1787. Goethe felt that his life was being entangled and stifled in Weimar; and in serious moments the disturbing thought pressed upon him that the pyramid of his life might remain an unfinished torso, thwarted by the stagnation in which he had too long dallied. He was growing visibly restless and unhappy, a gnawing discontent, an increasing disillusionment set in with this little state, which had showered upon him its highest honours and saddled him with its onerous responsibilities. Moreover, having successfully educated his master into a ruler who was beginning to take his duties seriously, Goethe became apprehensively conscious that a rift had opened up between them. Karl August did not, in fact, develop into an ideal head of a state such as Goethe looked for. He always dreamed of playing a bigger rôle in German and European politics than was allotted to him or the resources of his little duchy permitted; in particular, he developed military ambitions which were to prove particularly disastrous at a later date. Against Goethe's wiser counsels Karl August let himself be drawn into the orbit of Frederick the Great. That monarch came forward as a champion of the unity of the Empire against the disintegrating insubordination of the Austrian emperor, Joseph II, and Karl August was eager to espouse the Prussian cause. No doubt the situation was difficult: Weimar was between two fires, Austria on the one side, Prussia on the other. But Goethe was not at all enamoured of Frederick's political ambitions, and would convince the duke that the most prudent course was to keep free from all such entanglements. He tried to show him that his true rôle as a ruler was to be a patron of learning, a Mæcenas of the arts. But this was not at all to Karl August's taste; he was more at home with his tiny army than with his poets; and he had his way. A gulf opened up between the ruler and his poet-minister which nothing in future years ever bridged. Prussia, meanwhile, played the part of the wily tempter. She helped the duke out of his chronic money difficulties, he being always reprehensibly extravagant. The upshot was that on August 29th, 1785, a treaty was signed whereby Weimar entered the Fürstenbund under Prussian leadership. This step was responsible for much of Goethe's growing restlessness.

The other tie that bound him to Weimar was weakening too, even if he did not yet admit it to himself: his love for Charlotte von Stein. That love had carried him over many a dead point and softened many a disappointment, but it was now beginning to wear threadbare; there came moments when he saw it plainly for what it was, a mere sentimental dalliance. Escape he must, if he would not renounce for ever that poetic mission which, he felt, was placed upon his shoulders; if he would ever bring to completion the pyramid which, he had once fondly thought, he could build on Weimar soil. He must wrench himself free while there was yet time; launch out into the full tide of European life, if he would become, as in his growing strength he felt he could, a great European among Europeans. " I cannot and will not bury my talent." Such was the prelude to the flight to Italy.

Goethe's journey to Italy was, indeed, a flight. After having, on the day preceding his departure, obtained the duke's consent to an indefinite leave of absence, he stole away from Karlsbad, where he had been spending the months of July and August. This was on September 3rd, 1786. Under an assumed name—no one knew of his intentions except his secretary—he set out in all haste by way of Regensburg to Munich; and from Munich he proceeded to Innsbruck and the Brenner Pass. After a brief rest of a night and a day, on the summit, the journey was continued " with terrific speed ", and in the darkness of the night through glorious mountain scenery which might well have tempted the most insensitive of travellers to linger, down into Italy. Goethe seemed haunted by the fear that a courier might overtake him and the realization of his plans once more be thwarted ; indeed, he did not venture to write to the duke or Charlotte until he had reached Verona. As the southern beauty of the valley of the Adige unfolded itself to him in the dawn, his delight was unbounded. He reached Bozen at nine on the morning of September 10th. And what a joy to hear on all lips the liquid Italian speech, with which he had been familiar since his childhood ! He was in Trento a bare week after he had left Karlsbad ; and on the shores of the Lago di Garda he put the first strokes to his final revision of *Iphigenie auf Tauris*. Verona was reached on September 14th, and its amphitheatre, the first great monument of antiquity he set eyes on, held him a willing and entranced prisoner for several days. In Vicenza he was held longer by the strange fascination which the architecture of Palladio —in our modern eyes no genius of a high order— exercised upon him. There was, indeed, something ominous in this experience that befell him on the threshold of Italy ; for Palladio seemed to narrow down and warp his whole outlook on Italian art, to put those classic blinkers on his eyes which he wore to the last. From Vicenza he passed to Padua, where palm trees threw a new light for him on the problem of plant metamorphosis, and then to Venice. "It was written on my page in the book of fate that on September 28th, 1786, I should see Venice for the first time." But even Venice soon began to pall ; it was not the goal ; and after seventeen days here the journey was continued. The attraction of the great magnet, Rome, proved the more irresistible the nearer he approached it ; he felt no rest until he had set foot in the "capital of the world". The feverishness with which he had set out returned with redoubled force ; through Fer-

131

rara, Bologna, across the Apennines, with only the
briefest of pauses, the journey was continued. Perugia
and Terni were rushed through—even for Florence he
could spare but three hours! "If I yielded to my
impatience, I should look at nothing on the way, and
only hasten forwards. Another fourteen days and the
longing of thirty years will be stilled! And I hardly
feel yet that it is possible!" And again: "I have
still three days to travel, and it seems as if I should
never get there". From early dawn to late in the night
he travelled on, not even taking time to remove his
clothes to sleep. "Rome! Rome! Two nights
more, and if the angel of the Lord does not bar our
way, we shall be there!" And then to Charlotte
von Stein: "Yes, I am at last in the capital of the
world. My second word shall be directed to you,
after I have fervently thanked Heaven for having
brought me hither." "Now I am here, and calm,
calm as it would now seem, for the rest of my life."

> From now begins, I may well say, a new life; I now
> see with my own eyes the whole, of which I had only
> known before the parts. I behold now in living form all
> the dreams of my youth. . . . From the day I entered
> Rome I count a second birthday, a rebirth. I am healed
> from a monstrous passion and sickness. Had I not taken
> the resolution which I am now carrying out, I should
> have perished, become incapable of achieving anything.
> Rather dead than live again as in these last years.

And indeed Rome was still, in the eighteenth century,
the capital and mistress of the world; her domination
was none the less real because it had ceased to be
political, ceased also for the northerner to be religious.
She was the symbol of that century's dream of a golden
age of taste; the portal to the classic beauty of antiquity.

Goethe's first residence in Rome lasted nearly four
months, busy months spent in methodical and systematic sight-seeing; guide-book in hand, he visited

the recognized sights. Meanwhile he maintained his incognito and kept—an unusual thing for him—very much to himself; his intercourse in Rome was restricted to the little circle of German artists, chief among them Johann Heinrich Wilhelm Tischbein, who painted the familiar picture of him sitting like a pasha among the ruins of Rome, and later, Angelica Kauffmann. He made the acquaintance of the painter-poet, Friedrich, or, as he was usually called, Maler Müller, of Heinrich Meyer, the Swiss art-historian, who was to become so intimate a friend of his later years, and of Karl Philipp Moritz, whose work on German prosody was helpful to him in putting the final rhythmic polish on his *Iphigenie auf Tauris*. That work was completed on the 12th of December. Apart from the task of revising and completing his earlier writings for publication, Goethe's main and, indeed, sole interest in Rome was art; this was what had drawn him to Italy. "On this journey", he had written in his diary before he left, "I hope to calm my mind concerning the fine arts, stamp their holy image deep on my soul, and preserve it for quiet enjoyment."

On February 21st, 1787, Goethe, accompanied by Tischbein, set out for Naples, where he spent over a month, luxuriating in the sunshine and delighting in the naïve life of the people. His geological interests led him to make no less than three times the ascent of Vesuvius; and looking out on the Bay of Naples, the momentous thought first flashed upon him that all the organs of the plant were but modifications of the leaf as it appears in the first cotyledons. Pompeii, the existence of which had only been discovered some twenty years before, opened a new chapter in Goethe's knowledge of antiquity. From Naples he crossed to Palermo—a four days' voyage!—with, as travelling companion, the early fragment of his drama of *Tasso*; in Sicily he read the *Odyssey* with new understanding, and planned a Homeric drama round the figure of

Nausicaa. But again it was the luxuriant bounty of Sicily that impressed him most deeply; Sicily the granary of Rome interested him more than the beauty of the Sicilian towns. In the middle of May he was back again in Naples—the return voyage was still more adventurous, for it all but ended in shipwreck—and a few weeks later, he had settled down to his second residence in Rome, which lasted from June until the April of the following year, 1788. Here *Egmont* was finished, *Torquato Tasso* planned in its new form; and in the gardens of the Villa Borghese was written that very un-Italian scene of *Faust*, the " Witches' Kitchen ", where Faust finds the rejuvenation his creator had himself undergone under the Italian sun. In Rome Goethe enjoyed his freedom to the full; he gave himself up to life's pleasures with an abandon impossible at home; for free enough as Weimar was in its countenance of mild amours, it was governed by a straight-laced enough etiquette. There were many light-o'-loves in Goethe's Roman life; and for one, " the fair Milanese ", a certain Maddalena Riggi, or Ricci, he seems for a time to have cherished something of the more sentimental passion of his youth.

But the break had at last to come, and on the 23rd of April, 1788, in passionate sorrow and regret, Goethe left the Eternal City by the Porta dei Popoli, by which he had first entered it eighteen months before. He journeyed back by way of Florence, where he made amends for his hasty flight through it on the outward journey; and in Milan he completed his conversion to the gospel of classic beauty by a final repudiation of that Gothic, which in earlier life had opened up to him such wide spiritual horizons; Milan Cathedral is now to him merely " a mountain of marble in the most tasteless shapes ". He travelled across the Splügen into Switzerland, and then, by way of Constance, Augsburg and Nürnberg, back to Weimar.

On the evening of June 18th, 1788, he was home again. Such is, in brief outline, the story of Goethe's journey to Italy.

More than a quarter of a century later Goethe put together out of his letters to Charlotte von Stein and Herder and his Diary, the volumes of his works which bear the title *Italienische Reise* (1816-17). This is a collection of documents which bear witness to Goethe's many-sided interests; it is, in parts, as delightful a record of travel as one could wish to read. But it is not so much a book as materials for a book; and although Goethe gave it the sub-title *Aus meinem Leben*, it cannot be regarded as, in any real sense, a continuation of *Dichtung und Wahrheit*. The *Italienische Reise* is, in fact, lacking in that quality which makes the Autobiography so precious to us, namely, its " Dichtung ", its power of rising superior to the facts and distilling from them their spiritual essence; it is not *the* book we should have liked Goethe to write about the culminating experience of his life.

As his account of his visit to Switzerland in 1780 already testified, Goethe was a good traveller; " zum Sehen geboren ", he had in a high degree the power of seeing things as they actually were; and this objective vision reaches its full power in Italy. He gave himself up without reservations or prepossessions to the impression of the moment; he never failed to establish the bond of sympathy between himself and the people among whom he moved, sharing their outlook and entering into their life. But our pleasure in the *Italienische Reise* is tempered by impatience with its many tedious pages; it is often disappointingly informative about many matters which we would rather seek and could easily find in guide-book or encyclopedia. A monument to Goethe's wide sympathies, it suffers, too, from the discursiveness which such latitude brings with it. We pass confusingly from scientific record to art criticism, from observation to often irrelevant enough reflection. There is a kind of latent struggle throughout the book between science and art—the old dualism of Goethe's mind in still another form. And the record of scientific facts has, on the whole, the better part; it encroaches more and more as the work progresses. To the sensitive reader it comes, for instance, as a douche of cold water, when, after his expectations have been raised to a high pitch by the feverish haste of Goethe's journey to Rome, he is treated to the kind of record, which any traveller might make, of a round of sight-seeing. With all respect for Goethe's marvellous and saving interest in concrete things, we would willingly have sacrificed his matter-of-fact accounts of his experiences for more enlightenment on the spiritual significance of Italy to him. It is not the traveller's notes we seek from Goethe, but the co-ordinating and harmonizing vision of the artist and the poet. Interesting as his account is—and it contains shrewd observations of men and things—of how he spent his days in Venice, it would have been much more interesting had Goethe vouchsafed to reveal to us what it meant to him when, from the tower of St. Mark he, for the first time in his life, set eyes upon the sea—the open sea! How gladly we should have welcomed it had he, instead of in leisurely detail describing to us the Roman carnival, told us of the new spiritual horizons he owed to Rome! We should have liked to hear more of the inspiring beauty of Sicily, which brought Homer near to him as never before, and less statistics of Sicily's contribution to the economic wealth of Italy.

There is disappointment, too, in store for us when we face honestly what Goethe has to tell us of Italy. His journey to the south was, like his own Faust's, a quest for an ideal beauty; but he entered this Land of Promise with strangely limited vision, limited by his own humanistic education and approved by the classic tastes of the Weimar court. He, the heir of centuries of humanism, went to Italy, like Winckelmann before him, burdened with all the preconceptions of his century ; he went, not to seek, but to find the glory that was Rome ; and apart from his pleasure in the sunshine and the Italian people, he had little eye for anything but the vestiges of antiquity. To us moderns, who have seen Italy in the light of another century, and of a wide and catholic Romanticism, the reflexion is inevitable : how very little of Italy and Italy's art Goethe actually did see ! The resplendent Italy of the Renaissance was a closed book to him ; it is true, he speaks with warm admiration of Michelangelo and Raphael ; but the great quality in these masters which he appreciated was their fulfilment of the promise of antiquity. It was a similar kind of antiquity-ridden appreciation to that which Lessing had shown for Shakespeare. One has, indeed, sometimes the impression that Goethe, confronted with the riot of colour in the Italian painters, was colour-blind ; insensitive to it. All his life long, indeed, Goethe's outlook on art was sombrely influenced by a grey tradition ; he studied it through the medium of austere engravings and marble-cold casts. The great house in Weimar was full of such things.

And for a poet how little the great poetry of Italy meant to Goethe ! For Dante, we know, he always had an aversion ; this was a natural consequence of his pagan dislike of the ascetic, which prejudiced him against the crucifixions and martyrdoms of the religious art of Italy. But even Ariosto and Tasso seem, as far as the record of the *Italienische Reise* goes, to have meant little more to him than they had meant to Addison at the beginning of the century. His reading of Italian books, his visits to Italian theatres, are rarely recorded, and then with little understanding or warmth ; they clearly touched no responsive chord in his own poetic nature. He spent days in Verona, without ever remembering that two of the immortal lovers of all poetry had shed a lustre on that city before which even the Amphitheatre itself grew pale; and when he visited Ferrara, he was content to set down a few conventional phrases about its literary past, forgetting that he had in his trunk the beginnings of a drama which was concerned with that very past.

In a letter to the Duke of Weimar, subsequently to be quoted, Goethe declared that in Italy he had "found himself as an artist". But surely he was under a delusion here, or his conception of "artist" was envisaged all too narrowly as his theoretic attitude to art. Had he said: In Italy I have stripped myself of the confusing and disturbing *naïveté* of my earlier poetic method, and disciplined myself in objectivity; I have broken with the unbridled realism that found expression in my former works; I have repudiated the fantastic absurdities of the Gothic and all that was Gothic in me, and taken to my heart the sublimer art of Michelangelo and Palladio; I have lived down my confused German past, and acquired the possession of a pellucid classic style—all that would have been true. But that the renunciation of this past meant "finding himself" as an artist was, as the barren years that were to come only too plainly show, an unfounded hope. Rather might we say that the Goethe who believed that he had at last entered into the Holy of Holies of the artist's calling, ceased from now on to be a creative artist at all. Thus for Goethe the poet the Italian journey was no unmixed blessing; it would have been truer had he told his duke that in Italy he had found himself as a man of science. The palm-tree of the Padua garden that set him thinking about the metamorphosis of plants, a specimen of mica spar, the structure of the lava of Vesuvius, meant more for him than all Italy's poetry. It is significant that one of the most promising conceptions of the Italian period, the drama of *Nausikaa*, should have had in Palermo to yield before the superior claims of botanical theory: "My good poetic intention was disturbed; the garden of Alcinous disappeared, and a world garden opened before me." With all respect for Goethe's scientific zeal and achievement, one cannot help feeling that the world has been thereby the loser.

These are disappointing aspects of Goethe's Italian journey. But his record of it is not to be thus negatively dismissed. The truth is, it was with Goethe in Italy much as it had been with his own Wilhelm Meister: he went out to seek his father's asses, and he found a kingdom; went out to find the realization of classic beauty, and found himself not as an artist, but as a man. The true significance of this supreme event of his life has to be read between the lines of the printed pages. In Italy Goethe attained an objectivity in his attitude to his own personality that he had never known before. He was able to look upon himself—as once, on his ride home from Sesenheim in 1772, he had imagined that he saw his double coming towards him—as a being apart. Free from Weimar ties and Weimar provincialism, he stood upon a vantage-ground from which he saw backwards upon his past, weighing and judging, and forwards into his future, planning and hoping. His spiritual and intellectual life was ordered and stabilized; the confusing emotional factor was, if not eliminated, at least subdued; he attained at last a vision of that harmony in the greatest of all the arts, the art of living, which had ever been his goal, and was to be his goal until the end. The Italian journey has to be looked upon, not as the opening of a new epoch in the poet's life, but rather as the culmination and the close of the process of liberation from subjectivity, which had set in in his early Weimar years. In Italy Goethe made up the reckoning of his past and, that reckoning closed, he was able to face the future with resolution. The attainment of inner harmony, the conciliation of the two souls within his breast, the elimination of disturbing " personal equations ", were thus the greatest gains Goethe owed to Italy. From now on he no longer lived unreflectively in the moment, but consciously and with wise foresight; subjective individualism has given place in him to an impersonal objectivity.

CHAPTER IV

THE REVERBERATION OF ITALY:
"TORQUATO TASSO"

IN spite of the wealth of new experiences that crowded on Goethe in Italy, there is very little to chronicle in respect of new literary plans or works ; the poetic conceptions that did occupy his mind—*Iphigenie in Delphi, Nausikaa*—did not get beyond the initial stages ; it was clearly much harder for Goethe to bring anything new to completion now than even in the early Weimar days. Instead, he busied himself with his older uncompleted works, and that under pressure from without ; for, before leaving Germany, he had made arrangements with the publisher Göschen in Leipzig for the issue of an edition of his writings in eight volumes. In this activity, at least, the instinct of the poet asserted itself over the dead hand of antiquity and the living hand of science. *Egmont,* that political drama which had been begun in his days of Shakespearean enthusiasm, and had benefited by the staider political experience acquired by the poet as minister of state in Weimar, received in Rome its finishing touches. *Iphigenie auf Tauris,* also, as we have seen, conceived in that early time, had vacillated between prose and verse, without receiving the stamp of finality ; and now it was taken in hand with a new enthusiasm born of immediate contact with the great monuments of antiquity. The elimination, or apparent elimination, of the turbulent element has been effected almost alone by the magic of rhythmic form, by the transformation of the original prose into deathless Italian iambics that leave no stain. Other works which he had hoped to complete were in a less forward condition. *Faust* had advanced little beyond the magnificent fragment he had read to the admiring ladies of the Weimar court soon after his first arrival there ; and *Faust* was the hardest nut of all to crack. Commentators like to talk of an " Italian " *Faust*, although the only additions which we know to have been made in Italy were the " Witches' Kitchen ", written in the garden of the Villa Borghese in Rome, and the scene " Forest and Cavern ". Both seem to have been produced by a kind of wrench, a forcible setting-back of himself into a mood anterior to and out of harmony with Italy. Still, in Italy was, no doubt, ripening the great new thought which was to convert that work into a modern *Divine Comedy*. But there is no work of Goethe's that can be called solely and definitely Italian : even *Torquato Tasso*, the most Italianate of his dramas, was not completed until 1790, after he had returned to Weimar ; and the *Römische Elegien* were almost exclusively written there, although clothed in the cherished memories of the Eternal City.

Balzac once expressed, through the mouthpiece of his " Modeste Mignon ", the opinion that " not *Faust*, nor *Egmont* "—as Ampère had asserted—was " Goethe's masterpiece, but *Torquato Tasso* ". And there are many admirers of Goethe's genius—more perhaps outside Germany than within it—who would still subscribe, in large measure, to this verdict of the French romantic age. One of the most finely strung Austrian poets of the last generation, Hugo von Hofmannsthal, has, indeed, claimed *Tasso* as Goethe's " most perfect dramatic work of art ". There is much justification for this high claim. Other works of Goethe's appeal to us at one stage or another of our lives ; they have their day with us and pass into the undisturbed repose of accepted masterpieces whose virtues we do not question ; but we leave them behind us. But the great achievements of Goethe's middle period—from

Iphigenie to the First Part of *Faust*—hold us fast ; their immediate and living appeal remains. They are free alike from the unclarified subjectivity of his early work and the chilling objectivity of his later classicism. Above all, *Iphigenie* and *Tasso* must be thought of together ; they may well be regarded as the culmination of the whole classic movement in European literature ; the final links of a chain of endeavour which begins with the Renaissance in Italy, to reconquer for the modern world the " beauty that was Greece ". But while *Iphigenie* is still in virtue of its theme dominated by the great classical tradition, still looks backward in the pride of royal lineage, *Tasso* stands freer, looks forward into the future. It foreshadows the psychological evolution of dramatic poetry which is the nineteenth century's chief contribution to this art.

Judged by the traditional standards of dramatic form, *Torquato Tasso* is a weak and ineffective play ; Lewes had no difficulty in dismissing it as a work that contained great poetry but had no claim to be regarded as a drama. And indeed if drama is essentially concerned with " happenings ", *Tasso* is seriously wanting ; for there is no action in it : at most, when the poet draws his sword on his supposed enemy and when he takes the princess in his arms. All else is merely talk. A deaf spectator could draw little pleasure from it ; and it is the last play in the world to tempt the maker of scenarios for the cinematograph. The scene is laid at the court of Duke Alfonso II of Ferrara ; and the play opens at the moment when Tasso has completed his great epic *La Gerusalemme liberata*. The duke's sister, the Princess Leonora, celebrates the event by crowning the poet with a laurel wreath. To Antonio Montecatino, the duke's secretary of state, this honour appears merely fulsome flattery ; he accuses Tasso of courting a comparison with Virgil and Ariosto. The morbidly sensitive poet is deeply wounded. The princess pours balm on the wound and the duke endeavours to act as a wise arbiter; but the breach between the poet and the man of the world only grows wider. Ultimately, Tasso so far forgets himself as to draw his sword on Antonio. The duke places him under arrest, but subsequently bids Antonio restore Tasso his freedom and his sword and seek reconciliation with him. As proof of Antonio's sincerity Tasso asks Antonio to obtain the duke's permission for him to go to Rome, and Antonio reluctantly consents. Distracted by the prospect of his separation from Ferrara and the princess, Tasso again forgets himself, and confesses to her his love. This presumption is his final undoing; and in his despair he turns to Antonio to find in this man of practical common sense a real friend. Can one wonder that a spectator of the older generation, unable to anticipate the subtle change to be effected in the drama by Hebbel and Ibsen, whereby an intense psychological action takes the place of an outward and visible one, has relegated *Torquato Tasso* to the closet?

From Goethe's diary and his letters to Charlotte von Stein we know that he was engaged on a drama of *Tasso* between the end of March, 1780, and November, 1781. But the temptation is great to trace the beginnings of the drama back to Goethe's Frankfort days; for there are obvious ties that link up *Tasso* with *Werther*, ties which Goethe himself acknowledged. In later life he recalled with approval that Ampère had called his drama " ein gesteigerter Werther ". When, however, we turn to the original text of Ampère's criticism, we find that he did not at all say what Goethe attributed to him; his statement is merely that in *Tasso* " there is something of *Werther* " : " dans cette poésie si harmonieuse, si délicate, il y a du Verther ". It is thus Goethe himself who calls *Tasso* " ein gesteigerter Werther ". Thus we have the poet's own authority for bringing the two works together. The Lotte whom Werther loves in the novel is as much beyond his grasp as the princess is beyond Tasso's ; Werther, like Tasso, reaches a point when, throwing prudence to the winds, he openly confesses his passion ; and he, too, like Tasso, is rejected. Werther makes shipwreck on his passion ; his life is snuffed out in unmitigated tragedy. Had Goethe written or even thought of a *Tasso* at the time he was engaged on *Werther*, might not it, too, have been tragic ? Possibly, indeed, the play might then have closed, in accordance with history, by commitment of the unhappy poet to the madhouse of St. Anna.

We like to think of the *Tasso* on which Goethe was engaged in the years 1780 and 1781 as standing in a similar relation to that in which the early forms of *Faust* and *Wilhelm Meister* stand to these works as we know them. But behind the *Tasso* of 1781 there is a large point of interrogation ; for we do not possess a line of it. All we know is that the poet seems to have carried it as far as the second act. It was then laid aside and not looked at until some seven years later when he had been several months in Italy.

To define the character and scope of Goethe's drama as he planned it in Weimar, is thus purely a matter of speculation. The chief source of Goethe's knowledge of Tasso's life at that time was the biography of the poet published by Giambattista Manso in 1619, or rather the abridged German translation of this biography by Jacobi which Wilhelm Heinse inserted in 1774 in his journal *Iris*. From this work we are able to form a reasonably conclusive guess at the kind of drama Goethe might have welded out of it. We should have seen Tasso in love with the duke's sister, the Princess Leonora, and concealing his love by allowing suspicions to fall on other less highly-placed ladies at the court who bore the same name as the princess. The action might have been initiated by an enemy crossing Tasso's path, a minister of the Duke of Ferrara, who maligns the poet at court, and betrays the secret of his love ; who also perhaps criticises adversely his poetry ; in any case, endeavours to bring about Tasso's banishment from Ferrara. In Manso Tasso gives his adversary a box on the ears ; but Goethe, remembering, no doubt, the dust which the box on the ears in the *Cid* had raised, would have been chary of introducing such an incident. But an insult there must have been of some kind ; it leads to a challenge to a duel, whereupon the duke intervenes and Tasso is placed under arrest. With only Manso's materials to build on Goethe could hardly have got much further ; and it is admittedly difficult to see how he was to make a very satisfactory play out of them.

Under these circumstances it is not unreasonable to assume that Goethe looked about him to see how other poets had dealt with Tasso's life ; and he might well have sought guidance from a dramatic treatment of the Italian poet's love-troubles which was easily accessible : Goldoni's very popular comedy *Il Torquato Tasso*, produced in 1755. Here we find a number of traits which have no place in Manso, but which appear in Acts I and II of Goethe's drama, notably the two friendly Leonoras—one of them " d'allegro umore "— and the scene in which a Cavaliere del Fiocco offends the *amour-propre* of the poet by speaking slightingly of his epic. Possibly, too, Goldoni may give us a hint of how Goethe's drama was intended to proceed. The love-plot must almost inevitably have culminated in a scene between Tasso and the princess ; his open declaration is as essential to the theme as Werther's declaration of his passion for Lotte is to the novel. As this scene stands in the completed drama, it is usually held to be based on an episode described by Muratori. Goethe might have read Muratori's account of the matter, for it was published in the Venice edition of Tasso's works which was in Goethe's father's library ; but as he did not trouble to read Tasso's own poems and letters, it is improbable that he turned to Muratori's

introduction to the letters, where the anecdote in
question occurs. The most effective episode in *Il
Torquato Tasso* is, however, where the Marchesa
Eleonora—she is not a princess here, but the duke's
future spouse—summons Tasso to her presence and
urges him to receive her message manfully : she frankly
confesses her love for him and points out to him the
need and duty of both of them to renounce. Tasso is
overwhelmed, sinks back in his chair with the words :
" Son fuor di me ! " His nobler self is awakened :
he realizes that he must stifle his passion, and the comedy
closes with his departure for Rome. Keeping in view
the possible model, is it not a reasonable conclusion
that the plan of Goethe's earlier *Tasso* did not, after
all, differ very materially from that of the drama we
know ? As Iphigenie returns to Greece, so Tasso
might have departed for Rome ; and the Duke of
Ferrara, like King Thoas, have wished him God-speed
and a forgiving and friendly " Lebwohl ! "

This first Tasso was a legitimate brother of Werther,
but Tasso was what Werther had not been, a poet ;
and this opened up possibilities of a more intimate
" confession " than the novel offered. Unfortunately,
however, the drama did not take visible shape at this
time. Might it not be inferred that Goethe in his
groping towards an objective art, felt that the theme
touched the raw of personal suffering and conflict too
nearly to allow of completion yet ? Whatever the
reason, the tragedy of the " malheur d'être poète "
was abandoned, and the *Tasso* we possess was not
written until Goethe's experience had been enriched
by Italy.

The stimulus which led the poet to take his drama
up again in 1787 was less the fact that he found himself
in Tasso's Italy—he had, it will be remembered, to all
appearance forgotten his play when he visited Ferrara—
than the appearance of a new and fuller life of Tasso by
the Abbate Pier Antonio Serassi in 1787. This work

provided him with a wealth of Italian colour and with motives better suited to his purpose than the sentimentalities of the older tradition. But just as was the case with *Faust*, Goethe had considerable difficulty in grafting on to the youthful hero of his sketch the conception of the maturer, disillusioned and morbid poet of over thirty, of whom Serassi gave so vivid a portrait. The personage of the drama, however, who bears the plainest traces of changing plans is Antonio.

From the beginning there must have been an Antonio of some kind in the drama, an antagonist of Tasso, comparable to Mephistopheles, or to Don Carlos in *Clavigo*, otherwise there could have been no dramatic conflict. Now in Serassi's biography Goethe found an account of two statesmen at the court of Ferrara, Giambattista Pigna and Antonio Montecatino. Of these Goethe first selected Pigna whom Serassi describes as a man of great intellectual gifts, but hypocritical and envious. " Tasso had always paid court to him," he says, " and showed him all possible esteem even to the extent of recognizing him as his superior in matters of poetry. But Pigna never became his friend, or ceased to cherish malevolence towards him."

At a quite late date, however, Goethe went through his manuscript and everywhere substituted for Pigna Antonio, as being better suited to his purpose than the Pigna whom Serassi describes as an implacable adversary of the poet. In his final revision he also made some attempt to soften the asperities of the character.

Owing to this vacillation in the poet's intention with Antonio some bewildering inconsistencies have arisen. The new motive of reconciliation is introduced abruptly towards the close of Act V, and to make room for it, the course of events is rather violently disturbed. After the culminating scene with the princess the duke orders Tasso's arrest ; but, to our surprise, he is not arrested, and the duke suddenly and unaccountably withdraws—disappears from the play without a word of explanation. A little later we learn that he and the two ladies—contrary to their previous plans—have departed for Ferrara, leaving Tasso alone with Antonio, obviously to provide the opportunity for the concluding scene. The last additions which Goethe appears to have made to his drama, namely, the final scene, Scenes 4 and 5 of Act IV and the last scene of Act I, present, in any case, an entirely consistent Antonio, the calm philosopher of superior practical wisdom, who is clearly marked out to be the friend and support of the distracted poet. On the other hand, it is equally clear that Goethe's original Tasso could never have become reconciled with the Antonio (or Pigna) of the quarrel, or of the scene with Leonore Sanvitale in Act II. *Tasso* may be the most delicately harmonized of all his longer poems, but it has also suffered most from the wide gap that lay between its beginning and its end.

Once in 1827 Eckermann brought his talks with Goethe on to the subject of *Tasso* ; " What ", he asked him, " is the idea of the drama ? " Goethe replied :

> Idea ? What can I say ? I had Tasso's life ; I had my own life ; and in combining two such strange figures, the conception of *Tasso* arose in my mind. I gave him as a prosaic contrast, Antonio for whom I had also no lack of models. As for the other circumstances of a court, of love and life, they were to be found in Weimar as well as in Ferrara ; and I can say with justice that the drama is bone of my bone and flesh of my flesh.

No doubt the situation of the unhappy Italian poet at the court of Ferrara offered many temptations to Goethe to interpret it in the light of his own experiences in Weimar, his relations with the duke, his quarrel with the duke's minister Fritsch. But the subjective moment, the link between the poet's experience and its sublimation in poetry, lay deeper. As he once told Frau Herder, the real theme of *Tasso* is the " disparity between talent and life "; and it is in this wider sense that it is " bone of his bone and flesh of his flesh ". Tasso is unable to reconcile the ideal with the real ; he is the victim of his unbridled " Schwärmerei " for the unattainable. All Goethe's " Sturm und Drang " heroes had been afflicted with this " Schwärmerei ", and all had come to grief upon it. And when Goethe's rebellious mood yielded before the more balanced out-look on life of his Weimar years, the problem became for him—as it was to Wieland in his greater novels—how this " Schwärmerei " could be overcome and healed. Thus the education of Tasso, the cure of his morbid sensitiveness, is the main theme of the drama, just as that of *Iphigenie* is the healing of Orestes. *Iphigenie* and *Tasso* are " Bildungsdramen " as *Wilhelm Meister* is a " Bildungsroman ". The central idea of *Tasso* is to be found in lines spoken by the Gräfin Leonore which belong to the part of the drama written last of all :

> Wir wünschen ihn zu bilden, dass er mehr
> Sich selbst geniesse, mehr sich zu geniessen
> Den andern geben könne.

What, then, is the precise nature of Tasso's " Bildung " ? This is best answered by comparing the drama, not with the earlier *Iphigenie*, but with that other work in which Goethe has embodied the new ethical standpoint to which he attained in Italy, the completed *Wilhelm Meisters Lehrjahre*. To *Tasso* might be applied two sentences which concern that novel : one is Goethe's own dictum : " Man does not attain to happiness until his unconditioned striving has set a definite limit to itself " ; and the other the words with which Schiller summed up the novel : " Meister passes from an empty and undefined ideal to a definite active life, but without thereby losing his power to idealize." Tasso, too, Goethe will have us believe, passes from an undefined ideal, from unbalanced dreaming to a

positive, even if never practical outlook upon life ; he
goes through disillusionment, as Meister does ; he
" learns to eat his bread with tears " ; and his trials
come to an end, not as in Meister's case, with the
opening up of a life-giving practical activity, but rather
in the discovery that his salvation lies in the power of
giving expression as a poet to his griefs ; to " teach in
song " what he has " learned in suffering " :

> Nur Eines bleibt :
> Die Träne hat uns die Natur verliehen,
> Den Schrei des Schmerzens, wenn der Mann zuletzt
> Es nicht mehr trägt—Und mir noch über alles—
> Sie liess im Schmerz mir Melodie und Rede,
> Die tiefste Fülle meiner Not zu klagen :
> Und wenn der Mensch in seiner Qual verstummt,
> Gab mir ein Gott, zu sagen wie ich leide.

Everything in the drama centres in this " education "
of Tasso ; it is the care of the duke ; it is the dearest
wish of the princess ; it is the purpose, if less conscious,
of Leonore Sanvitale ; and the instrument of that education is that spirit, " der stets das Böse will und stets das
Gute schafft ", Antonio. This is the most satisfying
interpretation of Goethe's *Torquato Tasso* ; and perhaps
in respect of its story, the mature drama does not differ
very essentially from that which the poet had been
minded to write in 1781.

Thus *Tasso* is no tragedy. But is this true ? May
not the drama, in spite of all Goethe's efforts and pro-
tests, be a tragedy after all ? The great works of
poetry have a way, once created, of living their own
life ; and if they do possess this independent life, it is
for us to judge their issues by our own light, just as
we judge the facts of biography or history. No reader
of Goethe's drama can be satisfied or convinced in his
own mind that its close, the reconciliation of the poet
with Antonio, will result in permanent harmony.
Rather do we feel, given the character of Tasso, that

an ultimate tragic issue is inevitable. Goethe's new optimism is in conflict with his old realism; but the inexorable logic of life still triumphs over his constructive interpretation of it.

The Tasso Goethe has created is no hero; he breaks the rules of propriety unheroically, not from strength but from weakness; he is the victim, not the master, of his foolish passion; he meets adversity unheroically; unheroically resigns himself to his fate. Is his life anything but one long tragedy, and a tragedy without the katharsis of pity and fear? Tasso's love is a tragic failure; his efforts at friendship are ineffectual. Endowed with an insatiable hunger for human sympathy, he can find no mistress; and he could find no friend. His supersensitiveness will always sooner or later raise obstacles—it may be only pride, it may be innate antipathy. Can the end of such a "problematic nature" be anything but tragic? There is—there can be—no promise of permanence in the patched-up friendship of Tasso and Antonio; for the antagonism between the two men is deeper than the mere failure to form a particular friendship; it marks Tasso's condemnation to that solitude from which he would fain escape. We know that, before many days pass after the curtain falls, the antagonism will have broken out afresh, more bitterly perhaps than ever. In fact, Tasso's clinging to Antonio is only one more of the many aberrations of his unhappy life, and he will assuredly waken on the morrow to realize that this friend whom he believes he has found, is no refuge for his shipwrecked soul, and can be none. Tasso is not "saved" by his genius; he does not reach the goal Goethe has marked out for him. He sees his fragile bark shattered by the buffeting waves of reality:

> Zerbrochen ist das Steuer, und es kracht
> Das Schiff an allen Seiten. Berstend reisst
> Der Boden unter meinen Füssen auf!

But there is no rescue. Thus, in spite of Goethe's untragic intention, his *Tasso* is a tragedy, and a deep tragedy; moreover, it is not merely the tragedy of a half-insane court poet, who through foolish blundering destroys his life-happiness; it is at the same time the tragedy of the over-sensitive human soul in any environment; of genius in conflict with life. Tasso is confronted by a Hamlet-like struggle with his fate—a fate which is too heavy a burden for him to bear; and to him, too, might well be applied the image of the oak-tree in the costly vase.

Torquato Tasso is, after all, an unreal drama, a dream-play—a poet's dream of " might have beens ". And is not just this unreality its most subtle charm? The world of the drama is as remote from common experience as that of the pastoral recalled by the opening scene. The crude sounds, the garish colours of reality are excluded; no breath of everyday is allowed to penetrate the magic gardens of Belriguardo. Indeed, one might well believe that there was no world at all outside the play—no city of Ferrara in the background with its prosaic, workaday population; Belriguardo might be some enchanted castle, whose inmates have all been sunk in magic sleep, all except the five figures of the drama—and a single page. And these figures flit across the picture like incorporeal shadows; they speak and move and act as in a dream. The two ladies, masquerading as fantastic shepherdesses, seem embodiments of " il Penseroso " and " l'Allegro " in this make-believe world; the Duke and Antonio are hardly more living figures; and in their midst Tasso himself—the only personage in the poem in whose veins the blood runs red—struggles towards the light of common day; struggles only to fall back, baffled and dismayed; ultimately to fade away, like Helena in *Faust*. And Tasso's friendship with Antonio?—that, too, is only make-believe; it will be shattered at the first breath of reality. Rome—the Rome which stands

153

in Tasso's soul as a symbol of the great Reality—is a goal which he never reaches, not, at least, within the compass of the play. Rome *this* Tasso, we know, will never see; he can only wander eternally amidst the bloodless ghosts of Belriguardo.

In Boccaccio's *Decameron*, written four hundred years before Goethe's poem, a company of exquisite souls met in an Italian garden to tell each other finely chiselled tales and bandy wit and jest. So here a choice company meets once more in an Italian garden, to discuss the finer emotions, and to dream beautiful dreams; here, too, as in the perfect art of Boccaccio's tales, we catch a glimpse of a more exquisite harmony and a more perfect blend of thought and form than the drab world of reality can attain:

> So scheint es mir, ich sehe
> Elysium auf dieser Zauberfläche
> Gebildet.

But alas, the real world existed all the same; even if Goethe, like Boccaccio, would put it out of mind and sight—the world of disappointment, of sorrow, the world of tragedy. Outside the Florentine garden of the Italian raged the terrors of the plague; and outside the idyllic garden of Goethe's Belriguardo the old world was rushing to its doom in the great cataclysm of the French Revolution.

The other work on which the stamp of Italy is deeply graven is the collection of twenty *Römische Elegien*; they, too, were largely written when Italy had ceased to be an immediate experience and had become a memory. They embody, moreover, erotic experiences which, as will be seen, belong to Weimar, and only by poetic licence are grafted on to Goethe's Roman life. But the *ars amoris* is still Roman; passion is here a naïve, sensuous, unsentimental thing, such as rarely, in so naked a form, flamed up in Goethe's life. It is, indeed, a far cry from the love of Werther to that of the Roman

Goethe! No work of our poet has so purely Latin a
stamp as this—Latin alike in its classic form and
equally classic contents. But the best that Goethe
owed to the " capital of the world ", its revelation to
him of unperturbed serenity and classic beauty, is
concentrated here :

O wie fühl' ich in Rom mich so froh ! gedenk' ich der Zeiten,
    Da mich ein graulicher Tag hinten im Norden umfing,
Trübe der Himmel und schwer auf meine Scheitel sich senkte,
    Farb- und gestaltlos die Welt um den Ermatteten lag,
Und ich über mein Ich, des unbefriedigten Geistes
    Düstre Wege zu spähn, still in Betrachtung versank.
Nun umleuchtet der Glanz des helleren Äthers die Stirne ;
    Phöbus rufet, der Gott, Formen und Farben hervor.
Sternhell glänzet die Nacht, sie klingt von weichen Gesängen,
    Und mir leuchtet der Mond heller als nordischer Tag.
Welche Seligkeit ward mir Sterblichem ! Träum' ich ?
    Empfänget
    Dein ambrosisches Haus, Jupiter Vater, den Gast ?
Ach ! hier lieg' ich, und strecke nach deinen Knieen die
    Hände
    Flehend aus. O vernimm, Jupiter Xenius, mich !

CHAPTER V

AGAIN IN WEIMAR

1788–1794

THE freedom of Italy was over; Goethe returned with extreme reluctance to Weimar; and had it not been for the lack of funds, he would probably not have returned so soon. After the happiness and hopefulness of the months in the south, when, in self-detachment, he had looked backwards and forwards, had seen his life, as it were, mapped out beneath him; after the delight with which he had revelled in the objectivity and clarity of antique beauty, disappointment with his German home was inevitable. The disappointment was the greater, as Goethe's wonted prescience and foresight seemed to have deserted him; he did not fairly conjure up to himself the peculiar disillusionment which Weimar had in store for him. He had forgotten that the old friends at home could not have moved and grown with him, and would be necessarily out of sympathy with him. The letter—a quotation has already been made from it—which Goethe wrote to the duke before his return, shows plainly that Goethe cherished hopes of Weimar which it could not realize:

> My desire—with this strange, unsubduable spirit of mine, which even in perfect freedom and in the moment of enjoying the earnestly desired good fortune, has brought me much suffering—my desire is, at your side, among your subjects, in your land, to find myself again; to cast up the account of my journey, and to gather together in the last three volumes of my works, the mass of many life-memories and meditations on art. I can say to be sure:

" In these eighteen months' solitude I *have* found myself " ;
but in what sense ? " As an artist." All that I am over and
above the artist it will be for you to criticize and make use
of. By your continuous active life you, as I can see from all
your letters, have been always widening and refining your
knowledge of the uses that can be made of men ; I submit
myself gladly to your judgment. Receive me as a guest,
let me by your side fill out the whole measure of my existence and enjoy life ; and thus my force will be like
a newly-tapped, concentrated, purified spring, easy to
guide from its source hither or thither as you desire.

Thus hopefully he wrote ; but he did not consider
how difficult it would be, after Rome, to reconcile
himself to the narrower world of Weimar, even if the
duke relieved him—as he magnanimously did—from
the tedious round of official duties. As the truth
forced itself upon him, a sense of emptiness, a blight-
ing discontent took possession of him, difficult to
explain in a poet of supreme genius in the prime of
life.

From Italy so rich in form, [he wrote], I had returned
to a formless Germany, to exchange a serene sky for a
gloomy one ; my friends, instead of consoling me and
drawing me to them again, brought me to despair. My
delight in very remote things, my suffering, my lament
over all that I had lost seemed to hurt them ; I missed all
sympathy ; no one understood my language.

Goethe turned his back on life ; withdrew in proud,
disconsolate self-sufficiency into himself. The biographer is not prepared for the collapse, or, at
least, the sustained collapse under which Goethe
suffered in these years ; and the whole period that lies
between 1788 and the beginning of the friendship with
Schiller in 1794 is something of a psychological enigma.
Its solution is perhaps to be sought outside Goethe's
personality, in the conditions to which he returned, in
his own distractions, and in that general out-of-jointness

157

of a world which stood on the brink of the great Revolution. Whatever may have been its cause, Goethe in these years passed into the winter of his discontent—paralysing discontent; it came over him like a premature climacteric which dulled his poetic faculties, an experience he had known in no previous period of his life. For although to this time we owe the completion of *Tasso*, as well as the *Römische Elegien*, these were no fresh imaginings, but only a rounding-off of the great Italian experience. And it is perhaps also to be put down to the jaundice which had crept over Goethe that, when, two years later, he had the opportunity of revisiting the Italy of his heart's desire, he found himself unable to recall the first fine rapture of his earlier journey.

He had ceased, in accordance with his wish, to take an active part, as member of the Council, in the government of the state; but he still remained, behind the scenes, the trusted councillor of the duke himself. In an informal way, indeed, he was consulted about most things, and ultimately, in 1791, when the duke established a court theatre on a permanent basis, Goethe was induced to be its director. Goethe's adage: " What one desires in youth, age brings in abundance " becomes irony when we see how, when the opportunity at last came to realize the dream of his early *Wilhelm Meister*, that dream had ceased to have vital interest for him. Nor is it possible to speak very warmly of his theatre management in these years; the means at his disposal were very limited, his actors inadequate and wretchedly paid. The public, too, which could patronize the theatre was so small that frequent repetitions of a play were out of the question. Thus it is hardly to be wondered at that the repertory he provided did not differ conspicuously from that of other German theatres of the day. The Goethe of 1791 was in any case in no mood to be a reformer.

His dissatisfaction with Weimar politics was as great

as ever. The martial zeal which had drawn the duke into the wake of Prussia was increasingly distasteful to him as its detrimental effects upon the little state became the more apparent. To this were added friction and discord within the ducal house, when the duke paid undue attention to an English lady, a daughter of Sir Charles Gore; and Goethe's powers of mediation and conciliation were put to a severe strain. What Weimar could offer in the way of sympathetic cultured inter-course was deprived of one of its attractions, when Herder—strained as the relations between the two men sometimes were—shortly after Goethe's return, set out on his Italian journey. And Charlotte von Stein?

It has been seen how Goethe's love for Charlotte, already overripe in 1787, had been gradually dying in Italy; the more earthly passions to which he had given himself up there, had reduced it to the temperate level of a friendship. But, once back in Weimar, Goethe felt that this friendship, like all else in Weimar, was a turned page in his life; in the new consciousness of his own spiritual strength, which he had acquired in the south, he had no further need for such companion-ship as Charlotte had to give him. There was some-thing callous in the way in which Goethe avoided her on his return, in the trivial excuses he made for not visiting her; if he did see her, it was usually in the company of others. His isolation had made him peculiarly vulnerable to a new attack by Eros, his old enemy. One day, only a few weeks after his return from Italy, a young girl, Christiane Vulpius, accosted him in the park and presented him with a petition on behalf of her brother, a struggling *littérateur* who hoped for help from Goethe's influence. The daughter of a minor town official, she earned a small livelihood by making artificial flowers. To the surprise and scandal of Weimar society Goethe took Christiane into his garden house as his mistress and subsequently established her in the mansion on the Frauenplan. It was clearly a case of quite earthly attraction that led the poet to transfer this " forest flower " from the wilds to his own trim garden :

> Ich ging im Walde
> So für mich hin,
> Und nichts zu suchen,
> Das war mein Sinn.
>
> Im Schatten sah ich
> Ein Blümchen stehn,
> Wie Sterne leuchtend,
> Wie Äuglein schön.
>
> Ich wollt' es brechen,
> Da sagt' es fein :
> Soll ich zum Welken
> Gebrochen sein ?
>
> Ich grub's mit allen
> Den Würzlein aus,
> Zum Garten trug ich's
> Am hübschen Haus.
>
> Und pflanzt' es wieder
> Am stillen Ort ;
> Nun zweigt es immer
> Und blüht so fort.

Such is, in poetic transfiguration, the sum of the most enduring of all Goethe's amatory experiences. To the poet, back in his chilly northern Weimar after months in the Italian sun, Christiane with her fresh colour and luxuriant brown hair, had made a peculiar appeal ; she was a warm-blooded, Dionysiac little creature, whose passion, devoid of the old sentimental wrappings of the *Werther* time, fitted exactly into the mood of the *Römische Elegien*. But when the passion of the moment died down in Goethe, a very real affection for her, it must be admitted, took its place ; his letters to her are always full of affectionate tenderness, even if it is the condescending affection one shows to a child. And

GOETHE'S HOUSE IN WEIMAR
By O. Wagner, 1827

[*face p.* 160

to Christiane's credit it must be said that she brought a new element into Goethe's relations with women; she kindled in him a love for home. This was something new to Goethe—perhaps a portent of the growing years; he had never felt it for the home of his childhood, nor for the Weimar of his earlier life. Thus was forged a new link, and a stronger link than either the duke or Charlotte von Stein had been able to provide, which held him prisoner in the little Saxon capital. As time went on and the "forest flower" became an unprepossessing, stout little woman, with a marked propensity for good living and drinking and an inordinate love of dancing, she still remained, in all the material sides of life, a very real helpmate to Goethe; she made his life easy and comfortable by administering humbly to his needs and comforts. And all this although Goethe did not remove the stigma upon her by making her his lawful wife, until the insecurity of life during the Napoleonic invasion and the insults of French soldiers forced the step upon him. Goethe's marriage offers baffling problems to the biographer. If we pass in review the many women that flitted through the poet's life, from Annette Schönkopf to Ulrike von Levetzow, we cannot but feel that hardly one was less worthy than Christiane Vulpius to fill the place of honour she filled; no manner of apology— and Christiane has her apologists—can convince us that she was the right mate for the greatest mind of Europe. Remembering the peculiar aptness with which all Goethe's loves fitted into the mood and situation of the moment, an explanation and exoneration of his choice might be found in the fact that he had turned his back on Weimar; a breach had been opened by Italy between him and his old friends; and by taking Christiane to fill that breach he gave expression, as it were, to the situation in which he found himself; he set up a barrier between himself and the polite society of Weimar which was insurmountable.

Christiane embodied Goethe's relations to Weimar now, as Charlotte von Stein had embodied them to the pre-Italian Weimar. But it is the permanence which Goethe gave to the union that puzzles us. It was, indeed, a union that carries us back to a primitive conception of marriage, when spiritual and intellectual comradeship, even a very modest level of taste and culture—one stands aghast at the illiterateness of Christiane's letters—were of no account in marriage at all. For his work, for poetry of any kind, she had, as Goethe himself frankly admitted, no understanding. If Christiane did not wholly fail, it was due to the fact that the great man made, in this respect, no demands upon her, and to the humble self-effacement with which she fulfilled her lot. But the gods are not so easily appeased ; Nemesis is not to be circumvented. There *was* tragedy in this union which brought bitter misery upon the old poet's last years ; that tragedy was the son Christiane bore him on Christmas Day, 1789.

Charlotte von Stein did not learn of what had happened until months later, for during the summer she was mostly absent from Weimar. When the affair ultimately did reach her ears, her indignation and recriminations were bitter. Goethe's reply to her reproaches in a letter of June 1st, 1789, is worth quoting for the light on his mood at this time :

How much I love you, how well I know my duty towards you and your Fritz [her son in whose education Goethe had interested himself] I have proved by returning from Italy. If the duke had his will, I should still be there. Herder was going to Italy, and as I did not see how I could be of use to the hereditary prince, I had hardly anything to consider but you and Fritz. What I have left behind me in Italy I need not repeat : you have received my confidences on that score with sufficient unfriendliness. Unfortunately, when I came back, you were in a strange mood, and I confess frankly that the

way in which you and others received me pained me very
much. I saw Herder and the duchess depart; I saw
in the carriage an empty place which I was urged to take.
I remained for the sake of my friends, as for their sakes I
had returned; and at that very moment I had to hear it
persistently repeated that I might very well have stayed
away altogether. And all this before there could be any
question of a new relationship which appears to wound you
so much. And what kind of relationship is it? Who
is made the poorer by it? Who claims the hours that I
spend with her? Ask Fritz, ask the Herders, ask every-
one who is intimate with me, whether I am the less willing
to hear confidences, less willing to confide, less active on
behalf of my friends than before. Whether, on the contrary, I do not now for the first time belong to them and to
society in the best sense. And it would have been a
miracle had I lost only the best and deepest relationship
of all—that to you. How vividly I felt it still existed
when, on one occasion, I found you willing to talk with
me on interesting subjects. But I confess frankly that
the way in which you have hitherto treated me I cannot
endure. Whenever I was disposed to talk, you closed
my lips; when I was communicative, you blamed me
for my indifference; when I was active for my friends,
you accused me of coldness and neglect.

And in a second letter of a week later he begs her to
help him " not to let the relationship which fills you with
so much repugnance degenerate, but continue as it is ".
Charlotte's comment on the first of these letters was the
" O! " she wrote upon it. Such was Goethe's final
reckoning with the love of more than ten of his best
years. The breach was complete; not until long
afterwards, when both Goethe and Charlotte von
Stein were old and grey, did something of the old
friendliness return again.
   More than once the dowager Duchess Amalia, who
had been living in Italy since the autumn of 1788,
had pressed Goethe to join her; and in March, 1790,
he once more crossed the Alps, arriving in Venice on

the last day of the month. But the disillusionment
which is apt to dog the steps of the ordinary mortal
who revisits places associated with great happiness,
also befell Goethe. The old rapture was not to be
recaptured, and in the many weeks he had to wait for
the arrival of the duchess he grew very weary of this
" nest of stone and water ". Two of his experiences
in Venice stand out, however, with peculiar significance,
if not for Goethe the poet, at least for the critic of art
and the scientist. It will be remembered how indifferent he had been on his first visit to the artists who are
the particular glory of Venice ; how, with a kind of
colour-blindness, he had passed by the gorgeous can-
vases of Titian, Tintoretto, Giorgione and Paolo
Veronese. Now, thanks, no doubt, to the guidance
of his Swiss friend, the artist Heinrich Meyer, whom the
Duchess Amalia had brought with her when she
arrived on May 6th, he learned to regard them with
more seeing eyes. This new appreciation was a
powerful stimulus to those studies on colour which
he was now beginning, and which were to occupy
him so intensively in the coming years. The other
experience had bearing on his anatomical studies.
A sheep's skull, accidentally picked up in the Jewish
cemetery on the Lido, inspired him with a great new
thought which furthered materially his theory of
organic evolution : as the plant structure is a development of the leaf, so the skull, it flashed upon him, is
the development of the uppermost vertebra. And
in Venice he wrote the epigrams—some hundred in
all—which are known as *Venetianische Epigramme*. It
is instructive to read these side by side with the *Römische
Elegien*, into which, hardly two years before, he had
distilled the quintessence of his pagan love for Italy.
Here one sees the full brunt of the disillusionment
which his second visit brought with it :

Schön ist das Land ; doch ach ! Faustinen find' ich nicht wieder.
Das ist Italien nicht mehr, das ich mit Schmerzen verliess.

Frankly, there is something almost inexplicable in this
sudden change of attitude.   Surely the weeks of bored
idleness in Venice could not have been responsible for it.
Rather might it be attributed to the new life that had
begun for him in Weimar ; the tugging at his heartstrings of wife and child :

> Südwärts liegen der Schätze wie viel !   Doch einer im Norden
> Zieht, ein grosser Magnet, unwiderstehlich zurück.

A warmth came into Goethe's whole attitude to Weimar,
which had become invested with a quality it had never
possessed before for him ; for the first time it stood to
him for home.   And of his duke, without whom this
happiness would not have been possible, he could only
think with gratitude :

> Klein ist unter den Fürsten Germaniens freilich der meine ;
>   Kurz und schmal ist sein Land, mässig nur, was er vermag.
> Aber so wende nach innen, so wende nach aussen die Kräfte
>   Jeder ; da wär's ein Fest, Deutscher mit Deutschen zu sein.
> Doch was priesest du Ihn, den Taten und Werke verkünden ?
>   Und bestochen erschien' deine Verehrung vielleicht ;
> Denn mir hat er gegeben, was Grosse selten gewähren,
>   Neigung, Musse, Vertraun, Felder und Garten und Haus.
> Niemand braucht' ich zu danken als Ihm, und manches bedurft'
>   ich,
>   Der ich mich auf den Erwerb schlecht, als ein Dichter,
>   verstand.
> Hat mich Europa gelobt, was hat mir Europa gegeben ?
>   Nichts !   Ich habe, wie schwer ! meine Gedichte bezahlt.
> Deutschland ahmte mich nach, und Frankreich mochte mich
>   lesen.
>   England ! freundlich empfingst du den zerrütteten Gast.
> Doch was fördert es mich, dass auch sogar der Chinese
>   Malet, mit ängstlicher Hand, Werthern und Lotten auf
>   Glas ?
> Niemals frug ein Kaiser nach mir, es hat sich kein König
>   Um mich bekümmert, und Er war mir August und Mäcen.

But, rightly read, there is more in these lines—as in the
Venetianische Epigramme as a whole—than a reviving
love for the Weimar that had so often hemmed his

flight. There is a note of resignation and self-imposed limitation. The Titan in Goethe is dead.

After visits to Padua, Vicenza, Verona and Mantua, the party reached home again on June 20th. This time Goethe returned to Weimar a more contented man than ever before. But his rest at home was brief; for the duke, who had been made a major-general in the Prussian army, desired him almost immediately to accompany him to Silesia, where Prussia was organizing a kind of military demonstration against Austria to prevent her entering into an alliance with France. During his stay in Silesia, where he had never been before, Goethe had an opportunity of learning to know the Slav peoples; Cracow was visited and the mines of Bohemia and Galicia, the latter being interesting to the Weimar party in view of the failure to make the Ilmenau mines remunerative. And both going to and returning from Silesia Goethe renewed his acquaintance with Dresden which he had not seen since his Leipzig student days. Altogether the journey was an interesting experience; but amidst all the military bustle he seems to have been chiefly engrossed with his botanical and anatomical theories. And in Breslau a new idea had presented itself to him in connexion with his other scientific interest, optics. In casually handling some prisms he had noticed that the refraction into the colours of the spectrum which they produced only took place at the edges of the ray of light where it merged into darkness; and, rather rashly, he leapt to the conclusion that this phenomenon upset the whole Newtonian theory of light. From now on optics usurped the place of biology in his scientific studies.

Meanwhile, the out-of-jointness of the great world outside was becoming increasingly apparent; all Europe was breathlessly watching the course of the French Revolution, as it plunged deeper and deeper into anarchy and bloodshed. Goethe's attitude to its terrible events was characterized by a balanced insight, and even foresight, which none of his contemporaries in the literary world shared. To say that he regarded the Revolution from his aristocratic standpoint as merely an unmitigated evil would be far from the truth. He had not, in the beginning, shared the exultation of all who were then young in the new gospel of the " Rights of Man " and when, after the storming of the Bastille, the Revolution degenerated into orgies of crime, he still maintained a certain balance of judgment. For Goethe it was one of those great world happenings —as Napoleon was a little later—which are foreordained and inevitable, and which have to be regarded without indignation and borne with seemly fortitude. His own firm stand-by in the welter of political confusion was the political ideals of the *ancien régime* as he had helped to perfect them in Karl August's little kingdom ; he had always advocated a wise anticipation of the terrible lessons the Revolution was to teach, by lightening the burdens and sweetening the lives of the governed. But for the " subject " he had nothing but the undemocratic and quietist doctrine of abject submission to authority, of unconcern in the affairs of government. It was enough for him that each man should " sweep before his own door ".

The Revolution gave the Duke of Weimar the opportunity he ardently sought of indulging his martial ambitions. Recognizing the dangers of an armed intervention from the east, the French forestalled such plans by declaring war on Austria in 1792 ; and the German world was moved to take action. The Duke of Weimar joined the Prussian contingent which was preparing to defend German hearths and homes against the pestilence from the west, and he again desired Goethe to accompany him. As before, the latter obeyed the summons with reluctance, for he was at the time deep in his new optical studies. But it was a great experience ; he had a taste of war, and, indeed, a very real one ; for

167

he deliberately exposed himself to cannon fire to see what impression it would make upon him. It is, however, a curious illustration of Goethe's powers of mental detachment that in the midst of the stirring happenings in the field, his optical interests were always uppermost.

On his way to join the army he spent a few weeks in Frankfort where, after an interval of twelve years, he again saw his mother, who had been extraordinarily staunch in her attitude towards her son's unsanctified union; she was pleased to have a grandson, even if she did regret that the birth could not " be put in the papers and properly celebrated ". Even the most sympathetic of Goethe's biographers has a difficulty in exonerating his lukewarmness in his relations to his mother. After all, Frankfort was not very far from Weimar; and there had been frequent opportunities for revisiting it. But not even when his father died in 1782, had he seen her; and after his long residence in Italy it would have been natural that he should have made the small detour by way of Frankfort on the return journey. Behind the present visit may have also been an ulterior motive, a vague suggestion that Goethe might cut the ties—no longer very binding— with Weimar, and return permanently to a responsible position in his native city. But this, he soon saw, was only a dream.

At the end of August Goethe joined the Prussian camp at Longwy. Verdun fell on September 2nd. So far, the issue was hopeful for the German allies; but unfortunately they did not—or owing to incessant rain, could not—take advantage of their initial success; they proceeded down the valley of the Aisne too leisurely, and the revolutionary forces had time to retrieve their strength. On September 20th took place the battle of Valmy which ended in the retreat of the invading Germans and the virtual end of the disastrous campaign. In the evening after the battle Goethe

made the oracular, if somewhat cryptic remark:
" From this place and day begins a new epoch in
history, and you may say that you have been present."
Did he mean more than that the campaign was hope-
less, and that the Revolution must triumph? Or was
there perhaps a dim hint in his words of the coming
of a democracy, when a nation's fate would lie in its
own hands and not in those of a professional soldiery?
Or did he merely over-estimate the significance of an
engagement that left no particular mark on the history
of Europe? That night Goethe and the duke slept
in their cloaks in the trenches. Little over a week later
the Germans were in full retreat, a wet, cold retreat full
of privations, sickness and discontent. Goethe was
induced to separate himself from the army, and proceeded by way of Longwy to Trier which he reached on
October 20th; he then, after a few days' rest, sailed
down the Moselle to Coblence. Once here, he took
the opportunity of paying a visit to Düsseldorf, and
in Pempelfort he saw again Jacobi, only to discover how
wide the gulf was that had opened up between them
since the old days. In the beginning of December he
spent some days with the Princess Amalie von Gallitzin
and her catholic circle in Münster, which was followed
by an interesting correspondence in the months to come.
After all the adventures and discomforts of the campaign it was a very real pleasure to be welcomed home
at midnight on December 16th by the mistress of his
house on the Frauenplan, which, in his absence, had
been undergoing considerable alterations.

The story of this chapter in Goethe's life he has himself written for us in that vivid description of the
military adventure which, however, was not published
until thirty years later, *Campagne in Frankreich*.
Meanwhile the French revolutionaries advanced into
German territory; they had not only military success,
facilitated by the want of agreement among the German
states; but their propaganda was spreading. Mainz

was occupied and even Frankfort. In the following year, 1793, he was present with the duke at the siege of Mainz by the German forces, a kind of aftermath of his martial experiences in France. On this, too, he wrote a book, *Die Belagerung von Mainz* (1822), but it is of inferior interest to the *Campagne*. The siege, moreover, was a very protracted operation and not successfully terminated until July 23rd. The little state of Weimar had paid dearly for its espousal of the Prussian policy and the military ambitions of its duke; and it was a great satisfaction to Goethe that, when the latter ultimately returned, disillusioned and embittered, he was firmly resolved to have nothing more to do with armies and war. He resigned his generalship in the Prussian army.

These were barren years in Goethe's poetic life; the great stimulus of Italy had, as we have seen, been sufficiently powerful to carry *Torquato Tasso* and the *Römische Elegien* to a successful conclusion; but it failed conspicuously when it was a question of completing *Faust*; of new creations there is little to record. He turned—as he always did when poetry lost savour with him—to an objective, impersonal task, which had in it a certain element of the mechanical; he made an admirable modernization of the old Low German beast epic of *Reineke Fuchs*, attuning it to the political temper of his own age. This was published in 1794.

The Revolution colours all Goethe's thought in these years; and it leaves its imprint on his writings from the *Venice Epigrams* of 1790 to *Die natürliche Tochter* of 1804. It is a tribute to the staidness of Goethe's outlook on world affairs that his standpoint and attitude, as they are to be seen in the last of these works, do not differ materially from those in the first. The precipitate of the Revolution in Goethe's literary work is admittedly an indifferent one; but that is less to be attributed to lack of inspiring materials, than to the atrophy of Goethe's own poetic genius in these years. *Der*

Grosskophta (1792), a dramatization of the notorious Diamond Necklace story, is one of the most trivial of all Goethe's pieces : a mere intrigue drama of a kind which dozens of purveyors for the German theatre of the day could have turned out. There is little of the Revolution in it, although Cagliostro's swindles might well have been brought into relation with the break-up of the old social order in Europe. *Der Bürgergeneral*, a one-act comedy written in 1793, is on a slightly higher level, but it, too, is an inconsiderable satirical trifle tossed off in three days. A village barber Schnaps gets possession of a French uniform, and poses as an emissary of the Jacobins ; the rogue escapes punishment by the intervention of the squire of the place who pleads that such things in a land undisturbed by the revolutionary upset need not be taken too seriously. Goethe evidently intended to handle the Revolution in a more serious spirit in an unfinished play *Die Aufgeregten*, which might have been a *Bürgergeneral* turned into tragedy ; and perhaps a still more valuable tragic contribution would have been *Das Mädchen von Oberkirch* of which we only possess a sketch. It is hardly possible to offer a very serious apologia for these pieces now. The language in which they are couched is in more than the literal sense the language of prose ; the thoughts that inspire them are, when they are not merely trivial, crudely political rather than poetic and interpretative ; and the men and women that people them live only the artificial stage-life of the comedies of Iffland and Kotzebue.

CHAPTER VI

GOETHE'S FRIENDSHIP WITH SCHILLER

THE friendship of Goethe and Schiller—one of the dreams of literary history come true—is the visible symbol of the culmination of that classical literature which they had the main share in creating. There is no chapter of German literature on which one dwells with more satisfaction than that which describes this brotherhood of genius ; the more so as it was not one of those happenings which are to be taken as a matter of course. For Goethe and Schiller were too different in temperament and mentality to be suited to become friends ; and had the approach been initiated by Goethe, we might be tempted to see in it the working of that instinct which always led him to select antipathetic people as his associates—men like Behrisch, Merck and Herder in his earlier life. But the choosing was rather on the part of Schiller. As a schoolboy in Stuttgart, he had, it will be remembered, first set eyes on Goethe, on the occasion of the visit paid by Goethe and his duke to the Military Academy in 1779 ; and since then he had looked up to him as one to whom had fallen the good fortune which had been cruelly denied to himself. The elder poet—and Goethe was ten years Schiller's senior—had, he enviously felt, never known the adverse fortune which had so far been his own lot.

In July, 1787, Schiller, then still homeless and with a very uncertain future, paid a visit to Weimar; he was oppressed and irritated to find the atmosphere of the town impregnated with adulation for Goethe who was, of course, at the time absent in Italy. He was by no means at first disposed to bend the knee, and expressed himself with some acrimony to his friend Körner in Dresden. Still, he had words of admiration for *Iphigenie auf Tauris*. It was not in Weimar, but in the house of Schiller's future mother-in-law, Frau von Lengefeld, in Rudolstadt, that the two poets met in the following summer, a few weeks after Goethe's return. By this time Schiller had grown visibly warmer in his attitude, probably influenced by the fact that Frau von Lengefeld was a friend of Charlotte von Stein's. In September, 1788, they met again and Schiller described this meeting with some cordiality to Körner on the 12th :

My first glimpse of him considerably lowered the high opinion which I had been led to form of his attractive and handsome figure. He is of medium height, carries himself stiffly and walks also with some stiffness ; his face is uncommunicative, but his eye is very expressive and bright, and one hangs with pleasure upon his glance. Although full of earnestness, his expression has much benevolence and kindness. His complexion is dark, and he seemed to me to look older than, according to my calculation, he can actually be. His voice is exceedingly agreeable, his discourse flowing, genial and vivacious ; one listens to him with very great pleasure, and, if he is in good humour, which this time was generally the case, he likes to talk, and talks in an interesting way. We soon became acquainted and our conversation was quite unconstrained ; the company was, of course, too large, and every one too jealous of his attention, to allow me to be much alone with him, or to discuss anything but generalities with him. He speaks willingly and with impassioned recollection of Italy, and what he told me of it gave me a most striking and living picture of the country and its people. . . . On the whole, my really high idea of him has not been lessened by personal acquaintance, but I doubt whether we shall ever get very near to each other. Much that is still interesting to me, much that I still wish for and hope for, has had its day with him ; he is so far ahead of me—less in years than in self-development and experience of life—that our paths can never meet. His whole nature is fundamentally different from mine in its constitution, his world is not mine, our ideas seem essentially at variance. Nothing, however, is definitely and finally settled by such a meeting. Time will show the rest.

Meanwhile Goethe's opinion of Schiller was not unfavourable, and when an opportunity occurred, he recommended him for a professorship in the university of Jena. It may have been that this recommendation was not entirely disinterested, a motive being perhaps that he wished to keep Schiller, the inconvenient rebel of *Die Räuber*, at some distance from Weimar. But to Schiller the appointment was a boon in those days when he was looking forward to marrying Charlotte von Lengefeld, even if he had good reason to be disappointed with the meagre income it brought in. In the next few years the two poets did not get much nearer to each other : Schiller had hoped that Goethe's interest in him might have been the beginning of a closer friendship, whereas Goethe seemed to forget all about him. To Körner Schiller wrote again on February 2nd, 1789 :

To be often with Goethe would make me unhappy ; even towards his nearest friends he has no moment of effusion ; one cannot, as it were, seize hold of him. I believe, in fact, that he is an egoist to an extraordinary degree. He possesses the talent of captivating people and of binding them to him by little attentions as well as great ones, but he always keeps himself free ; he makes his existence known by kindly actions, but only as a god, without giving anything of himself. This seems to me a consistent and well-planned line of action, entirely calculated to afford the highest enjoyment of self-love. People should not allow such a nature to rise up round them. For this reason I hate him, although I love his spirit with all my heart and have a high opinion of him. It is a very strange mixture of hatred and love which he has awakened in me, a feeling which is not dissimilar to that which Brutus and Cassius must have cherished towards Cæsar ; I could destroy his spirit and yet love him again from my heart. It is Goethe's influence, too, which makes me wish to have my poem [*Die Künstler*] very perfect. I attach very great weight to his judgment. He has criticized *Die Götter Griechenlands* very favourably ; he only found it too long, and in this he may not be wrong. His mind is ripe and his opinion of me is unfavourable rather than favourable. Now I only desire to hear the truth about myself, and consequently just this man, of all whom I know, can do me this service. I will surround him with eavesdroppers, for I shall never ask him about myself.

And then in a burst of candour a few weeks later :

I have to laugh when I think of what I may have written to you of and about Goethe. I am sure you must have seen me in a proper state of weakness and have laughed over me in your heart ; but, be that as it may, I am willing to let you know me as I am. This man, this Goethe, is, once for all, in my way, and he reminds me too often that fate has treated me harshly. How lightly has his genius been borne aloft by his destiny and what battles I have still to fight, down to this very moment !

In October, 1790, Goethe visited Schiller in Jena and they discussed Kant together, which gives the younger poet another opportunity for a penetrating glimpse into Goethe's way of thinking :

It is interesting to observe how he clothes everything in his own style and manner and gives back in a surprising way what he has read. But I would rather not discuss with him things which interest me very much. He entirely lacks a hearty way of admitting anything. For him all philosophy is subjective, and, with such an assumption, conviction and discussion both come to a dead stop. Nor do I wholly like his philosophy ; it takes too much from the world of sense, where mine draws from the soul ;

and, in general, his method of representing an idea is too concrete ; he feels and handles too much for me. But his mind works and searches in all directions and strives to build up for itself a whole—and that makes him in my opinion a great man.

The first letter which Schiller addressed to Goethe was a formal and tentative note of June 18th, 1794, inviting him to collaborate in a new periodical, *Die Horen*, which Schiller was preparing to launch. Goethe replied politely, and a meeting between the two men took place not long afterwards in Jena, when Goethe demonstrated his theory of the metamorphosis of plants, to be somewhat rebuffed by Schiller's assertion that this was an " idea " and not, as Goethe the realist would have it, a tangible fact that could be seen with one's eyes. Then came, in the end of August, that extraordinarily penetrating letter of Schiller's in which he accurately stated the antithesis between them, a summing-up which, one might well say, contains the essential substance of Schiller's important treatise *Über naive und sentimentalische Dichtung*, published in the following year. Goethe replied exceedingly warmly, and the letter was the beginning of the enduring friendship which was only cut short by the younger poet's death in 1805. Schiller saw in himself the philosophic, reflective poet who proceeds from the abstract to the concrete, sets out from the idea, and seeks to impose that idea upon phenomena ; while Goethe is the realist, who takes his stand on nature and the world revealed by the senses, allowing this world to interpret itself, as it were, untrammelled by abstract preconceptions of a purpose that lies behind. Nothing more illuminating has ever been written on Goethe's intellectual temperament, although by the time the friendship with Schiller was sealed, Goethe had, as has been already indicated, become in large measure faithless to the " naïveté " of his earlier writings on which Schiller had based his conception of him.

You take, (Schiller wrote to him), all nature together in order to obtain light on isolated phenomena ; in the totality of her manifestations you seek the explanation of the individual. From the simple organism you rise, step by step, to the more complicated, in order to reconstruct genetically from the whole edifice of nature, the most complicated phenomenon of all, man. By, as it were, creating as nature herself creates, you seek to penetrate into her most secret technique. A great and truly heroic idea, which sufficiently proves how your mind combines the rich whole of its ideas to a beautiful unity. . . . Had you been born a Greek, or only an Italian, and had, from your cradle onwards, a choice nature and an idealizing art around you, your way would have been infinitely shortened, perhaps it would have been quite superfluous. . . . But as you have been born a German, as your Greek spirit has been set in this northern world, you have no other choice than either to become yourself a northern artist, or with the aid of your intellect, to supplement your imagination by giving it, as it were from within, that reality which has been denied you, and with the help of reason, bringing to birth a new Greece.

There had been greater reluctance on Goethe's part to enter into the new friendship. He was in no mood to make new friends of any kind at this time, let alone such a friend as he believed Schiller to be. The post-Italian Goethe with his " Sturm und Drang " far behind him, and his mind attuned to classic harmonies, could not but profoundly distrust this younger poet, whose early dramas, not excepting *Don Carlos*, seemed to him reprehensible aberrations from good taste. But the first meeting between the two men in Jena, and the letter which has just been quoted, removed the more serious obstacles. Both poets allowed themselves to be convinced that, despite all intellectual disparity and antagonism, they were at bottom seeking the same goal, approaching it from different sides.

The history of the friendship between Goethe and Schiller is contained in the thousand letters which the two poets interchanged between 1794 and 1805. It is the most " literary " of all the collections of Goethe's correspondence; indeed, it is almost exclusively literary. On the human side, the letters are disappointing; they throw strangely little light on the more intimate personality and life of either poet in these ten years. One obvious reason was that Christiane presented an obstacle—Schiller's wife in particular would not countenance her—which restricted the intercourse of the two poets to their professional interests as men of letters. Besides this barrier, which Goethe tacitly, and probably not unwillingly, recognized, there was a distinct disinclination on his part to be communicative, even where his work was concerned. It is doubtful, indeed, whether he ever overcame his original distrust of Schiller; ever accepted him quite unreservedly as his brother-in-arms. The latter's frankness certainly contrasts pleasantly with Goethe's " buttoned-up " attitude and somewhat condescending tone. Goethe had, as Schiller anticipated before he knew him, no moments of effusion. He who had been so prone in early years to wear his heart on his sleeve, and who could still write openly about himself, his work and his plans to correspondents of much smaller calibre than Schiller, maintains, for the most part, a reserve that must have been chilling. There was, in other words, good friendship between the two men, but no deeper personal intimacy; they never got beyond the formal " Sie " in their mutual address.

In replying to Schiller's invitation to contribute to the *Horen*, Goethe had expressed his regret that he had already made arrangements for the publication of *Wilhelm Meister*; otherwise, that novel might have been published serially in the new journal. No doubt, this and *Faust* were what Schiller hoped to induce Goethe to give him. It was a pity for Schiller's sake that they were not available; for *Wilhelm Meisters Lehrjahre* might have staved off the failure of *Die Horen*.

As it was, that failure has in great measure to be laid at Goethe's door. What he actually did contribute, the *Unterhaltungen deutscher Ausgewanderten*—surely the least inspired of all Goethe's experiments in prose fiction—and the translation of Benvenuto Cellini's life, not only fell very far short of what Schiller might have reasonably expected from the greatest of his contemporaries, but they must also have been unattractive to the public to whom *Die Horen* appealed. Even the *Römische Elegien*, the only contribution worthy of him, were, owing to their unveiled tone, a somewhat dubious asset to a journal which catered for the general cultured public.

Although Schiller was debarred from publishing *Wilhelm Meister*, he took the greatest interest in it ; and through all these years his concern with Goethe's poetic work continued unabated, in spite of the *noli-me-tangere* spirit with which his criticism and advice were often accepted. This forms the most valuable part of the correspondence ; and it will always redound to the younger poet's credit that his pleading induced Goethe to take from his drawer the old yellowed manuscript of his *Faust* and resume work upon it.

Active collaboration between Goethe and Schiller began with the collection of epigrammatic distichs on the model of Martial, the *Xenien*, which were published in 1797, not, however, in the *Horen*, but in another periodical venture of Schiller's, a *Musenalmanach*. The motive which prompted the *Xenien* was, in the first instance, the discouraging reception of *Die Horen* ; but in a larger sense they voiced the resentment both poets felt at seeing the leadership in the literary world pass to the hands of the younger generation ; what hurt them was not so much that they had been attacked by that generation, as that they were being ignored. Satire does not seem the most helpful way of redressing such a balance, especially as it must have been patent to the two poets that they had only themselves to blame if they were being thus tacitly relegated to the shelf. Since *Don Carlos*, ten years before, Schiller had abandoned the drama, and we have only to put ourselves at the standpoint of 1796 to admit that contemporaries had every reason to think that his day was over. In Goethe's case the public had equally good grounds for believing that he had abdicated. The attack of the *Xenien* went forth, and seems—although it is a little puzzling for a modern reader to explain why—to have been effective. Schiller, no doubt, contributed most to this end, for his distichs have more sting in them than Goethe's. The latter also replied to belittlers in an essay entitled *Literarischer Sansculottismus*, which was published in *Die Horen* itself.

It is doubtful, however, whether the *Xenien* would have done more than raise a temporary dust, had not the two friends, satisfied that they had somehow rehabilitated themselves by their onslaught—as a matter of fact, they rather increased the number of their enemies,—settled down to serious work : the "Xenien-war" was the prelude to Schiller's *Wallenstein* and Goethe's *Hermann und Dorothea*. This was, after all, the only real way of putting themselves right with the public. Before, however, these works matured, the beneficial effects of the new friendship showed themselves in the series of ballads which the two friends composed in friendly rivalry in 1797. Here, again, was the front of the medal, of which the *Xenien* had been the reverse. Schiller's ballads with their picturesque dramatic settings and broad, simple moral, belong to the most cherished possessions of the German people ; Goethe's of this period—*Der Zauberlehrling*, *Der neue Pausias*, *Der Schatzgräber*, above all, *Die Braut von Korinth* and *Der Gott und die Bajadere*—may not have equalled them in widespread popularity ; the peculiar mental exclusiveness of the post-Italian Goethe stands in the way ; but they take very high rank among Goethe's shorter poems ; represent, indeed, a kind of high-water mark of the German classical ballad. But just this adjective " classical " reveals the wide gulf that lay between the Goethe of *Der Erlkönig* and *Der König in Thule*—which breathed the very spirit of Percy and Bürger—and the Goethe of 1797 ; once again, in fact, it is the antithesis of the " naïve " and the " sentimental " of Schiller's definition. The ballad as Goethe now cultivated it, is not, in respect of its æsthetic presuppositions, so very different from that in which Schiller excelled. And having thus, with Schiller's help, rediscovered his poetic genius, Goethe gradually found his way back to that " cloudy and misty way " which led to *Faust*.

Meanwhile, in these ten years of his friendship with Schiller Goethe's interests were directed rather to art and science than to poetry.

> My life (he wrote in 1800) is swept along, to all appearance with ever greater vehemence. The many threads I took up in earlier years—in the sciences, the arts, public affairs—run ever closer together. Poetry is again in danger of being neglected in favour of philosophy, physical science and their like.

One wonders, indeed, how in a life so preoccupied with unpoetic things, Goethe could have found time for a *Hermann und Dorothea* at all. We hear, however, little of these many interests in his correspondence with Schiller.

Undismayed by the disappointment of 1790, he again contemplated a journey to Italy ; and again the magnet was Italian art. Together with his friend, Heinrich Meyer, he had planned a great history of the art of Italy. The journey was put off from year to year, the reasons being, first his preoccupation with *Wilhelm Meister*, and then the disturbed political conditions ; and when it was actually undertaken in the autumn of 1797, it was restricted to Switzerland. Once again, and for the third time, Goethe reached the St. Gotthard Hospice ; but on Italy he was never to set eyes again.

On the way, as on his previous Swiss journey, he spent some weeks—Christiane and his eight-year-old son August accompanied him—in Frankfort, to the great joy of his mother. It was the last time he was to see her; she died in 1808.

After his return from Switzerland his life was very full—full and reasonably happy. It is true, things did not go as smoothly in the house on the Frauenplan as in the earlier years of Goethe's " conscience marriage ", for Christiane had asserted herself a little more and often filled his house with friends that were not to Goethe's taste. We find him with increasing frequency living by himself in Jena. His dominating interest was art; and the precipitate of this interest between 1798 and 1800 found its way into his periodical *Propyläen*, which, like his later journal, *Über Kunst und Altertum*, is a receptacle for often quite inconsiderable odds and ends; that mania for collecting which Goethe had inherited from his father, and which was to be his chief hobby in his old age, left its mark on both periodicals. It seems a pity that just in those years when Schiller—his *Horen* at an end—was throwing his full energy into poetry and giving Germany the master-works of her classic stage, Goethe, instead of seconding his friend's splendid efforts, should have wasted his powers on art criticism of transient value. He was, in particular, engaged at this time on his theory of colour, and in 1810 appeared the two volumes of his important work on the subject, *Zur Farbenlehre*.

Schiller died on the 9th of May, 1805. Goethe was at the time seriously ill, and it was not until the following morning that Christiane ventured to bring the dire news to his bedside. He turned away and wept. Even after months had passed, he could still tell his friend, the musician Zelter:

> Since I wrote to you, I have lost a friend, and in him half of my existence. Properly I ought to begin a new mode of life, but at my age that is no longer possible.

And so I only look upon each day that lies immediately before me, and do what lies nearest to me, thinking of nothing beyond.

And in 1806 he wrote the fine threnody, his Epilogue to the *Lied von der Glocke*, when that poem was presented in tableaux on the Weimar stage as a celebration of Schiller's memory. A nobler tribute has never been paid by one poet to another than the often quoted lines :

> Denn er war unser ! Mag das stolze Wort
> Den lauten Schmerz gewaltig übertönen !
> Er mochte sich bei uns, im sichern Port,
> Nach wildem Sturm zum Dauernden gewöhnen.
> Indessen schritt sein Geist gewaltig fort
> Ins Ewige des Wahren, Guten, Schönen,
> Und hinter ihm, in wesenlosem Scheine,
> Lag, was uns alle bändigt, das Gemeine.

Looking back on the friendship between Goethe and Schiller, it is not easy to endorse the view usually held that Schiller's influence was an unconditional gain to our poet. Its chief significance remains the fact that Schiller quickened and kept alive in Goethe an interest in poetry ; in his all too engrossing preoccupation with science and art, he might otherwise have neglected it altogether. This was, indeed, a gain ; but when we look into Goethe's reaction to his younger friend's virile intellect, the benefits are not so apparent. As his early antipathy to the poet of *Die Räuber* slackened, Goethe gradually lost sight of the essential antithesis between his own nature and his friend's ; or rather, he discovered that the antithesis was immaterial ; that they were both " approaching the same summit from different sides ". But was this not also an illusion ? Truer would it have been to say that they were climbing different summits, albeit summits of equally dominating eminence. The illusion had unfavourable consequences for Goethe ; for it prevented him understanding that Schiller's poetic method, transferred to himself, would only result

in barrenness. It was a misfortune that he allowed
himself to be drawn into Schiller's metaphysical and
rhetorical orbit. Schiller, who cherished equally er-
roneous illusions about Goethe, helped to complete the
alienation of his genius from actuality ; tempted him
to see more in the idea which his work was to express,
than in the plastic embodiment of the idea in the real,
where Goethe's strength had always lain. With his
wonderful idealizing mind, it *was* possible for Schiller
to create poetic masterpieces on abstract premisses ;
but when Goethe attempted it, the result fell far short
of what his genius, following its natural bent, might
have achieved. Thus, if a balance has to be struck, it
was undoubtedly Schiller rather than Goethe who was
the gainer by the friendship. To both poets it had
meant a return to poetry. But the magnificent series
of dramatic masterpieces from *Wallenstein* to *Wilhelm
Tell* is more eloquent testimony to this return—a
return in Schiller's case from historical and abstract
philosophical studies—than Goethe's disappointingly
meagre record in these ten years.

"WILHELM MEISTERS LEHRJAHRE", "HER-MANN UND DOROTHEA" AND "DIE NATÜRLICHE TOCHTER"

IT has always been known that Goethe was engaged on *Wilhelm Meister* years before his journey to Italy; and discerning readers have felt that it, like *Egmont*, *Iphigenie* and *Tasso*, links up Goethe's production with that of his "Sturm und Drang", and thus helps to establish continuity in his intellectual development. It was not, however, until 1910 that we obtained any clear idea of how much in the novel belonged to his first Weimar period. In that year, by a lucky chance, a manuscript copy of the first *Wilhelm Meister*, or, as it was then entitled, *Wilhelm Meisters Theatralische Sendung*, was discovered in Switzerland and has now its place in the poet's complete works. The case is parallel to that of the discovery of the first draft of *Faust*, and we have a similar difficulty in appraising the early *Meister* at its true value. In Goethe's case first thoughts may not have always been the best; and it cannot be gainsaid that the second thoughts in respect of *Wilhelm Meister*, whereby the hero's apprenticeship to the art of the theatre gave place to an apprenticeship to the art of living, raised the novel to a higher plane. On the other hand, the novel suffered, like almost all Goethe's greater works, from his unfortunate habit of spreading their composition over wide periods of time; moreover, what he added to *Wilhelm Meister* after his return from Italy is, in respect of vital poetic qualities, much inferior to the earlier parts. All that

is best in *Wilhelm Meisters Lehrjahre* in the imaginative
sense is to be found already in *Wilhelm Meisters
Theatralische Sendung.*

It is known from Goethe's diaries and letters that
the novel was begun in the summer of 1779; but it
had certainly been thought about much earlier, perhaps
even in the extraordinarily prolific Frankfort years.
The first book was completed in 1780. Then came a
pause. The second and third books were not written
until 1782; Books IV and V followed in 1784 and
1785; and on November 11th, 1786, the sixth book
was finished. These six books were ultimately condensed into Books I–IV of the *Lehrjahre.* The whole
work was originally intended—the plan was drafted at
the end of 1785—to extend to twelve books; it is now
reduced to eight.

Wilhelm Meisters Theatralische Sendung is a novel about
the theatre, and the theatre only. Wilhelm, son of a
well-to-do merchant, Benedikt Meister, is a youth of
the better middle class whose imagination as a child
is stirred by a marionette theatre. This is all related
at much greater length than in the completed novel
where it is described by Wilhelm in retrospect. As he
grows up, his interest in the real theatre is kindled by
a company of players in the town; and he falls deeply
in love with a pretty actress, Madame de B——, or
Marianne. Again, this love-affair, which culminates
dramatically in Wilhelm's discovery that Marianne is
unfaithful to him, appears in much greater detail in the
older novel. We learn, too, more about the antecedents
of Pfefferkorn who assumes the stage name of Melina,
and his runaway match with the citizen's daughter who
is to share with him the miseries of the actor's life.
Wilhelm is bitterly disillusioned by the issue of the
affair with Marianne; and although he continues to
write plays and study the drama, he is open to be convinced by his practically-minded friend and future
brother-in-law Werner that the counting-house has also

its ideal side. He is induced to take an active part in his father's business and sets out on a mission to collect debts. The novel thus slides into the form so congenial to the eighteenth century of the description of a journey, interspersed with motley adventure. In the course of his travels Wilhelm's latent interest in the theatre is reawakened by the amateur efforts of factory workers ; and a little later he falls in with a theatrical troupe directed by a Madame de Retti. Here he sees enough of the dark side of the actor's profession. With the money he has collected for his father's firm he comes to the rescue of the troupe, and makes Melina, who with his wife has joined them, its manager. The living and realistically drawn figures which people this motley world—Melina and his wife, the sprightly Philine, the amatory Friedrich and the cynical Laertes—are all already in the earlier novel ; so, too, are the romantic figures of the ethereal child Mignon, whom Wilhelm purchases from a troupe of acrobats, and the mysterious Harper— two figures that endeared the novel as no other feature in it to the new Romantic generation. And on Mignon's and the Harper's lips are put the immortal lyrics, *Wer sich der Einsamkeit ergibt*, *Nur wer die Sehnsucht kennt*, and, above all, *Kennst du das Land*. No poem Goethe ever wrote captured so completely the affections of the world as the last of these:

Kennst du das Land, wo die Zitronen blühn,
Im dunkeln Laub die Gold-Orangen glühn,
Ein sanfter Wind vom blauen Himmel weht,
Die Myrte still und hoch der Lorbeer steht,
Kennst du es wohl ? Dahin ! Dahin
Möcht' ich mit dir, o mein Geliebter, ziehn !

Kennst du das Haus ? Auf Säulen ruht sein Dach,
Es glänzt der Saal, es schimmert das Gemach,
Und Marmorbilder stehn und sehn mich an :
Was hat man dir, du armes Kind, getan ?
Kennst du es wohl ? Dahin ! Dahin
Möcht' ich mit dir, o mein Beschützer, ziehn !

187

Kennst du den Berg und seinen Wolkensteg ?
Das Maultier sucht im Nebel seinen Weg;
In Höhlen wohnt der Drachen alte Brut;
Es stürzt der Fels und über ihn die Flut,
Kennst du ihn wohl ? Dahin ! Dahin
Geht unser Weg! o Vater, lass uns ziehn !

The company of Madame de Retti undertakes to perform a tragedy by Wilhelm himself, *Belsazar*, which, it will be remembered, was the theme of Goethe's own earliest attempt at a drama of the higher kind. At the first performance the actor, a protégé of Madame de Retti's, to whom the principal rôle of Darius had been assigned, is found to be intoxicated, and Wilhelm is induced to step into the breach. He acquits himself with complete success ; but the substitution at the next performance of the original actor brings the company to disaster. In the completed novel Wilhelm's triumph in his own play is excised, Goethe having rightly felt that it anticipated and weakened his subsequent appearance on the stage as Hamlet.

Wilhelm, who has now forgotten his father's affairs, accompanies the troupe to the castle of a Graf. On their way thither they are attacked by robbers ; Wilhelm is wounded and left unconscious, to be taken care of by Philine and Mignon. He himself believes that he owes his life to a lady whom he calls " the fair Amazon ". All this and the lively experiences of the company at the castle, where the Gräfin takes a warm interest in Wilhelm, have passed over, with little modification other than condensation, into *Wilhelm Meisters Lehrjahre*. Here, too, the hero meets a Major Jarno who shows him the limitations of the French theatre and opens his eyes to the greatness of Shakespeare. The threat of war disperses the company and Wilhelm finds his way to what is obviously Hamburg, where his friend Serlo—Goethe is possibly thinking of the great German actor Friedrich Ludwig Schröder—directs the theatre. He is now introduced to a more stable

188

state of theatrical affairs; Serlo accepts him as a member of his company, and the manuscript of the *Theatralische Sendung* ends on the eve of his assumption of the rôle of Hamlet.

Wilhelm Meisters Theatralische Sendung is emphatically a book about real things and real people; its motley theatrical vagabondage is depicted with extraordinary vividness. Goethe has not yet to have recourse, as when he took up the novel fifteen years later, to schematizing and inventing, when, like so many great writers, he often lapses into stultifying artificiality. It is true the early *Wilhelm Meister* has no higher life-wisdom to inculcate; its sordid world is trivial enough compared with the subsequent symbolization whereby the hero's apprenticeship of the theatre—he does not appear more likeable or praiseworthy by the change—is converted into an apprenticeship to the art of life. At the same time we must not forget that the *Sendung* already contains the wonderful interpretation of Hamlet as a soul broken by a burden too heavy to bear, an oak-tree in a costly vase, which made the *Lehrjahre* a milestone in the critical appreciation of Shakespeare. If, however, we will envisage Goethe, not as a moralist, but as a creative artist, we cannot but regret that the old torso was not completed in the spirit in which it was conceived. In the vivid depiction of people and events our own great fiction of the eighteenth century contains nothing greater.

But how was the novel to be completed ? Whither was it all to lead ? Was Wilhelm's goal, the creation of a national theatre for his people, to be achieved ? Or was disillusionment here, too, to creep in and lead him to abandon his plans ? Against the latter view is the original title of the novel which was certainly not meant to be ironical. Again, it has been suggested that Wilhelm's adventures might have closed romantically with his flight with Mignon to the land of the orange and the myrtle ; but once more, one remembers how sympathetically the "fair Amazon" had been introduced, and feels that she was thus early destined to be Wilhelm's bride. Nor is Marianne forgotten in the story; Wilhelm learns that she has borne him a son, and that son could hardly have been omitted when the continuation was originally planned. Much, no doubt, that is now narrated in the fifth book belonged to the first draft, including the disclosure of Mignon's antecedents. We might go even still further and claim that, when Goethe as early as 1778 defined his ethical purpose in the words : " More definite sense of limitation and thereby of the possibility of a truer expansion," he was voicing an idea which casts its shadow not merely across the *Lehrjahre*, but across the *Wanderjahre* as well.

Goethe took *Wilhelm Meister* with him to Italy, and it is frequently mentioned in his correspondence; to the duke, for instance, he wrote in February, 1787, that Meister is forty when he proposes to end the novel, and that he ought to finish it before he had himself passed that age. Still, the right mood was difficult to recapture. He did not resume his work in earnest until he had finished *Tasso*; and in 1794 he brought pressure to bear upon himself by offering it to the Berlin publisher Unger. The task that lay before him was a formidable one. The old manuscript had not merely to be revised and condensed, but modified in accordance with his new standpoint, where the theatre was no longer the be-all and end-all of the book; even Schiller had complained as he read the manuscript, that it made the impression of being a book for actors rather than one about them. And, of course, it had also to be completed; for it is doubtful whether anything more than a rough plan existed of what is now the seventh and eighth books of the *Lehrjahre*. We may regret the disappearance, in the revision, of much realistic detail; but the novel has benefited by concentration; the characters have been polished and refined, Philine gaining particularly by the revision.

The *Theatralische Sendung,* as we possess it, had left Meister within sight of a climax in his relations to the theatre, namely, his performance of Hamlet. It is, however, improbable that this performance was to mark the end of his "theatrical mission". In the completed novel, however, it does end it. In resuming work Goethe lost no time in initiating the change ; we see it at once in the letters which Meister writes to his friend Werner at the opening of the fifth book. He says :

> In a word, the cultivation of my individual self—here, as I am—has, from my youth upwards, been constantly though dimly my wish and purpose. . . . The harmonious development of my nature which was denied me by birth, is exactly what I most long for.

This is not the old Wilhelm whose sole obsession was the theatre. To Goethe now the final goal is no longer the establishment of a national theatre ; art is not the end, but merely the stepping-stone to the higher life, a doctrine which Schiller had so eloquently and persuasively preached in his *Briefe über die ästhetische Erziehung des Menschen* (1795). The insufficiency of the "æsthetic education" as an end is indicated in the novel by the mysterious warning which Wilhelm reads on the veil of the ghost at the performance of *Hamlet* : "For the first and last time : Flee, youth, flee ! " Wilhelm had only turned to the theatre in his first enthusiasm—so Goethe regards it now—because he saw here an escape from the sordid world around him and a foundation for his own culture. The best the theatre had given him was to teach him to appreciate Shakespeare. Now the change comes ; not in the substitution of the ideal for the real does his aim lie, but in the subjection of the real to the ideal. The contemptuous irony with which the practical life was viewed in the *Sendung* compared with that of the theatre, is reversed ; indeed, so far from the artist's calling being the highest fulfilment of life, it is now shown to lead to its abnegation. Thus the theme of *Wilhelm Meister* becomes the development of the hero's personality; the " Theaterroman " has become a " Lebensroman "; and instead of passing to mastership, Wilhelm finds himself again an apprentice, but this time an apprentice to life.

With the death, after a performance of *Emilia Galotti*, of Serlo's sister Aurelie, the actress who had played Ophelia, is symbolized the final passing of the art of the theatre; in her Goethe had personified that art in its highest and purest form. She had, we learn, been seduced and deserted by Lothario, and we are at this stage given to believe that a child Felix is hers. On her death-bed Aurelie charges Wilhelm to seek out and avenge her betrayer, and she entrusts him with a manuscript, *Die Bekenntnisse einer schönen Seele,* which is inserted as the sixth book of the novel. These *Confessions,* for which Goethe utilized records and memories of the friend of his youth, Susanna von Klettenberg, are usually regarded, even by indulgent critics, as a stopgap, a device to obliterate, or at least make less noticeable the joining of the new plan to the old. The *Confessions* also provide a bridge linking up the new characters necessary to bring the novel to a conclusion, with those we already know. It has been contended by critics who would find a more organic reason for this sixth book, that Goethe intended here to stress the significance of religion in helping man to attain to spiritual freedom. The " beautiful soul " has sustained a harrowing disappointment in life by the loss of the man she had loved, and had thereby risen to a higher life; she had attained that personality which in Goethe's eyes was the highest of human virtues. But it is questionable whether the poet had any such subtle purpose in interpolating her life-history.

In Book VII the theatre has completely sunk beneath the horizon. Wilhelm finds himself in another world. His new friends, Lothario and Therese, are concerned not with the cultivation of art, but of the practical life. Lothario, essentially a man of action, has travelled widely; he has been in America, been involved in financial troubles; and now, matured by his manifold experience, has come to recognize that his activities may be unfolded as well at home as abroad : "Here or nowhere is America!" He devotes himself with enormous energy to the development of his estate, and brings his ripe knowledge to bear upon it. Therese, again, is the practical life in person; she devotes herself to the management of her house and the bringing-up of children : a world which presents the greatest possible contrast to the dream-world in which Wilhelm had hitherto lived. "Insight, order, discipline, command: that", she declares, "is my affair." Instead of faith she has insight, instead of love constancy, not vague hope but confidence. Jarno and the Abbé supplement these two as the exponents of the new culture. Jarno had formerly been a sceptical realist, inclined to cynicism; now he has developed into a man of penetrating understanding and practical zeal; while the Abbé, who had brought up Lothario and Therese, is the representative of a more contemplative culture; he has now the main share in the education of Wilhelm. These enlightened people form themselves into a secret society, the "Company of the Tower", suggested by the practices of freemasonry in which Goethe took so deep an interest. The Tower is a wing of the castle built by the Uncle, a mysterious building of secret passages and locked doors. This company is the directive force in Wilhelm's new life; it holds up to him new aims and high ideals of the brotherhood of man. "From our Tower a society shall go forth which will spread over all parts of the world, and of which people from everywhere may become members."

Thus Wilhelm is educated to an activity based upon a sense of duty to mankind. This achieved, he is admitted to the Company of the Tower, and his

apprenticeship is at an end. He receives a " Lehrbrief "
or indenture, the first part of which is concerned with
the false education of the artist, the second with the
true education in the art of life. Action, it declares,
lies within every one's grasp ; even the child learns it
in play, and imitation is inborn in all of us ; but
thinking is less easy, and to act with wisdom has to
be learned by bitter experience and disillusionment.
The true artist is a discoverer ; not to know what is
known, but with the help of the known to unveil the
unknown : this alone transforms the disciple into a
master. Thus the aim of all true education and culture
is to direct man's energies into the right channels of
activity. " Man does not reach happiness until his
undisciplined striving has defined its own limitations."
Or, as Schiller summed up the novel : " Wilhelm
Meister emerges from an empty and undefined ideal
into a definite active life without thereby losing his
idealizing power."

The novel closes with the death of Mignon, who is
now revealed to have been the daughter of an Italian
marchese, the Harper, by an incestuous union ; the
Harper himself ends in insanity. She is laid to rest with
much ceremony in the Hall of the Past, in which stands a
statue of its builder, the Uncle, bearing in its hand a scroll
on which are inscribed the words " Gedenke zu leben ! "
(" Think of living ! ") ; and over Mignon's bier four
youths sing : " Travel, travel back into life ! Take
with you holy earnestness, for earnestness alone makes
life eternity ! " This is the most vital ethical lesson
which *Wilhelm Meisters Lehrjahre* has to teach.

More than a quarter of a century later Goethe summed
up his novel to Eckermann in these words :

> This work belongs to my most incalculable productions
> for which I myself hardly possess the key. One looks for
> a central point, and that is difficult and not always good.
> I should think that a rich and manifold life, which passes
> before our eyes, is in itself something without an expressed

purpose, which, after all, only concerns the idea. But if you must have something of that kind, keep to the words which Friedrich in the end addresses to our hero; he says: "You appear to me like Saul the son of Kish, who went out to seek his father's asses, and found a kingdom." Hold by this. For at bottom the whole seems to say nothing else than that man, in spite of all follies and confusions, is led by a higher hand and does reach a happy goal.

In other words, this modern son of Kish who had gone out to find the art of the theatre, finds the art of life. And on the strength of this majestic idea—at bottom hardly different from that of *Faust* itself—the novel has been transformed into what has been well called an " Odyssey of culture ".

But there is a grave side to this development of the novel. In the vivid art which had been so manifest in the motley pictures of the *Theatralische Sendung*, the continuation which Goethe provided in these years is lacking; he seems to have lost his old magic life-giving power; and the new figures of the book, Lothario, the Abbé, Therese, the transformed Natalie, are only shadows, paper creations without real life. Moreover, they are linked up with each other by the absurd coincidences of kinship, of which the eighteenth-century novel was never ashamed; everybody turns out to be related in some degree to everybody else. Wilhelm himself, after being attracted by Therese, fulfils what was apparently the first intention of the *Sendung*, and chooses Natalie as his wife, while Lothario and Therese are disabused of the fear of too close consanguinity, and united. But all these happenings leave us cold; and even Wilhelm has become only a mannequin on whom Goethe drapes his ethical ideas; we can sympathize with Carlyle who in one of the many moments of impatience when he was engaged on his translation, called him contemptuously a mere " nose of wax ". And the world in which these new personages move is no real world. One is tempted to say that the art of the theatre, which *Wilhelm Meister* had been originally planned to exalt, took a cruel revenge upon her faithless devotee, and triumphed in the end. For what are all the settings and para- phernalia of these last books—the mysterious tower, the freemasonic mummery, the operatic ceremonies— but things of the theatre : artificially lit tableaux, pro- perties of lath and plaster, mere stagecraft ? The creator of the Wilhelm who had on the stage given life to Hamlet, is now powerless himself to recall the great Shakespearean art which had once been his, of en- dowing his creations with reality.

Is it too much to read out of the disappointing falling-off in *Wilhelm Meisters Lehrjahre* the conclusion that as Goethe grew in wisdom—and a wiser outlook upon life no man ever had than Goethe from his return from Italy until the end—it was paid for at the cost of his productive genius as a poet ? That seems to be the lesson of these years, the key to the understanding of the post-Italian Goethe : he who believed that he had " found himself " in Italy as an artist, had in reality there lost his artist's soul.

Critics have liked to dwell on Schiller's share in the transformation of the old theatre novel ; his letters to Goethe as he read the proofs of the first book and the manuscript of the remainder, are full of penetrating observations. And, after all, the new ethical ideas of the *Lehrjahre* were Schiller's own. But it is doubtful whether his co-operation was to Goethe's advantage. There was a kind of metaphysical incitement in Schiller's criticism which encouraged Goethe in his quest of ideas, and a corresponding neglect of the plastically real. It had a paralysing effect on his creative imagination, and helped to complete the descent from the heights he had attained in his earlier work.

Is it to be wondered at that *Wilhelm Meisters Lehrjahre* was received by those who knew Goethe's genius best,

Herder, Wieland, Charlotte von Stein, with no enthusiasm?—that it has never meant to the world what *Werther* meant; and that it belongs, even in Germany, to the category of masterpieces which are more often praised than read?

But it would be unfair to leave Goethe's novel on this negative note; for *Wilhelm Meisters Lehrjahre* does remain the central work of prose fiction in Germany's literature; it represents a type of novel that is peculiarly and nationally German. We may well see in it a kind of far-off event to which the fiction of the eighteenth century from Gellert through Wieland was dimly feeling its way—nay, more, as a descendant of the magnificent " Bildungsromane " of Germany's past, the *Parzival* of Wolfram von Eschenbach and the *Simplicissimus* of Grimmelshausen. And it is the fountainhead of the Romantic German novel of the nineteenth century down to the greatest of all Germany's Romantic novels, *Der grüne Heinrich* of Gottfried Keller.

Although the letters to Schiller throw disappointingly little light on the growth of *Hermann und Dorothea*, there is much to learn from them concerning the spirit in which that poem was planned and written. We see how completely Goethe had been won over to Schiller's idealistic approach to the problems of literary creation; and a tiny essay on epic and dramatic poetry, embedded in the correspondence, to which both poets attached their names, is equally applicable to Schiller's dramatic art and the art of *Hermann und Dorothea*. Schiller completed the process in Goethe's mind which Italy with her revelation of antique beauty had initiated: his conversion to an idealizing classicism; and once this classicism had taken root in him, it grew, as it grows in all minds that yield to its spell. The subjective realism of *Götz* and *Werther* had been long repudiated by Goethe as a thing of evil, a " Gothic " crime against the majesty of art, and now even the tempered and still subjective classicism of *Iphigenie* and *Tasso* had become a turned page in his life-book. The " great confession " of poetry, once in Goethe's mind the supreme end and essence of his own work, was now ruthlessly eliminated from it; experiences and emotions had to be sifted and sublimated before they were acceptable as even the raw materials of poetry; it was no longer, in our poet's eyes, legitimate art at all to transfer ordinary human beings into a poem, unvarnished and unidealized, unscrutinized for their general and universal aspects. Thus the classic veil was descending on this great northern mind; generalizing, typifying, ordering, were now the serious business of his genius; not, alas, creating.

Much of this development has, for good as well as for evil, left its mark on *Hermann und Dorothea*. For good, in so far as Goethe has abandoned the undisciplined and disturbing formlessness of his early work; *Hermann und Dorothea* is a " regular " poem, an epic idyll of surpassing formal beauty. Its balance and proportions are irreproachable, its contents are divided over nine cantos, each dedicated to one of the Muses—without, it is true, much relevance to the matter of the section over which each particular Muse is chosen to preside; and it is written in Greek hexameters magically adapted to the music of the German tongue. Such beauty of form is in itself a virtue of the highest order. But it is less easy to accept Goethe's commitment to the classic dogma, when one remembers that he had already given the world masterpieces of transcendent genius which were innocent of " classicism " in any form. *Hermann und Dorothea* is essentially a classic poem. Its hero, Hermann, is conceived on classic lines; that is to say, he is not a particular German youth, but a generalized type of German youth; Dorothea is a typical German maiden; and the host of the Golden Lion and his wife are equally representatives of their class. These figures have, so to speak, been rolled like pebbles in a brook, until all

their sharp corners are rubbed off, or they are—if one
may be anachronistic—the product of composite photo-
graphy. This process completed, the essence of the
type distilled, Goethe—having enough of his old sense
of reality left to appreciate the dangers of schematism—
proceeds to superimpose upon them a new realism ;
he takes his generalized portraits and touches in, with
the deft brush of the perfect artist, individualizing traits.
His skill is particularly noticeable in the subtlest figure
of the poem, the Apothecary ; and it tempts us to seek
a model for Hermann's mother in Goethe's own, and
Dorothea has even been associated with Lili Schönemann. It may well be that specific subjective traits
are not absent ; but the process by which the resem-
blance between portrait and model is achieved is
a very different one from that whereby Lotte Buff
passed into immortality in *Werthers Leiden.* The great
figures in the creations of Goethe's youth, Götz
and Weislingen, Clavigo and Don Carlos, Faust and
Mephistopheles, know nothing of the curry-comb of
æsthetic theory. Similarly, the background of the poem
has been invested with a semblance of particular realism
which has entrapped commentators into fruitless con-
troversies concerning the actual town of the Rhineland
in which Goethe laid his scene, whereas it is merely
a classically constructed, typical town built up from
innumerable memories.

The outline of Goethe's story came from a chronicle
which described how, some seventy years before,
Protestants had been harshly exiled from Salzburg by
an intolerant archbishop ; the poet transferred an
anecdote there related to his own time, and framed it
in the great Revolution. The Revolution, and the
Revolution alone, dates *Hermann und Dorothea* ; its
ominous rumblings form its dark background, as the
Thirty Years War was the " finstre Zeitgrund " of the
noble tragedy on which Schiller was engaged at the
same time. The lines which Goethe dedicates to the

Revolution contain the best that he had thought about it, and his idyllic scene is as a haven of refuge amidst the upset and turmoil of Europe at the century's end. In his sixth canto Goethe crystallizes and sanctifies with a halo of poetry his attitude to the passing of the old régime. The words are put upon the Judge's lips :

> Nicht kurz sind unsere Leiden ;
> Denn wir haben das Bittre der sämtlichen Jahre getrunken,
> Schrecklicher, weil auch uns die schönste Hoffnung zerstört ward.
> Denn wer leugnet es wohl, dass hoch sich das Herz ihm erhoben,
> Ihm die freiere Brust mit reineren Pulsen geschlagen,
> Als sich der erste Glanz der neuen Sonne heranhob,
> Als man hörte vom Rechte der Menschen, das allen gemein sei,
> Von der begeisternden Freiheit und von der löblichen Gleichheit !
> Damals hoffte jeder sich selbst zu leben ; es schien sich
> Aufzulösen das Band, das viele Länder umstrickte,
> Das der Müssiggang und der Eigennutz in der Hand hielt.
> Schauten nicht alle Völker in jenen drängenden Tagen
> Nach der Hauptstadt der Welt, die es schon so lange gewesen
> Und jetzt mehr als je den herrlichen Namen verdiente ?
> Waren nicht jener Männer, der ersten Verkünder der Botschaft,
> Namen den höchsten gleich, die unter die Sterne gesetzt sind ?
> Wuchs nicht jeglichem Menschen der Mut und der Geist und die Sprache ?

And after describing the avenging wrath of the German people, he points the moral :

> Möcht' ich den Menschen doch nie in dieser schnöden Verirrung
> Wiedersehn ! Das wütende Tier ist ein besserer Anblick.
> Sprech' er doch nie von Freiheit, als könn' er sich selber regieren !
> Losgebunden erscheint, sobald die Schranken hinweg sind,
> Alles Böse, das tief das Gesetz in die Winkel zurücktrieb.

And yet one feels that the French Revolution has not its place here by any natural right ; it is something of an obtrusion on a poem and theme which are classically timeless ; it is not vital to *Hermann und Dorothea*, and its removal would make no essential difference. Again, this was not the method Goethe employed in *Götz* or *Werther*, or even *Tasso*, where the theme grew out of and was dependent upon its *milieu*; here the *milieu* is, as it were, superimposed.

George Henry Lewes, it will be remembered, claimed *Hermann und Dorothea* as Goethe's most perfect creation; and, indeed, throughout the nineteenth century there was a general consensus of opinion to this effect. If we are less willing nowadays to concede to it this exceptional position, it is not because we are less sensitive to its wonderful harmonious beauty, but because we feel an element of calculation in its perfection; it is no living experience as *Werther* and the first *Faust* had been, a spontaneous tribute to the compelling power of genius. When—to use again the terms of Schiller's æsthetics—the great "naïve" poets of the world thus become "sentimental", they lose something of their power. Of no man of genius is this truer than of Goethe; for him the experience, and the experience alone, provided the life-blood of his creative work.

Hermann und Dorothea brought Goethe popular success, such as he had not known since *Götz von Berlichingen* and *Werther*; it rehabilitated him in the eyes of his own people, and to this rehabilitation the publication of the First Part of *Faust*, some nine years later, put the crown. But Goethe probably did not grasp, or, if he did, cared little wherein the success of his epic consisted. He did not see that the classical form was hardly a factor of moment in its success; in fact, the reading public stumbled over his hexameters, and would have taken the poem more readily to their hearts had it been couched in a simpler, less exotic rhythm; possibly, too, remembering the unvarnished realism of Goethe's model, Voss's *Luise*, they may have resented the Homeric turns and the didactic wisdom the classically polished talk put upon the lips of simple folk. They felt instinctively the fallacy of Goethe's view that there was anything Homeric, or suitable to be treated in the grand Homeric manner, in his sentimental story. But in spite of these disadvantages, *Hermann und Dorothea* did hold a mirror up to the life of its time; contemporaries recognized its types as their own; and above all, they delighted in its idyllic love-story that ended harmoniously with marriage bells. Goethe, misjudging their applause, accepted it as an encouragement, not to write another *Hermann und Dorothea*, but to proceed further on his Homeric way; to justify the thought that Schiller had instilled into him that he was a Greek born out of his time. In his *Achilleis*, which remained a fragment, he grappled with Homer on his own ground; and he carried his new generalizing art to its logical conclusion in *Die natürliche Tochter* on the one hand, and to *Pandora* and *Helena* on the other. Thus with *Hermann und Dorothea* opened the last phase of Goethe's classicism, which was only to find its close with Faust kneeling at the feet of the Virgin; neither the magic of the East nor the mysticism of Romanticism —the most potent forces on his late years—was able to shake this allegiance.

The last greater work which Goethe wrote during Schiller's lifetime was *Die natürliche Tochter*, planned as the first part of a trilogy of the French Revolution and published in 1804. On other works, as we have seen, the Revolution had thrown its shadow, but so far, it had evaded Goethe's full grasp. Here at last he believed that he had found a theme in which he could embody all his thought on the greatest political upheaval of his time. Towards the end of 1799 Schiller lent him the first volume of the *Mémoires historiques de Stéphanie Louise de Bourbon Conti, écrits par elle-même* (1798), and he read it with such pleasure that on the following day he borrowed the second volume. Here in this mediocre and unreliable autobiography of an illegitimate daughter of Prince Conti and the Duchesse de Mazarin he found what he sought. " In the plan,"

Goethe tells us, "I prepared a vessel in which I hoped to precipitate with becoming seriousness all that I had written and thought through many a year on the French Revolution."

Her story—how her father had promised to naturalize her, but had been prevented by his family; how she was incarcerated in a monastery, forced into a loveless marriage and was finally involved in the terrors of the Revolution—covered the entire course of the Revolution from its eve to the beginning of the Consulate. Goethe made slow progress with the execution of his plan, and the first part was not completed until November, 1803; the remaining two dramas were never written.

Probably no work of the poet's was ever so coldly received by his contemporaries as *Die natürliche Tochter*, no drama so emphatically rejected by the theatre. The philosopher Fichte stood alone in giving it the first place among his works. It is thus not surprising that Goethe was discouraged. The failure was largely due to his uncompromising classical theories. The drama is not wanting in great flashes of poetic diction, and it opens dramatically enough. Eugenie, hunting in a forest, is thrown from her horse. When she recovers consciousness, the King promises her legitimization and recognition at court; but the political unrest puts difficulties in the way. Meanwhile the Secretary, the agent of the family, carries her off by stealth to a monastery, in order to prevent the fulfilment of the King's promise; he reports to her father the Duke that she has been the victim of a fatal accident. She is now virtually dead to the world. In Act IV we meet her and her Hofmeisterin in an unnamed seaport where she is confronted with the alternative of marrying a commoner or being exiled. She accepts a judge in the town. That is all. Its human interest is of the slightest and of the French Revolution there is hardly a trace.

Die natürliche Tochter has been called " marble cold " ; it is less cold than colourless—colourless and timeless ; it might well play outside any definite epoch at all. This impression is accentuated by the fact that, with the exception of the heroine, the characters bear no names ; had Goethe called his king Louis XVI and his duke Philippe-Egalité the play would, no doubt, have met with a warmer response ; the public would at least have known that it was part of that " vessel " in which the poet hoped " to precipitate his thought on the Revolution ". As it is, Goethe seems determined to be classic in the most uncompromising spirit of that doctrine, to present his audience with types, not individuals, and thereby all nexus with historical reality is destroyed. And even the most inveterate hunter for empiric bases in Goethe's poetry has not ventured to suggest a living model for Eugenie. *Die natürliche Tochter* is thus a fatal illustration of whither Goethe's preoccupation with poetic theories was leading him ; it is the least successful of all his attempts in his period of classic aspiration to impose upon his literature an alien art-form.

CHAPTER VIII

THE FIRST PART OF "FAUST"

IN this period of Goethe's preoccupation with classic modes of literary expression—a preoccupation which to many young ardent souls in the age of Romantic revival seemed little less than abdication—a strange thing happened. In 1808 appeared the First Part of *Faust*, a work that could by no means be described as " classic ", and, indeed, was soon to be regarded as the very pinnacle of the Romantic poetry of Germany and the highest achievement of her national literature.

Faust has already been discussed in these pages, and it has to be discussed again ; for both symbolically and actually it is the work of the poet's whole life, the imaginative record of his spiritual development and the receptacle of his most vital wisdom.

In following its history subsequent to the wonderful Frankfort torso, a long period of quiescence has first to be recorded ; there was little in the first ten years of Goethe's Weimar life that was likely to stir the Faustian chords in him ; the discordances of the early drama ceased to trouble, for in Weimar he had found peace, and in his love for Charlotte von Stein emotional tranquillity. What first turned the poet's thoughts back to his *Faust* was the contract for a collected edition of his works to which we owe the completion of *Egmont*, *Iphigenie* and *Tasso*. In the prospectus of this edition (issued in 1786) it is stated that the seventh volume is to contain, besides two acts of *Tasso*, *Faust*, *ein Fragment*. It is natural, however, that he should also have had in view the completion of this fragment :

and his correspondence from Italy contains many hints of his intentions and hopes in this direction. A notable passage is the following from the *Italienische Reise* :

> First the plan of *Faust* was drafted, and I hope that I have succeeded in this operation. Naturally it is one thing to write out the piece now, and it was another fifteen years ago. I think it will not lose by the lapse of time, especially as I believe I have found the thread again. Also, as regards the tone of the whole, I feel consoled ; I have already written a new scene, and if I were to smoke the paper, I think no one would be able to pick it out from among the old scenes. As my long rest and isolation have brought me back to the level of my former existence, it is remarkable how much I remain myself and how little my inward self has suffered by the intervening years and happenings. The old manuscript gives me often much to think about when I see it before me. It is still the first manuscript ; in its chief scenes it was written off without a preliminary draft, and now it is so yellowed by time, so worn (the sheets were never bound), so brittle and rough at the edges that it really looks like the fragment of an old codex, and I who then transferred myself to an earlier world must now transfer myself into the early time which I have myself lived through.

But it was not to be : Goethe decided that the completion of *Faust* lay beyond his powers ; and thus the great drama was first presented to the public in the form of the *Fragment*. This is essentially the *Faust* whose acquaintance we have already made. But there are a few additions and omissions. Immediately following the scene with Wagner is inserted a dialogue between Faust and Mephistopheles which now, in the complete drama, follows the conclusion of the pact : it leads over to the old scene—shortened and modified—between Mephistopheles and the student. " Auerbach's Cellar " is turned into verse and, as has already been indicated, altered in order to transfer the main business of the scene from Faust to Mephistopheles: Faust himself only utters five words. Then follows a new scene, the "Hexenküche", which was composed in 1788; and after the scene "Am Brunnen" still another new scene written in Rome, "Wald und Höhle", was inserted. Following this, the *Fragment* contains only two short scenes, "Zwinger" and "Dom". There is no mention of Gretchen's brother; and the three supremely tragic scenes with which the original sketch closed are omitted.

The most important inference to be drawn from these changes concerns the omissions. Goethe could only have withheld the close of his drama for one reason: he hoped to find the way to a less ruthless solution whereby the tragic end of his hero might be avoided; Faust, as Lessing had felt before him, must be saved. Man is formed in God's image; God has endowed him with the divine fire of reason; he is essentially good. That spirit in him which bids him ever strive to a fuller life, greater knowledge and power, cannot be relegated to eternal damnation. As long as the divine spark of inspiration is not dead within him, Faust must not be represented as worsted in his conflict with the powers of evil.

It is, as we have already seen, not easy to infer what Goethe originally meant to do with the young Faust whom he had depicted in the opening scene of his Frankfort drama. Filled with loathing for the vanity of learning, bemoaning his wasted life, he had turned to his magic books; he hoped to find a panacea for all his ills in intimate communion with nature. He conjured up the Earth Spirit, only to meet with humiliating rebuff when he dared to assert his spiritual equality with that spirit. This episodic scene contains virtually all that we hear of the Earth Spirit; but it could hardly have exhausted Goethe's first intentions. The scene "Forest and Cavern", however, gives us some idea of how he once proposed to develop Faust's relations to the Spirit. We gather from this scene that, in spite of the failure of Faust's first attempt, the Earth Spirit, presumably summoned a second time, did assist Faust to that communion with nature for which his soul yearned, helped him to penetrate deeper into nature's secrets than is given to ordinary eyes to see. We learn, too, that it was the Earth Spirit who gave Faust as companion Mephistopheles: but this Mephistopheles did not merely, as the servant of the Spirit, further Faust's cravings for a more complete union with nature: he also stirred up in him baser desires, dragging him from one pleasure to another, without, however, succeeding in satiating him.

Thus "Forest and Cavern" clearly belongs to the older plan of the drama, in which the Earth Spirit was to play a decisive rôle. But we are left in uncertainty as to how Goethe intended to develop Faust's relations with the Spirit. Did he mean to introduce these before Faust meets Gretchen at all; or was their culmination to be reserved for a scene for which the "Walpurgisnacht" was at a later date substituted? Such a scene might well have provided the long "dwelling in the wilderness" which lies between Faust's abandonment of Gretchen and his return to find her as the murderess of her child in prison. It is impossible to say. But one thing is certain: there is little poetic justification for the insertion of "Forest and Cavern" either, as in the *Fragment*, after the scene "At the Well", or, as in the completed drama, after that in the "Garden Arbour". If "Forest and Cavern" is not to precede the appearance of Gretchen in the drama, its only possible place is surely after the issue of the duel with Valentin which compels Faust to flee. In the First Part as we know it, Goethe employs the scene, to all appearance, to mark the passing of time, and to account for Faust's absence and his ignorance of Gretchen's fate in the months that elapse between the " Arbour " scene and the tragic close. It is the absence of Faust that now matters, not his appeal to the Earth Spirit, which is only a vestige of an older and subsequently abandoned plan.

More important and fruitful was the second motive which appears in the scene " Forest and Cavern ", namely, the implication that Mephistopheles is unable to satisfy Faust, to stave off his disillusionment; the sensual pleasures in which he plunges him are powerless to effect such an end. With this motive is concerned the new dialogue inserted before the scene between Mephistopheles and the Student. We hear no more now of Mephistopheles's co-operation with the Earth Spirit in furthering Faust's communion with nature and of Faust's aspirations towards equality with that Spirit; indeed, in lines preceding the scene in question, and probably also written at this time, Faust frankly admits that he has nothing to hope for in this direction. The Faust of these added lines voices a new desire, and one that is but faintly adumbrated in the early draft, namely, to live the great, full life of humanity, to share the joys and sufferings of the race. Mephistopheles endeavours to dissuade him from this empty aspiration : to induce him to rest satisfied, as a " microcosm ", with those possibilities of unlimited personal enjoyment with which he is able to provide him. And then, harking back to the disillusioned scholar of the first soliloquy, Mephistopheles sums up the problem in its new form : " If thou wilt once despise reason and all the learning reason has built up, then art thou unconditionally my victim." Here is the kernel of the new ethical problem of *Faust*; and it holds within it the possibility of Faust being saved. There is little doubt that Goethe had in Italy at last come to grips with the conditions of the pact which his Faust was to make with Mephistopheles. If Faust is to win the wager, it must depend on Mephistopheles's inability to destroy his better nature and his respect for reason. Goethe did not include the actual pact in his *Fragment*—possibly he did not feel sufficiently sure of its actual terms, upon which so much depended—but the general character of the agreement must have been already clear to him when the *Fragment* was published.

Another change which Goethe introduced into his poem in Italy concerns the age of his hero. The youthful Faust of the first sketch gives place—without, however, any alteration of the original lines of the first scene—to an elderly scholar, more scholar than adept in magic, who looks back over a long span of life wasted in barren learning. The poet's motive for the change may have been the purely subjective one that he himself had grown older and sedater; or he may have desired to adapt his hero to the tone of the Volksbuch and to the historical tradition. An effort to introduce historical colouring, entirely lacking in the original draft, and make Faust definitely a personage of the sixteenth century, is noticeable elsewhere, more particularly, in the dialogue between Faust and Wagner in the scene "Before the Gate". Moreover, once Goethe had resolved to stress the motives of disillusionment and dissatisfaction, an elderly Faust was more suited for his purpose than a young man—more likely to sink into that pessimistic despair which makes him an easy prey to Mephistopheles's wiles. On the other hand, an older Faust could no longer find pleasure in the crude pranks of Auerbach's Cellar; and it became necessary, if he were to play the rôle of Gretchen's lover, already mapped out for him in the original drama, that he should regain his youth in the "Witches' Kitchen."

The next stage in the history of *Faust* is associated with Schiller, without whose encouragement and stimulus it is doubtful whether the work might have ever advanced beyond the stage of the *Fragment*. Schiller took the initiative in a letter to Goethe of November 29th, 1794:

But with no less desire I should like to read the fragments of your *Faust* which are not yet printed; for I confess to you that what I have read of the piece is the torso of Hercules. In these scenes there is a power and a fullness of genius which reveal unmistakably the master: and I should like to follow as far as possible the great nature that asserts itself in them.

To this Goethe replied on December 2nd:

Of *Faust* I can give you nothing now; I dare not untie the packet which holds it prisoner. I could not make a copy without working it out further, and for this I do not feel the courage. If anything can make it possible for me to do this in the future, it will certainly be your sympathy.

Schiller returned repeatedly to the attack. A letter to him from Wilhelm von Humboldt of July 17th, 1795, reveals a regrettable gap in our records: he thanks Schiller for detailed information about Goethe's *Faust*. "The plan is grandiose: it is only a pity that for that reason it will remain only a plan." The letter in question to Humboldt is lost; and we are deprived of what would have been the earliest indication of how Goethe intended to continue his drama. For, of course, only to such a continuation could the expression "grandiose plan" be applicable. Thus, thirteen years before the publication of the First Part, Goethe had apparently conceived plans for the sequel to that Part which he hoped to write. Meanwhile Schiller's insistent interest was bearing fruit, and Goethe seems in August, 1795, to have given some kind of promise that he would allow him to print parts of *Faust* in his journal *Die Horen*.

1797 is an important date in the history of the *Faust* composition. Goethe's lost confidence returned: he took up the old manuscript again, and set to work in earnest to fill the gaps. The weightiest evidence of his progress is to be found in the following passages from his correspondence with Schiller. On June 22nd he wrote:

> As it is very necessary that I give myself something to do in my present restless state, I have resolved to turn to my *Faust*, and if not to complete it, at least bring it a good way forward, by breaking up what has been printed, and arranging in large masses what is already finished or thought out, thus preparing more precisely the execution of the plan which is still really only an idea. Now I have just taken up again this idea and the form I propose to give to it, and I am pretty much in agreement with myself. I should like if you would, some time in the course of a sleepless night, be so kind as to think the matter over, tell me what demands you would make upon the whole, and, like a true prophet, interpret to me my own dream.
>
> The different parts of the poem admit, in respect of their tone, of varying treatment, as long as they are subordinated to the tone and spirit of the whole; the entire work, too, is subjective, and thus I can work at it at odd moments; and I am at present in the position of being able to achieve something. Our ballad studies have brought me again on this misty and cloudy way; and circumstances recommend me in more than one sense to wander for a time along it.

Schiller replied at once, on June 23rd, on which date is an entry in Goethe's diary: " Detailed scheme of *Faust*." Schiller wrote:

> Your request to me to acquaint you with my expectations and desiderata is not easily fulfilled; but as far as I can, I will try to pick up your thread. If I am unsuccessful, let me imagine that I have found the fragments of *Faust* by chance, and have to complete them. So much I will only remark here, that *Faust*, the piece namely, cannot, in spite of all its poetic individuality, repudiate entirely the demand that it should have symbolic significance; and that is probably your own idea. The dual character of human nature and the unsuccessful endeavour to combine the divine and the physical in man cannot be lost sight of; and as the story passes, and cannot but

pass, into the fantastic and the formless, it will be impossible to keep narrowly to the theme; you will be led from it to general ideas. In short, the demands on *Faust* are at the same time philosophical and poetic, and, turn as you will, you will be compelled by the nature of the subject to treat it philosophically; your imagination will have to be reconciled to serving a rational idea.

But I am hardly saying anything new to you; for you have already in a high degree begun to satisfy this demand in what you have already written. If you really now get to work on *Faust*, I have no more doubts of its ultimate completion; and this fills me with great pleasure.

Goethe thanked him on the following day and on the same date entered in his diary that he had written the "Dedication to *Faust*". Goethe's rapid progress with the poem at this time tempted Schiller to write to his friend Körner that Goethe would probably "finish his *Faust*" before long. The "Vorspiel auf dem Theater" was probably now written; possibly also the "Prolog im Himmel" planned, although the last touches could hardly have been given to it before 1800. That Goethe was able to tell Schiller in December that he had decided to insert "Oberons goldene Hochzeit" in *Faust*, implies a considerable approach to the completion of the First Part as we know it.

Schiller's hopes were not, however, fulfilled; the next three years were lean years in the composition of the poem: and in the early months of 1800 Schiller begged the publisher Cotta to bring some pressure on Goethe to complete his work. This was effective, and the "Walpurgisnacht" scene was elaborated in that year, besides much that is now relegated to the Second Part. Finally, in April, 1801, Goethe wrote to Schiller:

To *Faust* in the meantime, something has been done. I hope that soon the only thing missing from the great gap will be the Disputation scene. This, however, has to be regarded as a thing for itself, and it cannot be thrown off lightly.

The " Disputation " scene remained, however, only a plan; Goethe's notes and sketches, now published as " Paralipomena " to *Faust*, give us a rough idea of its scope. Where and how it was to be inserted in the poem are, however, not clear; its purpose in the economy of the action may have been to provide Mephistopheles, after his assumption of human shape, with a less abrupt entry into the drama than at present, and to lead up more gradually to Faust's pact with him.

Again, between 1802 and 1805, *Faust* was laid completely aside; and in the summer of the latter year Goethe arrived at the decision to publish only the First Part of the drama. In April, 1806, the manuscript was finally revised for printing. The publication was delayed owing to the unsettled conditions caused by the Napoleonic wars, and it did not appear until 1808.

In taking up the First Part of 1808, we are mainly concerned with the question: How did Goethe put into effect his new standpoint towards the tragic problem of *Faust*? The reader is not left long in ignorance of the nature of the change; for Goethe provided, as we have seen, his original tragedy with three prefatory poems or prologues, one of which leaves no doubt concerning the new plan. First, there is a purely personal Dedication of surpassing beauty which links up the poet's own present with his past; then comes a " Prolog auf dem Theater "—a kind of *Tasso* drama in miniature, which was suggested by the *Sakuntala* of the Indian poet Kalidasa. This work had been translated into German from the English in 1791. The " Prologue in the Theatre " has, of course, no connexion with *Faust*; at most, it reminds hearer or reader that the little world of the drama is but a stage, and its figures are merely players; while the third prologue, the " Prologue in Heaven ", shows us that these players are but puppets in the hands of an all-wise God. The last prologue is the most significant of all, for here the problem is given, once and for all, its new setting. The individual tragic fate of the man who dares greatly in the realm of the spirit, is framed in the Christian faith. God Himself becomes an actor in the tragedy, and the conflict ceases to be one between a mortal endowed with free will and the powers of evil, in which the mortal necessarily succumbs ; free will is, in fact, eliminated, and the Faust problem assumes gigantic proportions, indeed sublimity, as a conflict between the powers of good and evil in God's world. In this conflict the good necessarily triumphs—the optimist Goethe could see no other issue—or rather evil is bereft of its antagonism to good, and as it were, harmonizes and coalesces with it. Faust is thus, at the outset, exonerated from his tragic guilt ; the sting is taken out of his tragedy. "Knowst thou my servant Faust ? " the Lord asks Mephistopheles. "Fürwahr" is the answer :

Fürwahr! er dient euch auf besondre Weise.
Nicht irdisch ist des Toren Trank noch Speise.
Ihn treibt die Gährung in die Ferne,
Er ist sich seiner Tollheit halb bewusst ;
Vom Himmel fordert er die schönsten Sterne,
Und von der Erde jede höchste Lust,
Und alle Näh und alle Ferne
Befriedigt nicht die tiefbewegte Brust.

   Der Herr. Wenn er mir jetzt auch nur verworren dient,
So werd' ich ihn bald in die Klarheit führen.
Weiss doch der Gärtner, wenn das Baümchen grünt,
Dass Blüt' und Frucht die künft'gen Jahre zieren.

   Mephistopheles. Was wettet ihr ? den sollt ihr noch verlieren,
Wenn ihr mir die Erlaubnis gebt,
Ihn meine Strasse sacht zu führen !

   Der Herr. So lang er auf der Erde lebt,
So lange sei dir's nicht verboten.
Es irrt der Mensch so lang er strebt. . . .
Zieh' diesen Geist von seinem Urquell ab,

Und führ' ihn, kannst du ihn erfassen,
Auf deinem Wege mit herab,
Und steh' beschämt, wenn du bekennen musst:
Ein guter Mensch in seinem dunklen Drange
Ist sich des rechten Weges wohl bewusst.

The good man can never be blind to the true path;
all men must err on their dark way; and error is
neither guilt nor sin. Faust's destiny, we are assured,
lies in God's hands, and He will lead him to victory
against all the powers of negation. Thus the tragedy
of Faust has become a "Divine Comedy"; a message
to the tragic sufferer not to despair, for God is good.
The temptation of the devil—now no longer a devil
but a servant of God—is framed in a conception of the
world where sin and evil have no substantial existence.
No longer is the salvation of man bound up with the
choice between right and wrong; it cannot be denied
to the mortal who merely errs, error being but another
name for the inadequacy of human vision. It is made
dependent on the keeping alive within him of the spark
of aspiration, the power to strive, the will to " achieve
great things ". As long as man's will to realize himself is not dead, he remains God's servant; and God
will not let His servant fall.

The early *Faust* poem gives no indication of the
nature of the pact which Faust makes with Mephistopheles; it was not included in the *Fragment* either.
Everything obviously turned round the terms of the
agreement, and these were not lightly to be set down
before the whole problem of Faust's relations to
Mephistopheles had been solved. Doubtless the pact
was originally conceived on the traditional lines of the
Volksbuch. But the new wager had to be adapted
to the perspective created by that greater wager which
Mephistopheles has made with God. The condition
of Mephistopheles's triumph is no longer success in
the simple task of dragging Faust down into the mire,
of exposing him to temptations which he cannot resist

—in the legend and the original plan these were amply sufficient to bring about Faust's undoing—but in killing his soul, in destroying his better self, the godlike in him. Mephistopheles's task is not to "ruin" Faust, to involve him in sin and debasement, but to satiate him : to bring his soul into that apathetic equilibrium, when every desire in him is extinguished. On this condition the new contract is framed :

> Werd' ich beruhigt je mich auf ein Faulbett legen,
> So sei es gleich um mich getan !
> Kannst du mich schmeichelnd je belügen,
> Dass ich mir selbst gefallen mag,
> Kannst du mich mit Genuss betrügen ;
> Das sei für mich der letzte Tag !
> Die Wette biet' ich ! . . .
>
> Werd' ich zum Augenblicke sagen :
> Verweile doch ! du bist so schön !
> Dann magst du mich in Fesseln schlagen,
> Dann will ich gern zu Grunde gehn !
> Dann mag die Totenglocke schallen,
> Dann bist du deines Dienstes frei,
> Die Uhr mag stehn, der Zeiger fallen,
> Es sei die Zeit für mich vorbei !

Faust thus anticipates what the "spirit that denies" in his blindness to the divine impulses in man, cannot yet understand, the eternal and inevitable insatiability of the human soul. Mere pleasure, happiness, can never produce a stable satisfaction. The ultimate issue of the wager is whether Faust shall lose or gain his soul, or, in terms of the popular conception of the after-life, whether he shall or shall not end in the flames of Hell.

As we realize Goethe's difficulties, we begin to see why he has departed from a motive which was not merely inherent in the legend, but was also a constituent in his own first plan, namely, that Mephistopheles should undertake to satisfy Faust's desire for a fuller knowledge of and a more intimate communion

with nature : why, too, he should have—as already in
the *Fragment*—poured scorn on Faust's longings to
gather into himself the joys and sufferings of humanity.
Had Mephistopheles made it his object to satisfy
Faust's legitimate and entirely estimable desires for
knowledge—estimable, that is, in our eyes, however
damnable in those of the sixteenth-century chronicler
of the Volksbuch who regarded them as mere " Für-
witz " or over-curiousness—had he aided him in his
aspiration to become the equal of the Earth Spirit, the
ground for a real tragic conflict would have been
removed ; the spectator could not have admitted
that Faust's guilt demanded tragic retribution. Thus
Goethe was obliged to reduce the task of his devil to
undermining Faust's moral nature by sensual temptations, to making him " sink into sin ". But once
having admitted the essentially noble nature of Faust,
the difficulty of carrying out his conflict with Mephistopheles in the spirit of tragedy was great ; and when
at last Faust's earthly career is approaching its close,
he does admit his satisfaction, does bid the passing
moment stay, the devil has to be cheated out of his
stipulated reward, and the terms of the pact annulled
by the intervention of Divine grace. But this is a
problem which has to be considered later.

    With the formulation of the wager between Faust
and Mephistopheles and the solemn signing of the contract in Faust's blood, the purely dramatic interest in
Faust's ultimate personal fate ceases. We now know
the inevitable close : Mephistopheles cannot triumph ;
his undertaking to provide his victim with satisfying
happiness is doomed to failure. The drama becomes a
chain of futile efforts on the part of the tempter to
attain his end, first in the narrow world of personal
emotion, and then in the great world of a far-flung
activity ; and it is in these episodes, rather than in the
central problem of Faust's development and fate, that
the poetic interest from now on lies.

Having established the terms of the pact between Faust and Mephistopheles, Goethe was faced with a new difficulty : how were they to be grafted on to the original torso of the play ? How was the aspiring Faust of the opening scene of the drama to be brought into such a frame of mind that he should entertain at all the idea of a pact with the emissary of evil ? It might be said that practically all that Goethe added—in respect of the relations of Faust and Mephistopheles —to the *Fragment* of 1790 and to the First Part of 1808 is concerned with this problem.

The scene "Vor dem Tor" is neither in the first *Faust* nor in the *Fragment*: but there is a strong presumption in favour of its early conception in some form as a means of introducing Mephistopheles. As it stands, "Before the Gate" may have been given its present shape subsequent to Goethe's stay in Italy : in its typifying presentation of the Easter crowd and its choruses of citizens, girls, students, soldiers, it bears the stamp of the "classic" Goethe ; but surely much of the wonderful conversation between Faust and Wagner belongs to an earlier stage of the composition. The splendid poetry—some of the very finest that the First Part contains—in which Faust reveals the passionate distraughtness of his soul, could hardly have been written by the calm and optimistically-minded Goethe of the post-Italian time. The ideas which are expressed here are an amplification of the bitter discontent of the first soliloquy, the conversation is a natural continuation of the first conversation with Wagner ; we are here clearly in contact with an older stratum of the poem. At most, it might be admitted that those passages in which Goethe has something to say of Faust's earlier life, of his father and the efforts of father and son in combating the plague, may belong to that period when the poet was endeavouring to give his hero—already an older man—more definite root in the sixteenth century.

But " Before the Gate " only brings Goethe to the threshold of the real difficulty : the preparation of Faust for the signing of the pact in the second Study scene.   In the actual introduction of Mephistopheles, his first appearance as a dog, his transformation into the semblance of a wandering scholar behind Faust's stove, in the obstacle which the pentagram offers to Mephistopheles's departure, Goethe had made use of old, popular devil-lore.   But there is an inconclusive-ness and even a purposelessness in the introduction of these motives, which bear witness to the confusion intro-duced into this part of the drama by Goethe's chang-ing plans.   Even the beginning of the scene, Faust's preoccupation with the Bible, his interpretation of the " logos ", reads like the fragment of some undeveloped intention ; as it stands now, it serves no dramatic purpose beyond that of exciting the evil spirit behind the stove.   These scenes are only concerned with introducing Mephistopheles into the drama ; the diffi-culty which through long years had held up the com-pletion of the work was how to make Faust a willing victim of Mephistopheles's allurements.

Goethe soon saw that if the essentially noble and right-minded Faust of the maturing plan is to be rendered pliant, it could be only in one way : the pessimism and discontent of the early Faust must be intensified, developed into a withering and soul-de-stroying negation.   There can thus in this pact scene no longer be any question of Faustian aspiration to complete knowledge of nature, still less of an all-embracing sympathy with humanity.   Faust, if he is to give himself into the hands of Mephistopheles, must be reduced to passionate despair ; all the positive values of life must be wiped out for him.   This is the meaning and purpose of that terrible curse which Faust pronounces on all the good and noble things of human life.   " Thou hast destroyed the beautiful world," sing the spirits who, in spite of Mephistopheles's efforts to discredit them by claiming them as his own, might well be the voice of Faust's own better self. His utter abjection is now complete; the slate is clean for the new writing.

This " knot " was among the last—as it was the hardest—which Goethe had to unravel. Whether he has chosen the best way of doing it, that is to say, of leading up to the signing of the pact, criticism has never been sure; but, given the unalterable conditions laid down by the earlier plan of the drama, it is difficult to see how the object could have been more satisfactorily attained.

To a late date in the composition belongs the continuation of the first soliloquy of Faust, after the withdrawal of Wagner. No part of *Faust* shows more plainly the grafting of the new on to the old than just this scene. The mood of Faust is not and could not be materially different from that depicted in the earlier part of the scene; but the tone is new; Faust has become another and a maturer personality. Again he runs through the gamut of disillusionment and revolt, no longer primarily as the suffering victim, but rather as a representative of humanity undergoing a universally human fate. The passionate, petulant note of individual despair gives place to reasoned and reflective wisdom; the new Faust speaks calmly in measured iambic verse; " we " takes the place of " I ". He now seeks freedom from his tribulations and the hemming fetters of the earthly life in death, a step which the first Faust, even after his rebuff by the Earth Spirit, could never, we feel, have countenanced. When this mature and elderly Faust raises the poison vial to his lips, it is not in Werther-like repudiation of an intolerable existence; it is a calmly reasoned resolution to seek in death the portal to a higher life. And when the pealing of the Easter bells stays his hand, it acts like a conciliating message from heaven bringing him back to peace and harmony with himself. This

awakening optimism and faith in life are foreign to the
Faust of the First Part; and we hear nothing more of
them until they are intoned in full major harmonies in
the Second Part. No scene of the First Part foreshadows more clearly the sequel that was to be, or provides a clearer transition from the First to the Second
Part, than this continuation of Faust's first soliloquy.

Still another late addition to the First Part of *Faust*
was the " Walpurgisnacht ". How far the conception
of such a scene goes back to Goethe's first preoccupation with the subject it is impossible to say : it is con-
ceivable, as we have seen, that he may have early
entertained the idea of putting the crown to a devastat-
ing accelerando of sensual temptation by involving
Faust in the orgy of the Blocksberg ; but, as it stands,
the scene was composed in the years 1800 and 1801.
Its most apparent purpose in the economy of the drama
is to provide Mephistopheles with a last opportunity
of counteracting the uplifting force of Faust's love for
Gretchen. Mephistopheles's intention is thwarted by
the vision of Gretchen herself, with the red line of her
doom on her neck, which brings Faust headlong back
to her prison. The scene fulfils a similar function—
the separation of Faust from Gretchen—to that for
which " Forest and Cavern " may have been originally
designed. In Goethe's presentation of Faust and
Mephistopheles's ascent of the Brocken there is a splendid sweep of imagination, and that in spite of the somewhat chilling generalization in the classical style of the
phenomena there. But once the summit of the Brocken
is attained, the poet's powers seem to have left him
in the lurch. His plans for a grandiose culmination
in which Satan was to hold his court remained undeveloped : and the gap was filled by irrelevant literary
satire, and the equally irrelevant " Intermezzo " of
" Oberon and Titania's Golden Wedding ", the latter
not originally intended for *Faust* at all.

In the closing scenes of the drama, which must always

be numbered among the greatest tragic scenes in literature, Goethe wisely did not attempt to modify the poignancy of the human conflict or—apart from the last words of the drama—adapt it to his later standpoint; and in converting the final scene from prose into verse, his great art did not desert him. With the assurance of " a voice from above " that this most poignant of tragedies is no tragedy in the eyes of God, and with the departure of Mephistopheles and Faust, the First Part closes. With such fundamental changes in its spiritual vistas as the poem underwent, consistency or unity was unattainable; no explanation or interpretation could justify the incorporation of the ruthless tragedy of Faust's love for Gretchen in the new " world-drama ". Merely to provide that tragedy with a spacious framework of optimism could not mitigate the intense woe and suffering it contains; and it would have been small consolation to Faust and Gretchen to know that they were enmeshed in a net of evil devised —like the misfortunes and sufferings of Job—for their undoing by God Himself. Nor does it bring conviction to the harrowed beholder to be assured that this evil is but an instrument in the hand of the All Good; that all ways lead to goodness, to God. Goethe has not succeeded in harmonizing the tragedy with his later conviction of the insufficiency of tragedy; and indeed, the whole original *Faust* drama would have had to be recast to bring it into line with his new untragic attitude to life.

PART III

OLD AGE
1805–1832

CHAPTER I

AFTER SCHILLER'S DEATH

THE death of Schiller made a deep incision in Goethe's life, deeper perhaps than might have been expected in view of the limitations to their intimacy. But the stage of their friendship which meant most for both poets was obviously that of which the correspondence has little to tell us, the last years, when Schiller was Goethe's immediate neighbour in Weimar, and the need for letters had disappeared. Schiller did perhaps find his way to Goethe's heart to a degree which is not to be read out of their correspondence; his death certainly left a blank which no other of his contemporaries was able to fill. From 1805 onwards Goethe's life took on soberer hues; he began visibly to grow old. As we have seen, he had himself been seriously ill in those tragic May days when Schiller died; indeed, he had never been more perilously near to death's door since the catastrophe that brought his Leipzig student days to a close than he was now. Christiane was unwearying in her devotion to him; and he never forgot it. It helped to stay the widening of the breach between them. His recovery was accelerated by his old panacea for the ills of life: travel and change of scene. In the late autumn of 1805 he paid a visit to Helmstedt and Brunswick; he was accompanied by the author of the famous *Prolegomena* to Homer, Friedrich August Wolf, between whom and the poet a warm friendship sprang up; and on the way home he sought out the old patriarch of German letters, the poet Gleim, in Magdeburg. In the years that followed, Goethe was frequently and often seriously ill—he suffered from abdominal and kidney trouble—and in the summers he regularly betook himself to drink the waters at spas such as Karlsbad, Marienbad, and Teplitz. Here, too, away from Weimar, he was able to forget for a while in pleasant company the darkening political horizon; and in Jena, where he retained a room for himself, he constantly sought refuge from the irksome formalities and distractions of court life.

In these years political trouble loomed very large on the horizon of Europe; the even course of the eighteenth century, which had been broken by the Revolution, was giving place to something new, strange and enigmatic. Goethe, as nonplussed as any of his contemporaries, could not find the key to it. Whatever the future might have in store, it was increasingly clear that there could be no going back; the placid days of the *ancien régime* would never return. Goethe cherished fewer illusions on this score than the political prophets of his time. A sorely tried Europe, hardly extricated from the blood-bath of the Revolution, was confronted by what to most contemporaries seemed still more momentous changes. The new disturbing factor was Napoleon. From the quiet seclusion of Weimar Goethe had watched Napoleon's meteoric course with intense interest; even with respect and admiration. In this man Goethe saw the potential healer and restorer, the leader who was to bring Europe back to health and sanity. But the political situation assumed a new aspect when Goethe's little state was drawn into Napoleon's net. He had never approved of his duke's love of and reliance on Prussia; and now, as he had foreseen, Weimar had to pay the penalty. Events moved rapidly in the autumn of 1805. Ulm fell; Vienna capitulated and the battle of Austerlitz was fought; the old Holy Roman Empire crumbled to pieces. The invincible conqueror now opened his campaign against Prussia, the main obstacle on the continent to his progress. The Thuringian states had refused to enter the West German alliance which Napoleon had formed under his protectorate; they threw in their lot with Prussia. Prussian troops were hurried southwards, and billeted on Weimar; the menace, not merely to the amenities of life, but to its very security, was becoming every day more threatening. Then at last on October 14th, 1806, came the fatal battle of Jena. The court fled—all except the Duchess Luise, who played the only heroic rôle in the *débâcle*. She alone had the courage to confront Napoleon, and defend her husband for his loyalty to Prussia with a spirit that softened the emperor and called forth his admiration. The French soldiery threw itself on the defenceless town, pillaging, burning, and destroying. Goethe's house was invaded, and his life menaced by two drunken *tirailleurs*; the danger was only averted by the bravery and presence of mind of Christiane, whom Goethe saw insulted by French officers as his mere mistress. Partly this incident, and partly the general uncertainty of life and property, matured his resolve to give his union with her that legal sanction which would ensure her respect, and provide for her in the event of his own violent death. The very next day, October 19th, he took steps to have his marriage solemnized. On the whole, however, Goethe came off relatively well in these terrible days; for Marshal Ney, who was to have been quartered on Goethe's house, issued orders that so distinguished a man should be respected, and his property spared.

Peace came in 1807, a peace bought, as far as Weimar was concerned, at the cost of a humiliating and crushing indemnity of nearly two and a half million francs; the duke was compelled to enter Napoleon's Rheinbund. In the following year, on October 2nd, 1808, Goethe had his famous interview with the Emperor at the congress of princes in Erfurt. This meeting of two of the greatest men in Europe—Goethe was then fifty-nine, Napoleon forty—is one of those events which the biographer is tempted to invest with peculiar significance ; and for Goethe the meeting certainly had significance. He went, it is true, unwillingly to Erfurt, for only a few days before, the news had reached him of his mother's death ; but the duke sent for him, and he felt that it was his duty to accompany and stand by his master in a difficult and embarrassing situation. It is to be regretted that we have no reliable account of this historic interview, or of the subsequent meeting of Napoleon and Goethe at Ettersburg, near Weimar ; it would have outweighed many pages of Goethe's recorded conversations. Perhaps, however, Goethe and Napoleon had less to say to each other that mattered than we like to imagine ; weightier political questions may have been discussed at Napoleon's interview with Wieland, a poet likely to have been more after his heart than Goethe. The first meeting, we are told in one account, lasted a full hour ; in another, only a few minutes ; and if we are to judge by Goethe's own record of it—it was not written, it is true, until sixteen years after the event—it could not have taken very long. In any case, it was a very informal affair ; Napoleon was at breakfast, others were present, and interruptions frequent. The conversation was literary ; and political matters could hardly have been touched upon. The two men met, however, in high mutual respect. Ever since the days of his " Storm and Stress " Goethe had had unbounded faith in the thought which he has voiced in *Faust*, that what matters in the world is not the word, but the creative deed ; and Napoleon was pre-eminently a man of deeds, the living exemplar of genius militant. The emperor, on his part, knew by more than hearsay that Goethe was a writer of genius. He told him of his admiration of *Werther* ; how he had read that novel no less than seven times. He even ventured to criticize it, pointing out to Goethe how he had confused the issue of his hero's tragedy by introducing an alien and disturbing motive in the shape of ambition. And Goethe smiled and bowed, politely admitting the justice of the great man's opinion. Napoleon, however, apparently knew more of Goethe's work than *Werther*; he complimented him as a dramatist; possibly he had heard of *Götz von Berlichingen*, or it may have only been that he was informed at the interview that Goethe had translated Voltaire's *Mahomet*. At the later meeting he suggested to Goethe that he should write a tragedy on Julius Cæsar; he was confident that it would be better than Voltaire's *Mort de César* which they had just witnessed in the Weimar theatre with the great French actor Talma as Brutus.

> Ce travail pourrait devenir la principale tâche de votre vie. Dans cette tragédie il faudrait montrer au monde comment César aurait pu faire le bonheur de l'humanité si on lui avait laissé le temps d'exécuter ses vastes plans. Venez à Paris! Je l'exige de vous!

Napoleon's comment on the Erfurt interview: " Voilà un homme! " has become enshrined as a tribute to his insight into Goethe's genius.

In Goethe's attitude to Napoleon the factor of patriotism played no rôle at all. Not for a moment did Goethe see in him the enemy. If the thought crossed his mind, he, doubtless, brushed it aside with the reflexion that, after all, Napoleon had been fighting Prussia, and that his own little state had committed a fatal error in espousing the wrong cause. At no time of his life could the word patriot be used of Goethe. His fellow-countrymen are sensitive to this lack of national pride; outsiders, on the other hand— and with equal injustice—have regarded it as a virtue which stamped him as a " good European ". In point of fact, the want of patriotism in the German writers of the pre-Napoleonic time—and beyond a flickering pride in Prussia's national hero, Frederick the Great, none possessed any—was but a natural consequence of that thing of shadows, the Holy Roman Empire. One might feel oneself a Prussian, a Saxon, a Bavarian ; but the Holy Roman Empire could inspire no patriotism ; and in the cosmopolitan eighteenth century it was more uplifting to think of oneself as the citizen of an empire that knew no narrow geographical bounds or common language. Thus Goethe's cosmopolitanism, far from being a superior, theoretically acquired standpoint, was merely the consequence of his being the citizen of a conglomerate state which had no collective political consciousness, not necessarily a higher virtue at all. At the same time, this lack of patriotism had its advantages for a mind like his ; it prevented him from being too seriously obsessed by the narrow world of Weimar ; it had allowed him, in that brief and happy period in Rome, to feel less of an alien and a stranger ; it left him at liberty to admire Napoleon, and, in future days, to sympathize, without national bias, with French and English aspiration and achievement.

The return of peace in 1807 reacted favourably on Goethe's intellectual and imaginative activity. As, too, the sting of Schiller's loss became less poignant, he began to show something of his old resilience ; no doubt, the disappearance of the none too congenial metaphysical atmosphere which Schiller surrounded him with, left him freer to express himself in his own way, untutored, uncriticized, unhampered. The greater part of that year he spent away from Weimar. He went to Karlsbad in May and remained until September. During his stay there he took up again the plans for the continuation of *Wilhelm Meister*, writing a number of the short stories, which, often incongruously enough, swell the bulk of the *Wanderjahre*. More significant for his reconvalescence as a poet was a new emotional experience towards the end of the year. In November he betook himself to Jena in the hope of making less interrupted progress with his literary work there than at home; and, in the household of the publisher Frommann he found a congenial circle. Frommann had a foster-daughter, Wilhelmina or Minna Herzlieb, whom Goethe had known since her childhood; now, a girl of eighteen, she delighted him with her singing of the songs he had written in his youth. In those happy days and evenings when he could cast off the formality of the Weimar Geheimrat, the old emotional chords in him were set vibrating again. Goethe was again in love; but it was a quite unobtrusive rekindling of the old fire, this love for Minna Herzlieb; and from her side there could be no encouragement, for her heart was already engaged. It was only, moreover, a matter of a few weeks, for by the 18th of December he was back in Weimar. But in Minna's company the old poet became young again; an autumnal sunshine came into his life which awakened old memories, and stirred old dreams of the perfect life-companion which he had always sought and had never found.

The immediate precipitate of Goethe's interest in Minna Herzlieb was the series of sonnets which he wrote in December, 1807. The sonnet was a verse-form that had little attraction for him; Goethe was no sonneteer. He had been tempted to try his hand at it now in friendly rivalry with the dramatist Zacharias Werner, who spent several weeks in Jena at the end of the year. His sonnets are essentially of literary provenance; it would be unreasonable to look into them for that subjective emotion which surged through his verses to his early loves, Friederike or Lili. If there is passion in them, it is of a sublimated kind, and deliberately pruned and ordered, fitted into the Procrustean bed of Petrarcan form. Before the end of the year Goethe was back in Weimar. The dream— a dream that seemed fantastically to mingle with memories of Lili—was over; at least the sleeper had recognized that it was but a dream; he was once more immersed in the old round of social and official duties and functions. To the quickening of Goethe's emotional life by Minna Herzlieb we owe, however, two of his greater works, the novel *Die Wahlverwandtschaften* and the uncompleted drama *Pandora*.

Another interesting woman who came into his life at this time was Bettina Brentano, daughter of Goethe's old love of the *Werther* time, Maximiliane von La Roche. Bettina, who first visited him in 1807, has left us her record of him in one of the strangest and yet most fascinating books we possess about Goethe, her *Goethes Briefwechsel mit einem Kinde*, published in 1835. For the biographer, whose object is to arrive at facts and truth, it is a quite unreliable book, romantically imagined and romantically untrue. Its untruth begins on the title-page; for the twenty-two-year-old Bettina was anything but a child; and if the letters she wrote to Goethe are sometimes childish, that is but a part of her Romantic affectation. This particular fiction was due to its having come to Bettina's ears that Goethe had, some years before, compared her with his own Mignon. The lack of veracity—and, as we have seen, there is no lack of veracity in the delightful picture which the book conjures up of Goethe's mother—does not, however, affect its peculiar value and charm. If Bettina shares the unbalanced character of her gifted brother Clemens, she has also a goodly share of his genius; and the reflexion she has given us of Goethe in her Romantic mirror helps us to understand him in his relation to the dominant literary movement of the time. Goethe, for whom Bettina wrote her adoring " Dichtung und Wahrheit ", was no doubt attracted by her elfin ways and touched by her devotion, but otherwise seems to have regarded her with only amused tolerance. A year or two later their relationship ended in a shrill discord; Bettina, who had in the meantime become the wife of the Romantic writer, Ludwig von Arnim, allowed herself to speak insultingly of Christiane, and Goethe never forgave her.

The publication of the First Part of *Faust* in 1808 had inaugurated a period of Goethe's life which was quite unusually productive of literary work: in fact, not since the turbulent years in Frankfort had he given so good an account of himself as a man of letters. *Die Wahlverwandtschaften*, as we have seen, appeared in 1809; *Pandora* in 1810; his great treatise on colour, *Zur Farbenlehre*, which he always regarded as one of the highest of his achievements, also in 1810; and these works were followed in the next years by his autobiography, *Dichtung und Wahrheit*. Of minor writings, a life of the landscape painter Philipp Hackert (1809), one of Goethe's Italian friends of 1787 who had left him his papers, has to be mentioned. Lastly, among the smaller poems written in these years, which were, however, not very productive in verse of this kind, stand out *Ergo bibamus* (1810), *Gross ist Diana der Ephesier* (1812), and in the following year, *Die wandelnde Glocke*, *Der getreue Eckart* and *Der Totentanz*.

And yet in spite of this activity these were years of intense dissatisfaction and depression for the poet. Not merely were the political situation and his own ill-health responsible for this mood; he also felt that his work had no resonance in the minds of his contemporaries. With the exception of *Hermann und Dorothea* and *Faust*, it had been received with indifference, even with animosity. Bitterest of all the pills he had to swallow was the almost universal disapproval with which the treatise on colour was received by the scientific world. In point of fact, Goethe *was* out of tune with his age. A new era had been inaugurated in German literature which seemed to him little less than a challenge to his own and Schiller's supremacy: the era of Romanticism. No longer did the classic tranquillity and harmony to which he and Schiller had risen in the first lustrum of the new century, appeal to the generation that was young; they pinned their faith to a passionate mysticism; probed the unfathomed depths of the soul, blended man pantheistically with nature—a very different pantheism from Goethe's in earlier years; they preferred the boundless realm of darkness to the clarity of light and form. To Goethe on his classic heights this seeking after unknown gods spelled confusion, unbalanced thinking, undisciplined emotionalism and chaotic formlessness. The will-less resignation of the new Romanticism to an overhanging fate against which man's puny efforts were powerless—a conviction, no doubt, borne in upon the generation that had witnessed with consternation the inevitableness of Napoleonic conquest—and its consequent flight for refuge to the bosom of the Mother Church, were all in direct antagonism to his own serene Hellenic faith. Indeed, this new movement seemed to him little better than a return to the fantastic confusion of that " Sturm und Drang " from which he and Schiller had emerged into the serenity of classicism.

The world was out of joint in Goethe's eyes, and his imaginative work found in it no answering response.

CHAPTER II

" DIE WAHLVERWANDTSCHAFTEN " AND " PANDORA "

Die Wahlverwandtschaften is one of Goethe's works which has always received warm praise from his critics ; but at no time could it be called a popular book. Goethe himself placed it high among his works, and was disappointed by the less than lukewarm welcome with which it was received in 1809. No one, he insisted, had any right to express a judgment on it who had not read it three times, and to Eckermann he made the claim for it which he had also made for *Tasso* and *Faust*, that it was bone of his bone and flesh of his flesh.

It was originally intended to be one of those shorter stories which in 1807 he began to collect together and subsequently incorporated in *Wilhelm Meisters Wanderjahre*. The actual plan seems to date from April, 1808, and it was completed in its first form with unusual rapidity in the summer of that year. In 1809 he took it up again and expanded it beyond the limits of a short story. In this new form it was completed and published by the end of the year. As far as its narrative contents are concerned, it might well have remained a short story ; but Goethe, under the stimulus of the cross-currents created by his feelings for Minna Herzlieb, was fascinated by the marriage problem it presented and felt the need of probing deeper into its psychological problems.

The structure of the novel is of severely classic simplicity. Eduard and Charlotte had loved each

237

other in early life; but Eduard had yielded to the pressure of his family and married a woman of wealth; Charlotte, too, had married. But later when they are both free, they meet again. Charlotte unselfishly thinks of her young niece, Ottilie, still a girl at school, as a new mate for Eduard, but he has not forgotten his love for Charlotte and insists on marrying her. When the novel opens we find them living a happy quiet life of leisure in Eduard's castle. Eduard proposes to invite an old friend the Captain, who has fallen on evil, or at least inactive days, to live with them and assist in the management of the estate. Charlotte, filled with presentiments, is unwilling to see their peaceful life invaded by a stranger, but consents; and to console her, Eduard suggests that she might bring her niece home from school and give her a home with them. Thus the protagonists of the drama are brought upon the stage. Like four chemical elements, these four people are brought into intimate proximity with each other, and the purpose of the novel is to show the working of their " elective affinities ", the irresistible attraction which grows up between Charlotte and the Captain, and between Eduard and Ottilie. The suggestion of a chemical experiment is early introduced. In the course of a discussion in the fourth chapter the expression " Wahlverwandtschaft " is mentioned, and Charlotte expresses her curiosity about its meaning. The Captain explains. Substances, he says, have a natural affinity with themselves; drops of water unite to form a stream; but they have also affinities to other substances. They may mingle without difficulty, as wine mingles with water; or with the assistance of an alkali, as oil and water. This affinity may be so strong between different bodies that when they combine, the result is the creation of an entirely new body, as when sulphuric acid is poured upon chalk and produces two new products, carbonic acid gas and gypsum. There may even be a third degree of affinity, a double or cross one. Two pairs of elements, A and B, and C and D, may be closely united to each other ; but when all four are brought together, A may prefer to dissociate itself from B and unite itself to D, while B and C are similarly affected. Thus early, Goethe makes his purpose with his novel known ; he will translate A, B, C and D into human terms.

The source of Goethe's interest in this chemical doctrine has been definitely traced ; he found it, he told his secretary Riemer, in a work by a Swedish chemist, Torbern Bergman, who wrote a treatise where the expression first occurs, *De attractionibus electivis*, which was translated into German in 1785 as *Die Wahlverwandtschaften*. In fact, the Captain's disquisition is more or less to be found here, although its precise terms—the use of the letters A, B, C and D— point to another source, the *Physikalisches Wörterbuch oder Versuch einer Erklärung der vornehmsten Begriffe und Kunstwörter der Naturlehre* by the German physicist J. S. T. Gehler (1787-91). Probably Goethe's study of both works goes back to the year 1798.

The basis of the novel having been laid, it becomes a psychological study of emotional dissolution and attraction, an experiment in which human souls and their affinities are the material factors ; a study of the " daimonic " attraction which metes out their fates to men and women. *Die Wahlverwandtschaften* is thus a love story, as, indeed, only *Werther* among his earlier books had been ; but the contemplative Goethe of sixty is less concerned with depicting the irresistible sweep of passion than in analysing it and reflecting upon it. Although a book solely about love and marriage, the novel is primarily a metaphysical study of human relations, or at least a scientific attempt, based on a life's experience, to penetrate their ultimate mysteries. Not merely is the basis of the novel given, but also its ultimate issue. Charlotte finds a superior attraction in the Captain and a love for Ottilie is kindled in Eduard which blots out his affection for his wife. Remembering Goethe's instinctive unwillingness to treat tragic themes, one might have anticipated that he might here have found a way out, a justification for the reign of beneficent law in an all-wise nature. As no blame can be attached to the behaviour of sulphuric acid and chalk, so, too, he might have shown us that the reshuffling of human elements under the influence of affinities for which they have no responsibility, was merely a natural and blameless process which need by no means lead to misery and disaster. But no; the old optimist, who always eschewed tragic issues when he could, has here had the courage to face the ruthlessness of life; again, as in *Werther*, love is no kindly god, but a destroyer. Subtly and insidiously the elective affinities do their work; the victims of the experiment are as powerless to withstand them as are the figures of a Greek tragedy to escape the web of fate which the gods have woven round them. Of the two men, both of whom see clearly the dangers of the situation, the Captain hopes to evade these by a renunciatory act of will; Eduard, with that impetuosity which had laid traps for him in his previous life, accepts the situation, and frankly proposes divorce to his wife. But to escape his growing passion for Ottilie he goes abroad, joins the army and wins military glory. Charlotte still hopes that the machinations of the wrecking affinities may be countered; she opposes the separation and pins her hope on the coming of her and Eduard's child. The child is born, but it resembles the Captain and Ottilie, thus bearing witness to the love that had usurped in the hearts of the parents the love for each other. Ottilie, the most helpless and least conscious victim of the sinister powers, suffers most tragically of all; Charlotte's child is drowned by an accident for which she is responsible. Thus an unsurmountable barrier is raised between her and Eduard; she falls ill and dies—

dies in a halo of transfigured renunciatory sanctity—
and before the novel closes, Eduard, too, broken-
hearted, ends as the victim of his aberration.

This brief outline of the happenings of the novel
takes, of course, no account of the multiplicity of
subtle traits and motives with which Goethe renders
its course not merely probable, but also inevitable.
Clearly much intense thinking went to its construction;
on none of his books did Goethe expend such a wealth
of psychological realism as here. And yet, just in this
conscious and deliberate construction lies the reason
why the novel has never succeeded in bringing conviction, as a work of creative art, to the sensitive reader.
There are great literary artists who have given us
masterpieces of such constructive art, but Goethe was
not one of them; with him " man sieht die Absicht
und man wird verstimmt ". Not so were *Werther* and
the early *Meister* composed; Goethe is only supremely
great when he gives himself up to the inspiration of his
genius; not when he constructs in accordance with
a logical plan. His works are richest in ideas when
he lets the ideas emerge of themselves from the natural
sequence of events.

Die Wahlverwandtschaften has been associated with the
quickening of Goethe's feelings by Minna Herzlieb;
but it is difficult to see, in spite of his " flesh of my
flesh and bone of my bone ", how the novel may be
regarded in any literal sense as a " confession ". To
Eckermann he once said in his last years : " There is
not a stroke in *Die Wahlverwandtschaften* which has not
been experienced, but not one in the form in which
it was experienced." Thus if the word confession can
be used at all, it is only in a subtly veiled sense; the
reader who seeks biographical facts in the novel will be
hard put to it. The " experiences " of *Die Wahlverwandtschaften* are not its happenings; they are its
sublimated emotional content; its deductions from
experience and all the crowding throng of might-have-

beens which surged in Goethe's brain under the new emotional stimulus. Still less should we be justified in tracing portraits in it. Ottilie is not Minna Herzlieb, Charlotte certainly not Christiane, and it would be equally unreasonable to attempt to associate her with the Charlotte who for so many of the best years of Goethe's manhood had dominated his life. We may find much of Goethe in the characters of Werther and Clavigo; but to seek portrait similarities in Eduard is surely a straining of the subjective interpretation of literature. And, indeed, all such attempted identifications are irrelevant; Goethe had travelled a long way towards poetic objectivity since the days of *Werther*.

But might we not go further and question whether the characters of *Die Wahlverwandtschaften* live at all? Are they not mere pale shadows of men and women; puppets moved by the not always invisible wires of abstract theory? As Goethe grew old, the love of shadows and allegorical abstractions grew upon him, as it seems with the years to grow upon all minds of supreme genius. Never again was he to be the creator of men in man's own image; of life as it is; he was content from now on to depict only its abstraction, its "farbigen Abglanz", or coloured reflexion. Just as his characters in this novel bear no names, or at least no surnames, so they are without real, convincing personality; they have no souls. They are theoretical creations, constructively adapted to the rôle they have to play in the human-chemical experiment. The dialogue of these people is mere "paper" dialogue, unnatural and tediously informative. Assuredly Goethe never was an eavesdropper in the castle which he describes; he never heard his men and women talk at all; he merely put upon their lips the edifying things he wanted them to say. It adds no jot or tittle to the living contents of the work to be enlightened on the theme of estate planning; and the book is full of discussions which are anything but relevant to its purpose and meaning. Critics intent, at all costs, on instituting comparisons, have spoken of Ottilie as another Mignon interpreted by the light of classicism; but surely there could be no more damaging comparison. Mignon lives the eternal imaginative life not by keeping a diary crammed with her creator's life wisdom; but by arresting speech that reveals her soul, by songs that can never die. Like her immortal sisters Gretchen and Klärchen, she owes her life not to ratiocination, but to intuition and imaginative genius. These figures start, as it were, instinctively into life— we cannot say exactly why or how; and least of all could the poet himself have told us. Whereas the people of *Die Wahlverwandtschaften* are merely laboured constructions. Even a subordinate figure like Mittler in the novel, who has been compared with the apothecary in so " classical " a work as *Hermann und Dorothea*, comes badly out of the comparison.

A book planned and written on the scheme of *Die Wahlverwandtschaften* is necessarily a book with a purpose; the chemical experiment must prove or disprove the hypothesis which prompted it; and the result of such an experiment in the domain of the spirit is necessarily its moral. What is the moral of *Die Wahlverwandtschaften* ? In point of fact, many different morals have been deduced from or read into it. We are told that it is a defence of the sanctity of marriage in an age when, under the influence of Romantic emancipation, it had come to be regarded too lightly; that it is a vindication of the belated justice which, under the stress of circumstances, Goethe had meted out to his own Christiane. Other critics, again, have pronounced it a grossly immoral book. But the ethical bed-rock of Goethe's ripe wisdom is, no doubt, dimly visible below the conflicts and problems of *Die Wahlverwandtschaften*, that renunciation which, with increasing clearness, he saw as the gateway to the higher life.

But a work of the imagination never stands or falls by its morals; and if we will put Goethe's novel in its fairest light, it is unreasonable to dwell upon any purpose it may have. After all, might it not be best described as a book about the " amor che a nullo amato amar perdona ", about the inviolability of the Eros in men's souls? In Goethe's sixtieth year he learned again from Minna Herzlieb the old lesson that he had been taught so often before, and yet always had to learn afresh.

The other work which has been associated with the name of Minna Herzlieb is the " Festspiel " of *Pandora*, which was written, in the form in which we know it, prior to *Die Wahlverwandtschaften*. Its composition dates from those last months of the year 1807 in Jena when Minna came into Goethe's life : its completion, as far as it is completed—for it is only a fragment—was effected in Karlsbad in May, 1808. The outward occasion for the composition of *Pandora* was an invitation to contribute to a new periodical, *Prometheus*, founded by a Leo von Seckendorf and a Dr. Stoll, a journal the avowed object of which was to restore beauty to the world.

Pandora has, however, older and deeper origins than the stimulus of Minna Herzlieb. We may remember that one of the most grandiose conceptions of the young Goethe was a drama of *Prometheus*; and the fundamental thought of *Pandora*, the mission of beauty in the world of men, had long occupied his mind. The education of humanity by the beautiful was perhaps of all the contributions of Schiller to Goethe's ideas that which had taken firmest hold of him. And just in this age of disturbance and disruption, when Europe had been thrown by Napoleon into the melting-pot, Goethe was deeply concerned with the problem of reconstruction, of bringing back harmony and concord into the world. Might not the fervid gospel of the *Briefe über die ästhetische Erziehung des Menschen* point out the way

to peace ?   It would be fairer to regard *Pandora* less
as a tribute to Goethe's new love—which concerns
only a small aspect of the poem—than as applicable
to the happenings on the world's great stage :   as the
poet's panacea for the distraughtness of his time.

The poem was originally entitled *Pandoras Wieder-
kunft* ; its theme is the restoration of beauty to a
world from which the stern happenings of the
Napoleonic age had banished her.   Pandora has fled
from a state of things which has no use for her, taking
with her Elpore, her daughter and Epimetheus's.   She
is a symbol of the resilient and joyous hope in
human hearts for the coming of better days.   But
the drama is less concerned with her than with the
two protagonists, the brothers Prometheus and
Epimetheus : and, indeed, it might have been desig-
nated by the latter's name.   Pandora herself does not
appear at all in the fragment.

The two chief figures of the masque are Prometheus
and Epimetheus, magnificently hewn, gigantic figures :
and it is their relations and their contrasting characters
which form the chief contents of the fragment.   Prometheus is the embodiment of the creative deed, the
realist who, impatient of all idle idealism, looks to
unremitting toil for the regeneration of humanity.
Epimetheus, on the other hand, is the dreamer who
consumes himself in bitter regret for the loss of his
beloved Pandora, for the beauty that has passed out of
life.   Prometheus devotes himself to tangible problems
which he will solve in a practical way ; Epimetheus,
incapable of translating will into action, dreams of a
fairer day when the beautiful will once more be the
arbiter in the affairs of men.   From the indications
which Goethe has given us of the sequel of the drama
it would seem that Pandora is to give the world her
mysterious box ; but Prometheus to set his face against
its contents being disclosed.   The box, in the contents
of which Epimetheus shows less interest than in the

245

recovery of Pandora herself, was, we learn, to have been ultimately opened and mysteriously resolve itself into a temple, in which Epimetheus sees his dream of a new reign of art and beauty symbolized and realized. Perhaps here, too, as in the Helena act of *Faust*, Goethe was to pay his homage to the spiritual mission of that Romanticism which, for a time at least, he had regarded as a hostile antithesis to the Classic. There are other motives in the drama. Phileros, Prometheus's son, loves Epimeleia, the daughter of Pandora and Epimetheus, and, under a misunderstanding, attempts to murder her : he is banished by his father and attempts to drown himself, to be rescued by peasants and fishers. But what purpose these motives were to represent in the symbolism of the whole remains shadowy and uncertain : they find no development and no solution in the fragment as we possess it.

Thus *Pandora* is enveloped in an obscurity which students of Goethe have failed to dissipate ; it remains the least comprehensible of Goethe's greater poems, and is consequently banished from those smaller collections of his selected works which are familiar to the reading public. Unjustly, for it contains some of the stateliest and most carefully chiselled verse he ever wrote. *Pandora* is a noble expression of Goethe's classicism in its conciliatory apotheosis, when it sought harmony with the Romantic idea. It is not coldly classic as *Die natürliche Tochter* had been : and although the poet's classicism has not yet taken on the warmer colours with which Byron's love of Greece later inspired it in the second *Faust*, the poem is saved from the aridness of allegory by the new warmth and humanity which came into Goethe's life in the winter evenings at the Frommanns' house in Jena. The lament of Epimetheus for the lost Pandora bears traces of the old poet's renunciation of Minna, and the figure of Elpore is in its dim, allegorical way a personification of the happiness which he had missed. The rebellious Titan of the

Prometheus of his youth has given place to a Prometheus
who will build up, not defy and destroy : and who, we
feel, in the unwritten close of the poem would have
attained conciliation with the idealism of his gentler
brother Epimetheus. In *Pandora* Goethe rises to a
higher spiritual peace : and no other of his greater
works breathes a more jubilantly harmonious spirit
than this.

Merke :

Was zu wünschen ist, ihr unten fühlt es ;
Was zu geben sei, die wissen's droben.
Gross beginnet ihr Titanen ; aber leiten
Zu dem ewig Guten, ewig Schönen,
Ist der Götter Werk ; die lasst gewähren !

CHAPTER III

FROM 1811 TO 1817

THE years were moving on apace. When 1815 saw the final overthrow of Napoleon, Goethe was sixty-six. Yet this old man, in spite of a state of health that was far from robust, remained young in spirit; the only sign, indeed, of the encroachment of the years was an increasing tendency to indulge in retrospect, a growing desire to "sum up his existence". During the years of Napoleonic unrest his works had been published in Tübingen by Cotta in a stately edition; and it was, in the first instance, the wish to supply these works with a commentary and binding matrix that led to the writing of his Autobiography. Three volumes of that work appeared under the title: *Aus meinem Leben : Dichtung und Wahrheit*, between 1811 and 1814; the fourth and last was held back until the very end of the poet's life. Even in its completed form, *Dichtung und Wahrheit* is only an autobiography of the young Goethe; it closes with his departure for Weimar in 1775. Goethe had a peculiar reluctance to write about his Weimar life. As far as consideration for the living was concerned, he could have arranged—as he did in the case of his own correspondence with Schiller—for sufficient delay in publication that no susceptibilities might be hurt. But Weimar, his relations to the ducal house and Charlotte von Stein were apparently sacrosanct, not meant for the vulgar gaze; he could not bring himself to drag them into the light and present them from the personal angle which he had adopted in describing his earlier life.

248

By common consent *Dichtung und Wahrheit* is one of the great autobiographies of the world's literature; it remains to this day perhaps the most attractive and generally read of Goethe's prose writings, and that in spite of a heaviness of style—unpleasantly apparent as the work draws towards its close—and often garrulous irrelevancy to the main issues. But there are great pages in this book—greater Goethe never wrote—and their virtue lies, not in their unvarnished reproduction of the truth, but in the fact that that truth is gilded by poetry, the poetry which in the old Aristotelian sense is more truthful than history. When Goethe called his life-story *Truth and Poetry*, he did not, of course, mean to mingle fiction with fact, to romance about himself as Bettina had romanced about him in her *Correspondence with a Child*. On the contrary, we have evidence that he gave himself the greatest pains to tell the truth and nothing but the truth. This, however, was not easy; for when he published his first volume, he was already sixty-two, and was thus separated from the events he described by something like forty years. These years may have given him a vantage-ground of objectivity, and have allowed him to write about himself impersonally; but they also brought serious disadvantages. He was obliged to collect his materials as laboriously as if he were merely an onlooker and an outsider. This left room for inaccuracies when memory or the materials he had at his disposal were insufficient for his task.

It was not, however, to exonerate such possible " untruths " that Goethe introduced the word " Dichtung " into his title; he wished rather to indicate that he would interpret his youth by the light of the acquired wisdom of later years, and demonstrate how his life had been moulded and guided by a Higher Power. This did not involve the suppression of truth; but it did necessitate changes in the proportions and perspective of his narrative. Emphasis had to be laid upon happenings and experiences which, apparently of small significance at the moment, had acquired real or symbolic significance in the light of subsequent developments; while other things, apparently of greater moment at the time, are passed lightly over. Thus by virtue of the "Dichtung" in *Dichtung und Wahrheit* Goethe will eliminate, as it were, the seeming purposelessness in life, as it is lived, and bear testimony to "the divinity that shapes our ends, rough-hew them how we will."

The most serious disadvantage of Goethe's Autobiography in modern eyes is its lack of spontaneity; one misses the spirit of youth in this record of one of the most delightful youth-times in the annals of literature. The figures that appear in it seem too often to be moved like chess-figures across the board; its apophthegmatic dogmatism and its heavy periods are wearisome and often chilling. This is assuredly not Goethe's life as it was lived—for that we have to turn to *Götz* and *Werther* and *Clavigo*, and the early letters —it is only a meditated reconstruction of it. At the same time, the value of such a reconstruction is not to be gainsaid; for behind *Dichtung und Wahrheit* there is a great philosophy of life which is a rarer thing in autobiographical works than faithful impressionism. Thus if Goethe's autobiography may be a less personal and subjective book—it is, for instance, very much less intimate than Rousseau's *Confessions*—than might have been expected from a writer whose strength always lay in his subjectivity, it will always remain a great interpretation from within of a poet's life.

It had been clearly Goethe's intention that *Dichtung und Wahrheit* should be continued; the account of his Italian journey, published in 1816–1817, was definitely described as a continuation; and the other descriptions of journeys which he has left us, including such works as the *Campagne in Frankreich* (1822) and *Die Belagerung von Mainz* (1822), were all blocks which were, no doubt, intended ultimately to be built into the great structure. It is noticeable, however, that these supplements are mainly a record of outward happenings; they do not deal in the same degree as the Autobiography, with the poet's spiritual life and development. Still less can the matter-of-fact annals, *Tag- und Jahreshefte*, of Goethe's later years be regarded as a surrogate for the continuation of *Dichtung und Wahrheit*. That continuation we have to seek and distil from the more intimate records of letters, diaries and conversations.

Of such records we possess an embarrassing abundance. If we piece them together, there are days together when our knowledge is so full that we can follow the poet's life from hour to hour, when hardly anything that occupied him escapes us. We know, indeed, more of the intimacies—often trivial enough—of that part of Goethe's life which lay within the nineteenth century than we have ever known of any man's. And when one remembers that Goethe was a cynosure for the eyes of all Europe, and that all who came into personal contact with him felt the need of putting their impressions on record, one may fairly say that the fierce light that beats on intellectual thrones did not spare him. For the biographer this wealth of material is a doubtful advantage; it often confuses us rather than aids us in our efforts to interpret the poet's inner life; we miss, above all things, that guidance through the intricacies and details which the poet himself provided for the first twenty-six years.

During the stirring years of European history that saw the downfall of Napoleon, Goethe's life, upset by the general unrest, which was nowhere felt more acutely than in Weimar, passed through many crises and vicissitudes; ultimately, when peace returned, to pass over into that extraordinary Indian summer of lyric rebirth to which we owe *Der Westöstliche Divan*. Outwardly, however, his life was comparatively uneventful in the larger sense. He endeavoured to pursue his wonted way, to busy himself with his literary plans and scientific investigations; he spent his summers at the Bohemian spas, although sometimes the military disturbances made it difficult for him to get there. Of these happy summers, that of 1812 stood out in his memory as particularly pleasant, an oasis in the desert of unrest and anxiety. In that year he met at Karlsbad the Emperor of Austria, and subsequently at Teplitz his consort and her daughter, the Empress of France. The Austrian empress was one of his warm admirers, and she and her entourage provided a social intercourse and a rich and varied intellectual stimulus, such as he had rarely known. Again gracious and graceful ladies passed across his field of vision—Silvie von Ziegesar, Marianne von Eybenberg—and gave him a new zest for life. In that summer he wrote at the suggestion of the empress the little play *Die Wette*. Indeed, these visits to Bohemia in his declining years were a kind of second Italy to him.

In Teplitz the news reached him of the disastrous end to Napoleon's invasion of Russia. The following year which culminated in the decisive " Völkerschlacht " of Leipzig from the 16th to the 19th of October was one of deep anxiety and disaster for little Weimar. The town had to bear the full brunt of the military disturbance; troops were frequently billeted on the inhabitants; and they stood in anxious dread of the fate that might befall them in the event of the Leipzig battle proving adverse to the German cause. Even as it was, the town was converted into a military hospital, which brought with it the then inevitable sequel of disease and epidemic. That summer Goethe was unwilling to leave his valuable manuscripts and collections to the mercy of the possible invaders; but ultimately he was induced—after the most precious valuables had been buried—not to forgo the visit to Teplitz so necessary for his health.

The catastrophic issue of the Battle of Leipzig came

as a surprise, and perhaps, in his heart, as something of a disappointment to Goethe. He had stood aloof from the patriotic fervour with which the rising against Napoleon had been fanned by the younger generation; not one song did he contribute to the stirring poetry of the " Wars of Liberation ". He had no faith at all in the success of German arms. " Shake at your chains," he said to Stein and Arndt, " the man is too great for you. You will not break them." Nor was it merely a conviction of the invincibility of the Man of Destiny that inspired Goethe's political attitude; but also a genuine belief in the political wisdom of the French. He was no lover of Prussia and Prussia's ways. French domination meant to him an enlightened advance in good government and superior care for the spiritual welfare of the nation, compared with what the ramshackle Holy Roman Empire had provided. King Jérôme on the Hanoverian throne had by no means, like Frederick the Great, considered Frenchmen alone eligible for his higher posts. If Frederick had refused to appoint Lessing his librarian, Jérôme had at least summoned the great scholar Jakob Grimm in that capacity to Cassel. To Goethe Prussia's domination —and we are reminded that by the partition of Poland that country had acquired a large Slavonic influx— meant the tyranny of the hussar; and, instead of the liberty for which the younger generation were fighting, he believed that they were merely assisting at a revival of brutal repression.

Thus it must have been with mixed feelings that Goethe received an invitation from the actor Iffland, then director of the Prussian Royal Theatre in Berlin, to provide a " Festspiel " for the celebration of the victory over Napoleon. But he was ultimately induced to undertake the task, and wrote *Des Epimenides Erwachen*. This is a masque-like allegorical " Fest-spiel ", similar to those which he had frequently written for his own theatre in previous years. Epimenides of

Crete, who had been asleep for fifty years in the cave of Knossos, awakens to find that his kingdom has gone to ruin : similarly, Goethe's Epimenides, before whom in his sleep pass panoramic visions, tinged with the colours of Calderonian mysticism, of the world-events of the Napoleonic age, learns that the cause of which he had despaired, has triumphed. Epimenides was felt to be the old poet himself, and his patriotic admirers —the prologue seemed a frank admission that he had been wrong—drew consolation from his recantation : he had even made amends for his silence among the patriotic singers of the revolt by introducing echoes of the lyric which, on the lips of Körner, Arndt and Schenkendorf, had inspired the young fighters. It is difficult, however, to think that these allegorical shadows could have given satisfaction to the exultant mood of 1815 : and the play was felt, at its first performance on March 30th, to be tedious.

Goethe spent nearly four months in the latter part of 1814 on a visit to Frankfort and the Rhineland. Part of this journey is described with pleasant freshness in the first volume of a new periodical, *Über Kunst und Altertum* (1816–1832), which, as we have seen, served Goethe in these years as a receptacle for essays and reviews; it ultimately grew to six volumes, the last appearing in the year of the poet's death. His scientific miscellanies found a place in another journal, *Zur Naturwissenschaft überhaupt*, which appeared in three parts between 1817 and 1824. Goethe's account of the journey of 1814 has no light to throw upon two outstanding experiences of that time which he would assuredly not have glossed over, had it been a chapter of *Dichtung und Wahrheit*. One of these was his acquaintance with Sulpiz Boisserée, a young art-historian and collector of pictures from Cologne, whom Goethe met in Heidelberg, and between whom and the poet a warm friendship sprang up. Boisserée cautiously, and without offending Goethe's classical susceptibilities, interested him in the plans for the restoration and completion of the greatest of the German Gothic cathedrals, that of Cologne ; and he gradually convinced Goethe, who, a quarter of century earlier, had felt before the cathedral of Milan that he had done for ever with the Gothic, that there was some virtue in such monuments of German mediæval faith. Thus he opened Goethe's eyes to the significance, on which the Romanticists laid such stress, of the Middle Ages ; and Goethe read, we learn, the *Nibelungenlied* with interest. Boisserée brought him, too, to view the Roman Catholic religion with more sympathy and understanding. Thus were the barriers crumbling between Goethe's classicism and the new movement in German thought and letters.

The other great experience was his acquaintance with Marianne Jung who had been brought up by Johann Jakob von Willemer, a well-to-do Frankfort merchant, with his own daughters. She was of somewhat obscure Austrian origin, and had been for a time an actress. Shortly after Goethe's first meeting with her at the Gerbermühle, Willemer's country house near Frankfort, on September 18th, 1814, Willemer, a widower for the second time, made Marianne his wife.

Of the two types of women between which Goethe's taste vacillated, the restful and stately, and the mercurial, she belonged to the latter. She was no Charlotte von Stein, but a woman of very lively and facile spirit, a Mignon come to years of maturity, a passionate Christiane, but with all that Christiane lacked to make her the real companion of a poet : intellect and genius. And the old poet found his love for Marianne returned, and ardently returned. The lyric chord was set vibrating in him as it had not vibrated for many a year, and it kindled an unsuspected and rich vein of lyric genius in Marianne herself. An emotional warmth which had been so long absent from Goethe's verses, suddenly came back, and came back with the irresistible force of a flood that has broken its dams. To Marianne von Willemer belongs the credit of having inspired Goethe to write in his *Westöstlicher Divan* more poetry than all his other loves together. There is none of Goethe's passions on which one dwells with more pleasure than this; in none was the erotic element so spiritualized and clarified, so transfigured into an ideal as here. The old poet faced it with the consciousness that it could only be a dream, a dream without possible substance. The calm " Entsagung " of these latter years pervades it from the beginning, and resolves it into a harmony without a discordant note. In some ways Marianne was the best of all Goethe's loves; she stood to him in a mystic way for all that his marriage with Christiane had not realized; and which neither Friederike nor Lili, neither Charlotte von Stein nor Minna Herzlieb could ever have realized. If congenial temperament and poetic gifts of a high order—for some of " Suleika's " contributions to the *Divan* are not inferior in inspiration and beauty to the old master's own —could have made any woman a worthy life-partner to the great poet, that woman was Marianne.

In 1816 a new star rose on Goethe's horizon : Lord Byron; and from now until the tragedy of Missolonghi Byron's career and poetry were of paramount interest to him. For Goethe Byron is nothing short of the greatest of the moderns. His relation to the great English poet is one of the problematic things in Goethe's life. It would, of course, be absurd to claim that Byron was, or could ever have been, a sympathetic personality to Goethe. The two men never met, and had they met, they could not have become friends; the disillusionment on both sides would have been shattering. Neither poet understood the other; and Goethe's estimate of Byron's literary genius often puts our confidence in his critical acumen to a hard strain. The truth is, Goethe took Byron to his heart, not because he had any real sympathy for his unruly militancy; but rather because he fancied he

BUST OF GOETHE
By C. D. Rauch, 1820

saw in him a reincarnation of his own far-off youth ; he re-lived, as it were, his own past in him. More than this, Byron's meteoric career afford him a glimpse of a wider, larger life of the man of letters—something that had been denied him in his own youth, hedged round, as he had been, by the narrow provincialism and middle-class domination of his own land. This English peer, the poet as a man of action, lived the great life ; he was the embodiment of revolt ; he had suffered banishment ; and had finally given his life in heroic self-sacrifice for a great cause. Such was Byron in Goethe's eyes : a tremendous personality, a veritable Napoleon of poetry. And for Goethe, personality was always the highest thing in the world :

> Volk und Knecht und Überwinder,
> Sie gestehn zu jeder Zeit :
> Höchstes Glück der Erdenkinder
> Sei nur die Persönlichkeit,

he had sung in his *Westöstliche Divan* ; and in the notes to that work he had added : " Not talents, not skill in doing this or that, really make the man of action ; it is personality on which everything depends, not talents." Goethe's unbounded—as we may think, unjustified— admiration for Byron may also have been tinged, as so much that passed through Goethe's mind in these sombre years, with regretful reflexions of how much he had not been able to achieve in his own life; here, he felt, was the green tree of life, not the grey theory, amidst which so much of his own career had perforce been passed. This is some explanation of the extrava- gant pleasure—one of the greatest of his later years —which the old poet felt when Byron laid his homage at his feet with his dedication of *Sardanapalus* : " To the Illustrious Goethe a stranger presumes to offer the homage of a literary vassal to his liege Lord, the first of existing writers, who has created the literature of his own country and illustrated that of Europe." If there had ever been any danger of Goethe sinking into the spiritual quietism of the East, Byron brought him back again to Greece, that Greece in which his Faust and Helena had been for so many years languishing and waiting for poetic deliverance. And in Goethe's mind, Byron's death that Greece might be free, was perhaps a greater achievement for humanity than his own Faust's reclamation of land from the sea on which men might toil and live.

Goethe's political pessimism proved only too well justified in the disappointing settlement of the affairs of Europe by the Congress of Vienna. The overthrow of Napoleon only made room for Prince Metternich; and the real political freedom of the German peoples seemed as far off as ever. The Congress, it is true, conferred outward glory upon Weimar; the duchy was converted into a grand duchy and its territory was doubled. But this left Goethe cold. The duke was full of zeal to conform to the spirit of the time, and boldly gave his state a new constitution which made wide concessions to the rising democracy. But such measures met with no sympathy or approval from his quondam minister of state, who disliked with all his old eighteenth-century conservatism everything that savoured of majority rule. For Goethe the minority was always in the right; and many a bitter word escaped him in those days about the folly of allowing bakers and butchers and apothecaries to interfere in the high affairs of state. In particular, he disapproved of his duke's decision that, within his territory, the press should be unfettered. It may be disappointing to find Goethe's great mind on the side of reaction and opposed to what we recognize now as progress in human affairs; but unfortunately the course of events justified only too well his caution, and demonstrated the short-sightedness of the Duke of Weimar. For there were stormy days ahead. The Weimar state was seriously involved in the disrupting and revolutionary movements of the next few years; the freedom of the press—as was perhaps only to be expected when Weimar pursued a policy at variance with her neighbours—was abused, until it ultimately became necessary for Metternich to intervene and curb it; Jena became a hotbed of frothy demagogism, and the celebration of the Reformation festival in the Wartburg in the autumn of 1817 degenerated into a dangerous political demonstration. It cannot be denied that all this seemed to justify Goethe's unsympathetic attitude to political change. The truth is—and Goethe may have seen it in this light —that, however laudable Karl August's intentions were, it was only courting disaster to adopt a policy of freedom, and introduce reforms in accordance with it, while the states around him persisted in their adherence to the principles of the old régime. Here lay the wisdom of the old poet's opposition.

Thus Goethe was without any real understanding or sympathy for the new orientation in political affairs. While in poetry, in science and the arts, even, as we shall see, in the new problems of industrialism, Goethe did see further and deeper than most of his contemporaries, his eyes were strangely blinkered when it was a question of political foresight. He remained to the last, in his conception of the relation of ruler and ruled, a pre-revolutionary theorist. Much of Carlyle's intransigency came from the support he found for it in Goethe's conservatism. Goethe believed in the strong hand; and when he was himself in the position to wield it, he wielded it magisterially. At no time did he see eye to eye with his sovereign in the guidance of their little ship of state. In older days his opposition had been to the duke's policy of an alliance with Prussia, a policy which Goethe saw—and no doubt saw rightly—had its roots in the duke's insensate craving for military glory and for a wider sphere of action and influence in European politics; now it was opposition to what later generations are inclined to put to the credit of the duke, his endeavour to meet the new time half-way. In the personal relations of the two men the result was the same: their difference of outlook became ever wider and was even now wellnigh irreconcilable.

Disappointed and disillusioned by such developments, Goethe turned his reviving energies to those fields that were peculiarly his own: to the university of Jena and the theatre. This was now the more possible as his official position in the grand duchy was restricted to the functions of a " Kultusminister ", that is to say, minister of education and the fine arts. This still left him great powers and responsibilities, even if he were not concerned with politics in the wider sense. Perhaps even here, too, he was something of a drag on the wheel. In the matter of the university, things went fairly smoothly; for the poet had a free hand, the duke having little or no interest in education and learning. But the theatre provided many sources of irritation; for the duke's tastes had to be humoured; his mistress, Caroline Jagemann, and her friends to be favoured in the distribution of rôles. Very serious friction between Goethe and the duke on this score had broken out in 1808, and Goethe had already then threatened to resign his directorship. The duke's interference must have been the more galling, as Goethe turned with youthfully active, if somewhat tyrannical, zeal to the reform of the theatre; indeed, at no previous period had he regarded his functions as theatre director so seriously as now. Suddenly, however, into the midst of all his admirable plans to make the little Weimar theatre the worthiest in Germany fell a thunderbolt, which contributed more to the estrangement of duke and poet than all their political differences. A travelling company of actors wished in 1813 to perform a translation of a French *mélodrame* that had whetted the jaded appetites of playgoers beyond the French frontier: *Le chien d'Aubry*.

The main attraction of the play was not itself, but the appearance in it of a trained dog.   Goethe who, in any case, disliked dogs, indignantly refused to have his classic stage desecrated.   But the duke, whose tastes in theatrical matters were, in spite of his apparent pleasure in French classic tragedies, by no means so nice, did not see why there should be so much fuss ; he thought he would quite well like to see the dog. He issued orders accordingly.   Goethe fled to Jena, and a few days later, sent in his resignation.   So that dream, too—the dream that had once been Wilhelm Meister's—was over.   Could anything throw a sharper light on the hollowness of the relations between the poet and his prince ?   To dismiss—for the duke knew well that his action could only mean Goethe's resignation—the greatest poet of Germany from the post that he was best qualified to fill with honour, and all for the sake of a performing poodle !   Of all the petty annoyances and tyrannies under which Goethe suffered in these years, surely this was the worst !   For twenty years he had guided the destinies of the Weimar theatre, and although there may be much to criticize in his barren efforts to impose upon the living theatre the artificial style of an effete classicism—to turn back the hands of the clock—yet none could deny that in that long period he had given his theatre a place of honour in the world of letters.

Thus a greater gulf than ever opened up between sovereign and minister, a gulf that nothing closed again. If ever there was a time when Goethe's thoughts must have reverted to the first great crisis in his relations with Weimar, on the eve of his journey to Italy—it must have been now.   And yet Goethe did not—outwardly at least—take it so bitterly to heart as might have been expected ; the old eighteenth-century loyalty to princes which he had put on Tasso's lips, was in his blood.

The death of Wieland in 1813 brought poignantly home to Goethe the passing of the old Weimar to

which he had come in 1775; and in 1816 he suffered
a grievous personal loss by the death of his wife
Christiane. When the grave closed over her, he felt
that an epoch of his life had come to an end. It had
been a great experiment, this union; an experiment
the outcome of which no one, least of all Goethe
himself, could have foreseen, when he first found his
"forest flower" in the Weimar park after his return
from Italy. No love of Goethe's life gave less promise
of permanence than this, and yet it proved to be the
most lasting of them all. It could not be said that it
had brought real companionship, or any great or deep
happiness; at most, it gave Goethe a certain material
comfort, a home and a son. Now that death had rung
down the curtain, he saw Christiane only in the kindliest
of lights:

> Du versuchst, o Sonne, vergebens
> Durch die düstren Wolken zu scheinen!
> Der ganze Gewinn meines Lebens
> Ist ihren Verlust zu beweinen.

And in a letter two weeks later: "I will not deny to
you—and why should one pretend otherwise?—that
my state of mind was nigh unto despair."

Chapter IV

" DER WESTÖSTLICHE DIVAN " AND " WILHELM MEISTERS WANDERJAHRE "

Der Westöstliche Divan is the most considerable collection of lyric poetry which ever at one time came from Goethe's pen. The *Gedichte* which comprise all Goethe's other lyrics and occupy several volumes of his works, were, of course, written at widely distant periods and inspired by widely different occasions. In no previous year or two years had Goethe's lyric inspiration welled forth so spontaneously and continuously as now.

There is a tendency among Goethe's critics to lay more weight on the form than on the contents of *Der Westöstliche Divan*; to emphasize the " östliche " in the title rather than the " west ". Goethe, we are told, had always cherished a warm affection for the East. From the Bible stories he listened to at his mother's knee and his first attempt at an epic in *Joseph*, down to the reawakening of oriental study in Germany by the Romanticist Friedrich Schlegel, the fascination for the Orient was never far absent from his mind. Moreover, the oriental origins of the *Divan* were obvious enough : in the course of the year 1814 Goethe came upon the translation of the *Divan* of the Persian poet Hafiz by the Viennese scholar Joseph von Hammer-Purgstall, published a year or two before, and immediately his love for the East was stirred.

But the beginnings of *Der Westöstliche Divan* were not quite so simple as this : the extraordinary rejuvenation of Goethe's lyric genius is not so easily explained.

Certainly it was not contact with the East that brought it about. For the conception of the work, or at least its individual poems, date from the year 1814 at a time when the thought was still far from him to clothe them in the oriental garb supplied by Hammer-Purgstall. In that year, it will be remembered, Goethe made a journey to Frankfort and the Rhineland which was a peculiarly happy one, perhaps the happiest of all his many travels. He sought to forget in the changing scene the distracting political troubles of the time. The journey, too, was, like that to Switzerland in 1779, a journey into his own past. He renewed old ties, visited places of hallowed memories, above all, those associated with Lili Schönemann whose share in his life he was just at that time describing in the last volume of *Dichtung und Wahrheit*. It was a journey, too, on which he contracted new congenial friendships, notably that with Sulpiz Boisserée. The poems of the earlier part of the *Divan* were written originally as a kind of lyric diary of this journey and had no trace of orientalism about them at all. It was not until the ensuing winter of 1814–5 that Goethe was seriously engrossed by oriental studies and Hammer-Purgstall's translation of Hafiz was his constant companion. Then, and, it would appear, then only, Goethe took the resolution to clothe his poetical diary in the garment of the East; to transfer these records of experience which were at bottom a kind of refuge for him from his disappointment with the western world, to the unchanging East:

> Nord und West und Süd zersplittern,
> Throne bersten, Reiche zittern,
> Flüchte du, im reinen Osten
> Patriarchenluft zu kosten,
> Unter Lieben, Trinken, Singen
> Soll dich Chisers Quell verjüngen.

For the familiar landscape of Main and Rhine was sub-stituted the oriental scene, and a note of oriental quietism and fatalism introduced which, if not entirely foreign to the poems in their first form, was at least not conspicuous. These changes were not, however, effected without a certain loss of lyric spontaneousness ; for although Goethe's mind was always prone to fatalism, it had by no means relinquished itself to the confident fatalism of the East. He was tempted, too, by his Persian model to give his thought a cryptic and gnomic form which harmonized with a trait which was growing upon the old poet with the years ; concentrated reflexion took the place of the lyric effusiveness of earlier years.

Were this all that the *Divan* contained, it might have made but little appeal to his contemporaries. But into this reflective poetry entered in the " Buch Suleika " the emotional experience of the poet's love for Marianne von Willemer; the personal, subjective note, which was always the best inspiration of Goethe's poetry, was provided by it. He projected himself into Hatem, the old poet with the white locks :

> Nur dies Herz, es ist von Dauer,
> Schwillt in jugendlichstem Flor ;
> Unter Schnee und Nebelschauer
> Rast ein Ätna dir hervor.
>
> Du beschämst wie Morgenröte
> Jener Gipfel ernste Wand,
> Und noch einmal fühlet Hatem
> Frühlingshauch und Sommerbrand.

The youthful Suleika is Marianne : and indeed in a quite literal sense, for Marianne herself contributed, as we have seen, poems to the collection which rival in beauty Goethe's own, notably the beautiful " Ach, um deine feuchten Schwingen ". Goethe saw his Suleika for the last time in September, 1815 ; but she continued, in correspondence, to follow and contribute to the composition of the *Divan* for many months. Thus the love of Hatem and Suleika gave savour to the work, and held the balance with the poetry of reflective wisdom which forms so large a part of its contents.

This spiritual journey of Goethe to the East was one of the unexpected happenings in a life full enough of surprises. That he who had so long swathed himself in the stately robe of ancient Greece should now have put on the kaftan and the fez, have taken his water-pipe and sat cross-legged in Eastern bazaars, is surely one of the strangest transformations of all among the many costumes Goethe donned in the great masquerade of his life. One of the latest of his biographers has aptly described it as a kind of Italian journey of Goethe's declining years ; and rightly adds that it was the only one of all Goethe's journeys which brought no disenchantment, left no trace of disillusionment behind it.

And yet it may be questioned how far Goethe actually did in spirit make this adventurous journey. Did he whose soul, like his Iphigenie's, had so long " sought the land of the Greeks ", ever really pass beyond Hellas and penetrate into the limitless and un-Greek mysticism of the East ? Is the *Divan* not " eastern " merely in its outward costume and background, in its fiction of the love of Hatem for Suleika, while its spiritual contents remain essentially " western " ? In other words, was Goethe's orientalism really more than skin deep, in spite of all the learning which he displays in the notes to his volume ? At no time do we find Goethe expressing sympathy for the Eastern mind ; and in earlier life, at least, its mystic asceticism was as abhorrent to him as the similar element in mediæval Christianity. The years had, it is true, blunted something of this antagonism. Moreover, Goethe's own lyric art had been gradually taking on an almost oriental quality of concentrated, antithetic expression ; the verse in which he distilled the wisdom of his old age had oriental affinities ; and this it was, rather than any deeper sympathy for the oriental attitude to life, that led him half-way to meet Hafiz. Rich and spontaneous as was the lyric inspiration Goethe owed to Marianne von Willemer, it must be admitted that a great deal of *Der Westöstliche Divan* is not lyric poetry in the old sense at all. Nor can it vie with the kaleidoscopic variety of Goethe's earlier verse ; for it is all in one form and in one key. It flows easily and steadily ; but one lives through more emotional experience in twenty pages of the early *Gedichte* than in all this volume.

Wilhelm Meisters Wanderjahre can hardly be described as a continuation of the *Wilhelm Meisters Lehrjahre* of more than thirty years earlier. The plan of writing a continuation had, no doubt, been present in Goethe's mind from the first : he had mentioned it to Schiller in 1795 ; and, indeed, it is tacitly implied in the original title : apprenticeship could hardly be the end of a hero whose name is Meister. But when Goethe came to take up his task in earnest, it proved beyond his powers to accomplish, other than by objectively throwing himself back into the past. And this he was by no means minded to do : for the ideas he would embody in the novel were more vital to him than its story. *Faust*, moving symbolically in a transfigured poetic world, might be adapted to the changing horizons of the new century ; but a novel of essentially realistic content, framed in the social *milieu* of the pre-Revolutionary epoch, dealing with pre-Revolutionary ideas, could only with the greatest difficulty be adapted to the new era of the coming of steam and collective industry. Goethe soon saw that the problems of the nineteenth century were not to be solved by the simple formulas which had served him in good enough stead in the *Lehrjahre* ; and the whole framework of the old novel had to be discarded and forgotten. Thus he hardly makes any effort to link up the new book with the old : even when the characters of the *Lehrjahre* reappear, they reappear only in name. The old plan might have been retained, but Goethe had no use for it ; he himself no longer saw life with the eyes of 1796.

267

When the new work opens, we find Wilhelm Meister, accompanied by his son Felix, on those " Wanderjahre " which had been foreshadowed at the close of the first novel. He has now to learn the great lesson of renunciation and self-limitation—the second title of the book is *Die Entsagenden*—regardless of the fact that the learning of that lesson was the essential ethical purpose of his apprenticeship. Under a vow of constant movement, exacted from him by Natalie, he may rest no longer than three days in any one place. In the Alps he comes upon a carpenter and his family who live in a ruined monastery of St. Joseph ; and in this family he fancies he sees a replica of the Holy Family of the Gospel story. It is, indeed, almost as if Wilhelm had made a journey back through time similar to that which Faust makes to Greece. The idyllic life which this second Joseph lives in a little community devoted to simple handicraft, provides a framework for reflexions on the basic significance of such handiwork for the welfare of society. At the end of his three days with the carpenter and his community, Wilhelm proceeds further into the mountains where, amongst the mines, he finds again his old friend Jarno, now re-named Montanus. A more uncompromising realist than in the *Lehrjahre*, Montanus insists on limitation and concentration in human activity. Wilhelm resolves to profit by this good advice, and, if he can be freed from the three days' embargo, to become a surgeon—surely the strangest of metamorphoses in one who had set out in life with the purpose of giving his people a national theatre ! But neither his training for his new profession, of which we hear nothing, nor his subsequent practice of it, is anything more than an unsubstantial symbolical thought. There is no attempt to visualize his life as a thing of concrete and tangible happenings.

In the further wanderings of father and son, Felix finds in a basalt cavern a mysterious casket, a kind of

Pandora's box, the contents of which would seem to be symbolic of life itself. But the casket, which is not entirely forgotten later in the novel, remains unopened, the key breaking in the lock ; its secret is never revealed. Many such incidents and motives in the novel are left hanging in the air : their possibilities are unexplored and undeveloped : and any attempt the old poet makes later in his book to link back to them, are artificial and unconvincing. Wilhelm next finds himself in a great castle, the castle of the Uncle, whose life-philosophy reverses those doctrines of Schiller of which the other Uncle of the *Lehrjahre* had been the spokesman. The problem of the education of mankind had now ceased for him to be a simple progress, as Schiller had seen it, through the beautiful to the good : rather must humanity ascend through the useful to the beautiful. Wilhelm's next visit is to a niece of the Uncle, Makarie, in whose house we are introduced to still more ethereal-ized and shadowy personifications of life philosophies. Makarie herself is a kind of transfigured and super-human " schöne Seele " who has attained to the mature wisdom of life, and exercises it in a beneficent activity toward her fellow-creatures. A more human element is here introduced in the nephew of Makarie, Lenardo, who is in love with a certain " nut-brown maid ", daughter of a farmer whom the Uncle has deprived of his farm. The nut-brown maid has disappeared and Wilhelm offers to assist Lenardo in his search for her.

In the course of this search Wilhelm is recommended to visit the " Pedagogic Province ", which provides Goethe with a setting for a utopian dream of education, his contribution to a solution of the problem which, from Lessing and Rousseau to Pestalozzi, had engaged the best minds of the later eighteenth century. The Over-seer of the Province conducts Wilhelm over it and explains its mysteries and symbols : and to the " Three" in whom its control is vested, he entrusts the education of Felix. Of most interest here to later generations have been Goethe's thoughts on religious education : his explanation of the three reverences which is instilled into the pupils, " the reverence for what is above us, for what is beneath us, and what is in us, which in their union produce what may truly be called the true religion ". And in the picture gallery of the Province he is shown the illustrations by means of which the young minds are led from the " ethnic " religion of the Jews to the New Testament. The pictures from the latter do not, however, depict the life of Christ beyond the Last Supper ; the Crucifixion is excluded. To the final stage of religious initiation, the Sanctuary of Sorrow, Wilhelm is promised introduction when he returns to the Province after the lapse of a year.

Wilhelm's next journey, the nut-brown maid having been found, is again a journey into the past: he revisits Mignon's home in Italy. Old chords are set vibrating again in the poet's heart, memories of the brightest and happiest experience of his own life, now alas, how remote ! On his return to the Pedagogic Province which has been deferred for many years, he finds that Felix has chosen the rearing of horses as his allotted task : he, too, has learned to limit his activity within the bounds of the useful. There is informative talk with the Overseer on the value of acquiring foreign languages and on the study of the arts. He finds Montanus again in command of the mining department of the Province ; and the quarrel of the Neptunists and the Vulcanists concerning the origin of the earth's crust is discussed. In what remains of the novel the shadowy parallelism with the last two books of the *Lehrjahre*, which has always been dimly traceable, is revived again in the founding by Lenardo of a society or Bund in which reappear old friends of the *Lehrjahre*, Philine and Friedrich, now converted to the new gospel of the sanctity of work. But these figures, reduced to immaterial shadows, only serve to show how Goethe's once great art of creating men and women has melted away into the thin air of abstraction and allegory. The Bund sponsors another utopian dream ; it will create a new order of human society in America : and with the departure of a select company, including Wilhelm, and a pæan in honour of emigration, the novel moves to its close :

> Bleibe nicht am Boden heften,
> Frisch gewagt und frisch hinaus !
> Kopf und Arm mit heitern Kräften,
> Überall sind sie zu Haus.

The " Here or nowhere is America ! " of the *Lehrjahre* has been replaced by a new and cosmopolitan precept: "Wherever thou canst be useful, there is thy Fatherland."

Were this " story," which has just been lightly outlined, all that the *Wanderjahre* contains, it would have long since been relegated to the lumber of the unreadable books of the past. But it contains, besides, a host of strange, irrelevant and arresting things ; and it is these irrelevancies that make it still worth our while to turn to it now. It is, in fact, a receptacle into which Goethe threw the most varied collection of odds and ends of his work and thought. Separate stories are awkwardly and purposelessly fitted into its structure, and stories for the presence of which there is no cogent reason at all. The reader is not, however, likely to resent their intrusion, for some of them are fresh enough to relieve the narrative dullness of the main theme. These stories all date from earlier more imaginatively productive years of Goethe's life : *Die neue Melusine* we have already met with in Goethe's Sesenheim days ; *Die pilgernde Törin* is merely a translation from the French and dates from 1789 ; *St. Joseph der Zweite* was written in 1799 ; *Der Mann von funfzig Jahren*—one of the better of the stories,—*Das nussbraune Mädchen* and *Wer ist Verräter* were written respectively in 1807, 1810 and 1820 ; while finally it will be remembered that *Die*

Wahlverwandtschaften in its original form belonged to this group.

Volume I of *Wilhelm Meisters Wanderjahre* appeared in 1821 : a second volume was one of the tasks that remained to him to complete as his days were drawing to a close. The material he had collected seemed bulky enough to warrant a third volume; but when the third volume was printed, it was found to be disproportionately short. So Goethe gave Eckermann a bundle of miscellaneous matter, and told him to utilize it to swell the bulk of the third volume as he thought fit. These materials Eckermann arranged in two large groups which he entitled *Betrachtungen im Sinne der Wanderer* and *Aus Makariens Archiv*.

Thus in proportion as the *Wanderjahre* gave up its pretence to be a novel of a readable kind, it became a storehouse of Goethe's apophthegmatic wisdom. There is no other of his works in which he has dwelt at such length on questions of religion, education and social organization ; there is ripe wisdom behind all his utterances on these matters, even if it often takes strange, unacceptable form, and if he indulges in a utopianism which ignores the firm earth underfoot and loses itself in the sky. Perhaps in the end the most significant thing about the *Wanderjahre* is that Goethe has here succeeded in dissociating himself from his old eighteenth-century self : it is a tribute to the progressive and adaptable nature of his intellect, his ability to reason wisely—and strangely few men whose best years lay in the era before the great Revolution show this ability —on the problems of the nineteenth century, the changes brought about in the social fabric by steam and industrialism, and the new horizons opened up by the advance of science. We can even catch a glimpse here of an understanding for that new orientation of the world, to which Goethe's mind had seemed always most impervious, the coming of democracy. Thus, if *Wilhelm Meisters Wanderjahre* is the most lamentable of

Goethe's failures as a creative artist, it remains a book of contemplative wisdom. Indeed, it is a kind of supplement to the Second Part of *Faust*; for much that is there set forth poetically and symbolically, finds in the philosophy of the *Wanderjahre* its justification and explanation.

Chapter V

THE LAST FIFTEEN YEARS

Goethe's biographers, filled with admiration for the great Olympian, to whom it was granted to complete the magnificent pyramid of his existence, so boldly planned in young years, have dwelt on little else in these closing years but the triumphant consummation of his career. The patriarch of the world of letters, the Goethe who received the homage of all Europe, who lived to put the finishing touch to his greatest edifice, *Faust*, and who passed out in the odour of the highest wisdom with the words " more light " upon his lips —this is the Goethe with whom we have been made most familiar. What they have not dwelt upon is the sadness and even tragedy of the close of this great life. In these late years Goethe said to Eckermann : " I have always been praised as a man especially favoured by fortune ; nor will I complain and make reproaches about the course of my life. But at bottom it has been nothing but toil and trouble, and I may, indeed, say that in all my seventy-five years I have never enjoyed four weeks of real well-being." And in truth the last years were sombre. Goethe's many visitors—and there were numerous Englishmen among them, notably Henry Crabb Robinson who was in Weimar in 1801 and 1829, and who has left us the fullest record of the poet— dwell on the lordly mansion with its thirty rooms, its museum-like wealth of sculpture and objects of art, its scientific collections, its abundant testimony to a noble, cultured taste ; although they also dwell on the con- trast presented by the extreme simplicity of Goethe's working rooms.   They tell us of their courtly reception by the old monarch, pompously decked in his stars and orders, who, stiff and chilling, often treated them with very monarchical condescension.   But of what lay behind this outward glory, they know nothing.

The death of Christiane left a great gap in the house on the Frauenplan ; it made the old man the more anxious to find for it a new mistress in the shape of a daughter-in-law.   A bride was selected for August, Ottilie von Pogwisch, the daughter of a noble family associated with the Weimar court ; and the marriage, in which love had no share, took place in June, 1817. In the following April Goethe's first grandson, Walther, was born.   Goethe opened his heart to his daughter-in-law ; and for a year or two his home-life was sunny and pleasant ; pleasanter than it had been for some years back.   But this did not last ; the horizon began to darken again.   Beneath the surface, things were running far from smoothly in the Goethe household. Goethe's son August was a growing source of worry and anxiety ; he had inherited nothing of his father's stability of character ; his upbringing had been without method or discipline—strange, when one thinks how interested Goethe had been all his life long in problems of education !—and as he came to man's estate, his life became more and more an aimless drifting, which made him an easy prey to licentiousness and drunkenness.   His marriage to Ottilie, instead of restoring his equilibrium, seems to have completed his undoing. And Ottilie herself ?   She flits gracefully through the pages of Goethe's biographers as an engaging figure who presided charmingly at Goethe's table when he entertained his guests, who brought life and light into the old man's days.   But here, too, unfortunately, there was a reverse to the medal.   Under Ottilie's régime Goethe's house was hardly a pleasanter place than it had been in Christiane's days ; and more frequently than ever—until 1825 at least—he was compelled to seek refuge in Jena from the upsetting disturbances for which her mismanagement and frivolity were responsible. With as little character as her worthless husband, she coquetted with every acceptable male guest—and Englishmen seem to have been particularly favoured—squandered money on dress and finery, and neglected house and children. These children—there were three, two boys and a girl, of whom the last had certainly no Goethe blood in her veins—grew up untended, unchecked, noisy and unruly, a constant disturbance to their old grandfather who yet drew such consolation from them as he could. Goethe had sometimes to attend to the simplest domestic duties, while his daughter-in-law flaunted in Weimar society; and when the stately reception of his guests was over, his night was often rendered hideous by the brawls overhead between Ottilie and his drunken son. Orderly and punctual to excess in all things, how Goethe must have suffered under all this! There is a grim irony in the fact that, for the benefit of these worthless heirs, he should, in 1826, have successfully negotiated—Goethe was always a shrewd business man—a fifty years' copyright in his works. He was himself, of course, amply provided for in the years he had still to live; not merely had he a considerable income from the sale of his works; he also enjoyed what was then a princely salary from the State, in return, as he frankly put it to the duke, for the fame and distinction which his presence in Weimar conferred on the town. But under Ottilie's control of his house money was needed; and if he did not often himself entertain on a lavish scale, his son and daughter-in-law had no qualms about doing so on their own account.

Can it be wondered that the old man contemplated for a brief space a new marriage? The duke's services were called into requisition in the matter, and the plan, needless to say, was the occasion of a stormy scene with August and Ottilie, who saw themselves in danger of being cut out of their inheritance. In the proposed marriage love had its share. During the summer of 1821 at Marienbad, Goethe's fancy had been captivated by a young girl, Ulrike von Levetzow; and the acquaintance was renewed there two years later. Ulrike did not seem averse from the homage of the famous poet and the glamour of his great name; she was only nineteen, Goethe seventy-four. But, fortunately for Goethe as for Ulrike, nothing came of the foolish plan; and she, the very last link in Goethe's emotional life, lived on, unmarried, almost into the twentieth century. Her death occurred in 1899. To look upon this, Goethe's last passion, as mere senile eroticism is a little harsh; for behind it was certainly the practical consideration of giving his home, laid waste by August and Ottilie, a new head. But there is something finer and subtler to be read out of the wonderful *Marienbader Elegie* in the *Trilogie der Leidenschaft* (1823), his last tribute on the altar of Eros. Each of Goethe's loves, as we have repeatedly seen, may be regarded as the muse of a definite phase of his life; Ulrike does not belie this representative character; but she is less to be thought of as the love and the muse of a very old man, than as the personification of retrospect, of a passionate re-living of the emotional memories of earlier days. There was nothing in Goethe's fancy for this child to be compared with the last real flame that had warmed his old heart, the passion for Marianne von Willemer which has given us the *Westöstliche Divan*; rather did Goethe see in her, in his mystic, allegorizing way, the Phœnix of his dead past; in her blended the memory that refused most obstinately to be effaced, that of Lili Schönemann. Ulrike was the last phantom of a happiness that had always " drawn him upwards and onwards "—the " Ewigweibliche " of the closing lines of *Faust*; but a happiness that had always eluded his grasp. The three poems which make up the *Trilogie der Leidenschaft* are *An Werther*, suggested by a new edition of the

novel, *Marienbader Elegie*, and *Aussöhnung*. The last
was inspired by the playing of Madame Maria Szyman-
owska, a Polish pianist, who brought Goethe nearer to
the art of music than he had ever been before; and in
these years he was deeply interested in the musical
" Wunderkind ", Felix Mendelssohn-Bartholdy. The
Trilogie der Leidenschaft is the last of his great lyrically
inspired creations, and not far behind it stands the
beautiful *Paria* (1821).

It was indeed a lonely life to which Goethe was condemned in these last years. One by one, the old friends
were inevitably passing out into the great darkness;
literary links with the past were snapped by the deaths of
Fritz Jacobi—friend and adversary through long years
—and of Fritz Stolberg in 1819; Charlotte von Stein,
with whom something of a reconciliation had taken
place in the last years, died in 1827; the duke in 1828,
and the Duchess Luise, the last intimate link between
Goethe and the court, in 1830. There were very few
left now with whom Goethe could still exchange the
intimate " du ", and these not the worthiest of his
intimacy. Knebel, his senior, who also outlived him,
was perhaps the best of these friends; the ties with
him had gone back to the very beginnings of his Weimar
life; and they had never been really broken, although
often suspended for a longer time than the short
distance between Weimar and Jena warranted. But
Goethe's intimacy with the Swiss, Heinrich Meyer,
is difficult to explain, and still more of a mystery is
his long and faithful attachment to the Berlin musician
Zelter, with whom the poet carried on a voluminous
correspondence. With Duke Karl August Goethe's
relations had never been the same again after the
political differences of the Napoleonic time and the
affair of the performing poodle; but appearances were
kept up. Now that Goethe was relieved of all official
duties, there was little to bring them together; but,
no doubt, in these days of increasing isolation the

personal relations between the two men did take on a warmer colouring. When in 1825 the jubilee of the duke's accession was celebrated, he insisted on that of Goethe's entry into Weimar being associated with it.

A new generation had meanwhile grown up at court, and Goethe held himself stiffly apart from it; his attendances became increasingly rare. He even caused some jealousy by dedicating his Correspondence with Schiller, published in 1828 and 1829, to the King of Bavaria, who had bestowed a high order upon him. There was a similar estrangement between Goethe and the new generation of men of letters in Germany, none of whom approached him without some fear and trembling. Invested although he was by the new Romantic school as one of its high-priests, he had at heart little real understanding for their aims or their world; he who had dwelt on Olympian heights and dallied in Hafiz' garden, never penetrated far into the great Romantic forest, or felt the magic of the Romantic night. For the weary and the broken-hearted, the outcasts of genius, in the Romantic age, for distraught poets like Heinrich von Kleist, he could have no fellow-feeling or real compassion; the lyric genius of Heine—whose delightful story of his visit to Weimar, when he could talk of nothing to Goethe but the plums he had plucked by the wayside, is familiar—found no recognition; and even when Goethe's feelings were manifestly friendly, as in the case of the great Austrian, Grillparzer, his pompous and forbidding manner led to misunderstandings and discouragement.

And yet Goethe was not uninfluenced by the Romantic constellation under which his declining years were passed. Less apparently affected by its æsthetic doctrines than the quite unromantic Schiller had been, he had been more appreciative of its imaginative achievement. It would, indeed, have been strange had he been insensitive to the devotion of the Romanticists laid at his feet, and the incense they burned

before him ; and in the First Part of *Faust* he had, as
we have seen, given Romanticism a poem which may
well be claimed as the greatest of its monuments.   Nor
is it merely fancy to see in Goethe's preoccupation with
the poetry of the East a great Romantic adventure ;
for it was the Romanticists who had opened up this
wonderland to western Europe.   They, under Friedrich
Schlegel's guidance, had sought and found in the Orient
a surrogate for the traditional Romantic trappings which
had begun to wear threadbare by constant reiteration ;
and *Der Westöstliche Divan* was a work after their own
heart, as definite a landmark in the progress of Romanticism as any creation of a purely Romantic poet.   Of
deeper significance than such outward points of contact with the contemporary movement was the change
that came over Goethe in these late years in his attitude
to the spiritual and the unseen.   Not since his enthusiasm for Spinoza in early years had Goethe found a
thinker so much in harmony with his own thought as
the metaphysician of Romanticism, Schelling ; and the
" heathen " Goethe of the years of classical ascendancy
was gradually giving place to a Goethe who—even if it
might be still too much to call him Christian—at least
brought to the Christian tradition, and to the Mother
Church which had cast so compelling a spell over the
Romantic mind, sympathy and understanding.   Thus
Goethe was by no means so impervious to the spiritual
message of Romanticism as is sometimes thought ; and
that often quoted dictum of his : " The Romantic I call
the sick ; the Classic the healthy " was no unconditional
truth in the ageing poet's outlook on either life or art.
There are visible traces of Romantic ideas in *Wilhelm
Meisters Wanderjahre* ; and *Faust* itself closes with an
apotheosis which might well have been inspired by a
Romantic Catholicism.

Meanwhile a grander and lordlier cosmopolitan
vision had broken upon Goethe with his conception of
" Weltliteratur ". He had himself found inspiration

GOETHE IN 1832
By K. A. Schwerdgeburth

[*face p.* 280

in the Persia of Hafiz, and had been fired by the genius of Byron. In Scott, too, he was deeply interested, and when in 1825 the young Carlyle sent him his translation of *Wilhelm Meister*, followed by the *Life of Schiller*, which Goethe caused forthwith to be translated into German, a correspondence sprang up between the two men which is the most substantial link between Goethe and England in the nineteenth century. On his last birthday in 1831 it gave the old poet great pleasure to receive the letter of congratulation signed by fourteen eminent Englishmen. The Romantic movement of French letters he followed with even more intense interest; he was an eager reader of *Le Globe*, and was impressed by the genius of Balzac and Béranger; only for Victor Hugo could he feel no warmth. Italy interested him in the person of Manzoni; and the Polish poet Mickiewicz was an honoured guest in Weimar in 1828. Thus from his throne in Weimar the old monarch surveyed the literature of the world; in fact, it created some jealousy at home that he had a kindlier eye for the poets of other lands than those of his own.

To the intimates of Goethe's last years belonged the immediate entourage of his " house friends " and his helpers in the ordering and arranging of his collected works. These men, the Chancellor von Müller, the French tutor of the new duke, Frédéric Soret, whose interests were mainly scientific, Goethe's secretary Riemer and, above all, Eckermann, have left intimate personal records of their intercourse with him. Goethe's conversations, notably those with the last-mentioned, are, for the modern reader, among the most attractive of Goethe's " works ". Johann Peter Eckermann is a strange figure in Goethe's life. He came to Weimar in 1823 with the recommendation of having written a book, *Beiträge zur Poesie*, which contained a sympathetic appreciation of Goethe's genius. It is difficult to think that Goethe could have been much impressed by his visitor's personality; but he rightly gauged his devotion, and took advantage of that strain of vanity and egotism which displays itself unpleasantly in his records : Eckermann is childishly unwilling to put himself in an unfavourable light, and is always anxious to identify himself with his master's opinions. Eckermann was certainly no Boswell, and the veracity of the records he has left us in his *Gespräche mit Goethe*, published in 1836, is not always above criticism; indeed, the liberties he took in expanding the notes which Soret generously placed at his disposal for a supplementary volume of his *Gespräche* (1848), show how cautious we must be in accepting all that Eckermann tells us as the poet's *ipsissima verba*. But Goethe not merely talked to the young man for the benefit of posterity; he also shrewdly saw that he could make use of him. With a ruthless disregard of such chances as Eckermann had of making an independent career, Goethe chained him to his side, entrusting him with the main business of preparing the final edition of his works for after generations.

This edition " letzter Hand " was Goethe's main pre-occupation in these last years : the final " summing up of his existence ". All the old man's activities, even the letters he wrote and the conversations he held, seemed directed to this end, the rounding-off of his life. The years meanwhile were growing sombrer as the end approached: and in 1830 the heaviest blow of all fell on him, the death of his son. In 1829 Goethe had sent him, accompanied by Eckermann, to Italy; but, owing to disagreements, Eckermann left him in Genoa. August went on to Rome, where he caught scarlet fever. This aggravated the already precarious state of his health, brought on by his intemperance, and he died on October 27th. It was surely a supreme touch of irony that he should have died in that Rome which had once been for his father the portal to a higher life, and be buried at the base of the pyramid of Cestius, which Goethe had once hoped would be his own final resting-place. But his own end necessarily not far distant, Goethe was steeled against even the worst buffets of fate. He would not speak of August's death, or have it spoken of, and to Zelter he concentrated his attitude to life in the grim words : " Forward over graves ! " But in the months following his bereavement he drew nearer to Ottilie and the grandchildren ; they were his last resource in his loneliness. During the dark days of 1830—again Goethe was very seriously ill towards the end of the year—he took in hand the final volume of his Auto-biography, which had been held back as long as Lili, its central figure, lived. In that year she died, and he rapidly dictated the work to its close, that it might complete the picture of his pre-Weimar life. Still two works remained to be finished and incorporated in the great edition : *Wilhelm Meisters Wanderjahre*, of which a first volume had appeared in 1821, and the Second Part of *Faust*.

Outward world-happenings had ceased to interest Goethe in these last years. In the feverish days of the French Revolution of 1830, when all Europe felt itself standing on the edge of a volcano, the only volcano for which Goethe had thoughts was that which had broken out in the French Academy of Sciences, the controversy between Cuvier and St. Hilaire on the origin of the globe ; the latter championed that synthetic conception of nature which had always been Goethe's, against the theory of cataclysmic origin of his opponent. The poet's last birthday was spent in Ilmenau, and with tears in his eyes, the old man read the lines he had scratched on the wall of the hut on the Kickelhahn fifty years before : " Über allen Gipfeln ist Ruh." And when the final touches had been put to *Faust* and the manuscript packed up and sealed, to be published after his death, he said

283

to Eckermann: "My further life I can only re-gard as a pure gift; I am indifferent as to what I may still do or whether I shall do anything else at all."

The following year, 1832, opened comparatively well, but on March 22nd, after only a week's illness, Goethe closed his eyes for ever. Older biographers liked to dwell on the tradition that the old poet's last words were "More light". A cruel exactness has whittled down this poetic close to a great life into a request of the dying man that the blinds might be raised. But the symbolical application of the words remains: all his life Goethe had sought untiringly for "more light" on the riddle of the world; and he, like his Faust, passed out with his craving unsatisfied and the mystery unsolved.

Here, at the close of his life, it seems fitting to look back once more on the wide span of years it covered. Goethe's life is not merely a life; it is an epoch. It covers the whole vast development of Germany's rich literature—its golden age—in the later eighteenth and early nineteenth centuries. That life began in rococo Leipzig, when the new literature was in its infancy, passed through its stormy adolescence of Rousseauism, to attain its majority in the humane classicism we associate with Weimar. More than this, Goethe lived through the first third of the new century; he was a contemporary of the whole vast development of Romanticism on which the new century was reared; and when he died, that Romanticism had already, as far as his own people were concerned, become a turned page. Thus Goethe is—and it can be said of no other of his contemporaries with the same force—a denizen of two centuries. This is the highest tribute that can be paid to the breadth of his mind and sympathies, to his marvellous power of spiritual growth.

CHAPTER VI

THE SECOND PART OF "FAUST"

THE ultimate victory of Faust in his struggle with the powers of evil was, as we have seen, indicated clearly and definitely in Goethe's plan long before the First Part appeared in print.   Early in the nineties the poet already saw his drama stretching out far beyond the limits of the present First Part; indeed, no scheme which Goethe at any time contemplated for the completion of the *Fragment* of 1790 was limited in its scope to what is now contained in that Part.   The moment Goethe decided that his Faust was to be saved, the question arose : for what future and what ultimate fate ?   A general scheme for the continuation was planned, as has been shown, in the first year of his friendship with Schiller; and this scheme must have covered in at least its general outline the poem as we know it in its two Parts to-day.

With the maturing years Goethe's conception of *Faust* widened and broadened.   The hero of the First Part had already gone through the process which converted him from a youthful rebel of the " Sturm und Drang " into an elderly sixteenth-century adept and wonder-worker.   The third phase, the generalization of Faust into a representative of aspiring humanity, has also begun in those parts of the drama which were latest to be written ; but nowhere had this generalization proceeded so far as to make Faust the symbol we find him in the Second Part; nowhere were his activity and aspiration envisaged as merely allegory. On the contrary, the pact with Mephistopheles was a definite narrowing-down of Faust's life-problem from the original vaster plan to the very human conflicts that beset the " two souls " within his breast. Faust's original craving for limitless knowledge—as in the old Volksbuch—and for equality with the Earth Spirit are lost sight of in the terms in which he signs away his freedom to Mephistopheles. Thus the actual problem of the First Part does not get beyond the trial of strength between Faust and Mephistopheles, between tempted and tempter: and its purpose is to put to the test Faust's insatiability. The great thought which becomes more and more dominating as the Second Part progresses : " He who strives forward with unswerving will can find salvation," is intoned in the " Prologue in Heaven," but it had been entirely foreign to the First Part of the drama. Faust has not there begun to " strive " in the later sense at all ; and we only know from God's word that error is no crime involving punishment, but an inevitable and desirable concomitant of all noble effort. Faust's activity is limited to one of defence against the wiles of the tempter; and the issue depends on the ineradicable element of discontent in human nature, not on the fulfilment of a positive ethical purpose. The Faust of the Second Part, on the other hand, is no longer " dimly and darkly conscious of the true way " ; he lives and acts in full consciousness of his will and power, and in confident faith in the justice of God's ways to man. When Goethe conceived the First Part and formulated the pact with Mephistopheles, he did not yet know that Faust was to find the ultimate solution to the riddle of his life, not in mere dissatisfaction, but in altruistic activity, in a life devoted to the service and welfare of mankind. Of this ethical creed of Goethe's old age there is nothing in the First Part of *Faust*. As the hero of the Second Part drew to himself ever-widening attributes, as his activities spread to æsthetic preoccupation with classic beauty, to statesmanship, economics, politics, and even war, to end in the overlordship of land that he has won back from the sea, the symbol usurped the place of the reality ; the Faust of the Second Part is a mere allegorical shadow compared with the human and tragic sufferer of the First Part.

It has always been regarded as an especial favour granted to Goethe by the Higher Powers that he was permitted, before he closed his eyes, to put the finishing touches to his life-work. *Faust* was completed within a month or two of his death ; he was constantly revising it and filing it to the last. It is difficult to say exactly when the idea of a Second Part took definite shape in Goethe's mind. The association of Faust with Helen of Troy was, of course, a very old motive in the saga ; and Goethe could not but have considered from the beginning how she might be introduced into his drama. But there was no room for her in the First Part with its essentially realistic atmosphere. The necessity of a continuation must have risen definitely into Goethe's consciousness when the poem was provided with a new cosmic framework by the " Prologue in Heaven " and the pact between Faust and Mephistopheles. This happened, as we have seen, in the last years of the eighteenth century.

The basic idea of the Second Part is that the Faust who, in the First Part, had been shown struggling tragically with an adverse fate within the narrow sphere of his personal life, should in the Second Part be led out into the great world of political and social activity. It was obvious—and it must have been clear to Goethe at a very early stage of his plan—that the poetic method of the First Part was wholly inapplicable to the Second. Faust, idealized and generalized as the representative of aspiring humanity, moving in a sphere of manifold activities, could only be presented, not as a being of flesh and blood, but as a type. The growing tendency of Goethe's imagination to express itself in abstractions was, in fact, a more compelling factor in his change of method than the poetic requirements of the theme. Faust and Mephistopheles, in other words, underwent the same dehumanizing process to which Wilhelm Meister and his circle had been subjected; the shadow took the place of the substance.

When Goethe was gathering together the materials for the fourth volume of his Autobiography in 1816, he, having then no hope of ever completing the Second Part of his drama, drafted the plan as it presented itself to him—possibly as it had been in his mind for long years. It is worth while reproducing this draft here at some length; for it is unfamiliar to English readers, and in many ways it reveals the possibility of a continuation of *Faust* in more stylistic harmony with the First Part than is to be seen in the classic Second Part as we know it.

At the beginning of the Second Part we find Faust sleeping. He is surrounded by spirit-choruses who in visible symbols and pleasant verses conjure up to him the joys of honour, fame, might and domination. They conceal in flattering words and melodies their actually ironic proposals. He awakens and feels strengthened; all his previous dependence on sensuality and passion has vanished.

Mephistopheles appears to him and gives him a merry and exciting description of the Reichstag at Augsburg [in another reference to this first act Goethe says Frankfort, the occasion being the coronation of the Emperor], which Kaiser Maximilian has summoned there; he describes it as if everything were taking place on the square outside the window, where Faust, however, sees nothing. Finally, Mephistopheles says that he sees the Kaiser at a window in the town hall talking with another prince; and he assures Faust that the Emperor is inquiring after him, where he is and whether he could not be brought to the court. Faust lets himself be persuaded, and his mantle facilitates the journey. In Augsburg he and Mephistopheles alight in a lonely hall, and Mephistopheles goes out to spy the land. Faust falls back meanwhile into his old speculations and demands upon himself. Mephistopheles then returns; he reports the strange condition that he, Mephistopheles, must not enter the hall, but must remain on the threshold; further, that in the Emperor's presence there must be no supernatural trickery and illusions. To this he has agreed. We are now transported to a large hall where the Emperor, just rising from table, comes to the window with a prince; he confesses that he would like to have Faust's mantle in order to be able to hunt one day in Tyrol and be back again on the morrow for a meeting of the council. Faust is announced and graciously received. The Emperor questions him concerning earthly hindrances and how they may be removed by magic. Faust's answers indicate higher demands and higher means of achieving them. The Emperor does not understand him; the courtiers still less. The conversation becomes involved, and Faust in his embarrassment looks round for Mephistopheles, who at once comes forward and answers in his name. The conversation now becomes lively; several people join them, and everybody is pleased with the wonderful visitor. The Emperor asks for visions and he is promised them. Faust retires to make preparations. At this moment Mephistopheles assumes his form to entertain the ladies young and old; he is regarded as a priceless man, for by a light touch he cures a wart, by a vigorous kick of his concealed hoof a corn; and a blonde young lady does not despise letting her little face be dabbed by his lean and pointed fingers : her pocket mirror consolingly shows her how one freckle after the other disappears. The evening approaches; a magic theatre rises up of itself. The form of Helena appears. The remarks of the ladies about this beauty of beauties enliven the otherwise awe-inspiring scene. Paris then appears and the men comment on him as the ladies had commented on Helena. The pretended Faust tells them that they are both right, and a merry scene develops.

On the choice of the third apparition there is a difference of opinion; the conjured-up spirits become impatient; several important ones appear together. Strange happenings take place, until at last theatre and phantoms suddenly vanish. The real Faust, illumined by three lamps, lies unconscious in the background; Mephistopheles disappears; no one perceives the duplicity, and no one feels very comfortable.

When Mephistopheles again meets Faust, he finds him in a most disturbed state. He has fallen in love with Helena, and desires that the master-magician shall procure her for him and hand her over into his arms. There are difficulties. Helena belongs to Orcus; by magic arts she can be lured out, but cannot be held fast. Faust insists, and Mephistopheles undertakes the task. An old castle, the possessor of which is fighting in Palestine, is to be the residence of the new Paris; the castellan of the castle is a magician. Helena appears; her bodily substance is restored to her by a magic ring. She believes that she has just come from Troy, and is arriving in Sparta. She finds it very lonely and longs for company, especially for male company, without which she has, all her life, been unable to exist. Faust appears and, as a German knight, presents a very wonderful contrast to the antique heroic figure. She finds him horrible, but as he knows how to flatter, she gradually grows reconciled to him, and he becomes the successor of many a hero and demigod. A son is born from this union who, as soon as he comes into the world, dances, sings, and waves his arms in the air. Now we must think that the castle is surrounded by a magic boundary within which alone these half realities can flourish. The rapidly growing boy gives his mother much pleasure. He is allowed to do everything except cross a certain stream which is forbidden to him. One holiday, however, he hears music on the other side, and sees country-people and soldiers dancing. He crosses the line, mingles with them, gets involved in quarrels; he wounds many of them and is at last killed by a magic sword. The castellan-magician saves his body. The mother is inconsolable, and ringing her hands in despair, slips off the ring and falls into Faust's arms, who, however, only embraces her empty robe. Mother and son have vanished. Mephistopheles, who has hitherto, in the disguise of an old female housekeeper, been a witness of everything, seeks to console his friend and inspire him with a desire for possessions. The owner of the castle has died in Palestine. Monks wish to acquire his property, and their blessings destroy the magic circle. Mephistopheles advises physical force, and places at Faust's disposal three helpers, Raufebald, Habebald, Haltefest. Faust believes that he is now adequately strengthened, and dismisses Mephistopheles and the castellan, carries on war with the monks, avenges the death of his son and becomes the possessor of great estates. Meanwhile, he is growing old, and what happens subsequently will be made clear when we, at some future time, collect together the fragments, or rather the scattered passages of the Second Part that have already been worked out, and thereby preserve for the reader some things that will interest him.

No one will, of course, wish to claim that this crude outline of the possible continuation of *Faust* is comparable with the classic poem as we know it, lifted up, as Goethe said, " out of the rough old popular legends ". But it must at least be admitted that had he, thus utilizing motives from Germanic fairy-tale lore, completed his *Faust* in earlier years, there might have resulted a more harmonious whole, a Second Part less distantly recognizable as a successor to the immortal realism of the First Part.

But it was not to be. When Goethe was preparing the First Part for publication, he was already deeply committed to that classicism which had matured *Die natürliche Tochter*, the *Achilleis* and *Pandora* ; and such time as he devoted to the continuation of *Faust* was expended on the third, or Helena act. This he had already decided should be purged of its German fairy-tale elements and executed in the spirit of ancient tragedy. The *Helena* is first mentioned in Goethe's diaries in September, 1800 ; it made some progress then, but was not seriously taken in hand until 1825. Two years later it was published separately as *Helena : klassisch-romantische Phantasmagorie.* Other scenes of the projected Second Part were, no doubt, taken in hand from time to time : but it was not until the publication of the *Helena* that Goethe earnestly resolved to complete his poem with such strength as was still left to him. By that time, even the classicism of the *Helena* had become a turned page, giving place to the mystic abstractions of the poet's last years.

A long period has elapsed since the tragic happenings with which Part I had closed; and Faust's recovery under the healing powers of nature is symbolically set forth in a kind of prologue. The spirits have sprinkled him with the waters of Lethe; he lies sleeping in a kind of Arcadia. From this sleep the rising sun awakens him to new life and resolution; and the scene culminates in the splendid monologue, setting the key of the new poem:

> Des Lebens Pulse schlagen frisch lebendig,
> Ätherische Dämmerung milde zu begrüssen;
> Du, Erde, warst auch diese Nacht beständig
> Und atmest neu erquickt zu meinen Füssen,
> Beginnest schon mit Lust mich zu umgeben,
> Du regst und rührst ein kräftiges Beschliessen,
> Zum höchsten Dasein immerfort zu streben.

Faust resolves to look forward, not backward and to strive towards the highest life in a world, which is only made manifest to us in its "farbigen Abglanz", its coloured reflexion. This is the theme of the Second Part of the poem.

In Act I we find Faust at the court of the Emperor. He is accompanied by Mephistopheles, who takes the place of the court fool and undertakes to amuse the court. There is a difficulty, however, about money: the imperial treasury is depleted. Mephistopheles is ready with a remedy: he suggests that the Emperor should issue paper money on the strength of the boundless treasures which must lie hidden throughout the empire. Meanwhile he organizes an elaborate "Mummenschanz" or masquerade of the kind which was beloved at the court of Weimar. These diversions provide—as they had provided in the Volksbuch—the

occasion for linking up Faust's life with Helen of
Troy. Relieved of his financial troubles, the Emperor
demands of Faust that he shall show him the fairest
woman and the most handsome man that ever lived,
Helena and Paris. Faust undertakes the task. He calls
Mephistopheles to his aid. The latter cannot, however,
directly give effect to his wish, the heathen world of
antiquity being outside his sphere, but he instructs him
how, with the aid of the mysterious " mothers ",
keepers of the Platonic ideals of realities—Goethe seems
to have found the motive in Plutarch,—he may obtain
from them the tripod which will bring back Helena's
shade from the dark land of Persephone. Provided
with a magic key which Mephistopheles gives him, he
achieves his end. With his key he touches the smoking
tripod : from the vapour emerge Helena and Paris.
The idle courtiers are more amused than impressed by
the spectacle ; but Faust himself is seized with violent
love for the spectre of Helena ; he attempts to grasp
it, and is thrown violently to the ground by an explo-
sion. Mephistopheles carries him off to the old familiar
Gothic room where his life in the drama had begun.
Here Wagner has stepped into his master's shoes ; he
is now the great adept and wonder-worker whom all
revere ; while the former student who had timidly
consulted Mephistopheles, thinking he was Faust,
about his studies, has profited by the devil's counsels
and blossomed out into a boisterous philistine.
Wagner is engaged in that most ambitious of all
the experiments of mediæval alchemy, the creation
of life. He is on the point of success ; and when
they arrive, a small living being, a " Homunculus ",
takes shape—no doubt, with Mephistopheles's aid—
in his glass retort. And now this extraordinary trio,
Faust—who has but one desire, to obtain the real
Helena from the shades—Mephistopheles and the
Homunculus, set out on a journey back through time
to the Greece of Helena. The most romantic of

romantic poets never conceived anything so fantastic as the journey of this trio into the past, Faust on the quest of the supreme beauty of the world, and the little Homunculus in search of the soul which the art of the alchemist could not give him. In Greece they arrive to witness the "Classical Walpurgisnacht". On the anniversary of the battle of Philippi on the Pharsalian plains, which, in Goethe's mind, had marked the downfall of the classic world, the denizens of Greek mythology assemble, as the northern witches had flocked to the Brocken on the last night of April. This gives Goethe's luxuriant imagination the opportunity for another masque in which are marshalled before us the mythological figures of the ancient world. The scene is grandiosely opened by Erichtho among the sleeping tents, and from all the spirits as they appear Faust asks the way to Helena. At last on the advice of the Sphinxes, he seeks out Chiron the centaur who had borne Helena on his back when she was a child. Chiron brings him to Manto from whose temple leads a secret way to the kingdom of Persephone. Here Goethe had the intention of introducing a scene in which Faust, before Persephone's throne, should demand and obtain Helena. Unfortunately it was never written. But in this part of the poem the sensitive reader again feels, as in the opening prologue, the compelling power of the poet's genius ; in spite of much being " hineingeheimnisst " into the " Classical Walpurgisnacht " of little poetic relevance, such as the controversy—which he introduces repeatedly into his later writings—as to whether the globe arose by fire or water, the grey veil of allegory becomes more tenuous, and the realization of the ancient world more real. The act is full of resplendent poetic imaginings, none more resplendent than that where Galatea, who takes the place of Aphrodite, emerges from the sea, and the Homunculus shatters his glass prison against her chariot.

The latter part of the " Classical Walpurgisnacht " plays against the lovely background of the Ægean Sea and the Upper Peneio ; and now the action turns to the personal fates of Faust and Helena. The classical Goethe has written nothing more stately and serene than this third act of the Second *Faust* ; and if the idyllic love of Faust and Helena is transfused by an unclassic emotionalism, Byron surely deserves some credit for it. It was, as has already been indicated, Byron's ardent philhellenism which infused life and warmth into the marble-cold Greece of the eighteenth-century tradition with which Goethe had grown up. Helena has come back to life ; but she still lives in the past. Troy has just fallen, and Phorkyas, a witch whom she finds lurking in her palace at Sparta—it is Mephistopheles in disguise—recalls to her her past ; tells her of the wrath of Menelaus, warns her that the only hope of escape for her and her women is to flee for refuge to a castle in the mountains. Whereupon, as in a dream, they are transported thither. Here Faust awaits her. Lynceus, the watcher on his tower, is so blinded by the apparition of matchless beauty that he neglects his duty to announce her coming. Faust in the splendour of a mediæval knight descends to meet her. In this episode Goethe's allegory again triumphs ; for the Greek Helena and the northern Faust are clearly symbols of that Classic and Romantic which dominated literature in the early years of the nineteenth century ; by this union of Greek and German the poet's conciliatory mind sought to symbolize that harmonious fusion which he had so deeply at heart. But Menelaus is reported to be in pursuit ; a clash with Faust's forces seems imminent, when Mephistopheles sees to it that the danger is averted. It passes as in a dream, and we hear no more of it. The scene now changes to Arcady, where Faust and Helena live their idyllic life. A child has been born to them, Euphorion. We see him, already a youth, climbing the rocky cliffs, higher

295

and higher, until, able to ascend no further, he throws himself into the air to fall lifeless at his parents' feet. "In the dead youth we believe we see a well-known form; but the bodily form vanishes, the aureole rises like a comet to the heavens, dress, mantle and lyre remain on the ground." Helena melts into air, and her cloak envelopes Faust like a cloud and bears him away. The "well-known form" was that of Lord Byron: in Euphorion, the child of Helena and Faust, Goethe raised a monument to the poet whom he regarded as the greatest of the moderns. It was, as Goethe conceived it, Byron's mission to bring about the reconciliation in modern poetry; and, in justifying his Euphorion allegory to Eckermann, he said: "I could use no one as the representative of the most modern poetic era but Byron, who is, without question, to be regarded as the greatest talent of the century. And then Byron is not antique, and not romantic; but he is as the present day itself."

The fourth act of the Second Part of *Faust*, with its allegory of great world happenings, of war and strife, fails signally to grip our interest. Here, indeed, is the weakest part of the poem; but had Goethe not attempted the impossible? We are brought back to the northern atmosphere. A cloud rests on a high mountain, and Faust emerges from it. Mephistopheles, once more the northern devil, arrives in seven-league boots. He induces Faust to intervene again in the affairs of the empire, now distraught by civil war. With the aid of the three "mighty men" whom Mephistopheles places at his service, Faust assists the Emperor to assert his authority, and stipulates, as a reward for his services, for a strip of land along the coast.

Between Acts IV and V many years elapse. Faust has made good use of his fief from the Emperor by making it a basis for the recovery of a large tract of land from the sea—an idea which Goethe seems to have borrowed less from Holland than from the project of

land reclamation at Portmadoc in Wales. Faust has
now reached his hundredth year, and his great work is
all but accomplished. The act opens with the idyll of
Philemon and Baucis who live happy and contented
in their cottage which overlooks Faust's achievement; they watch the harbour and its ships. But
Faust desires just this plot of land to round off his
scheme. They are unwilling to be transferred elsewhere. Mephistopheles, who arrives in a ship, undertakes to carry out Faust's purpose; and their cottage
goes up in flames. Faust is seized by remorse for the
misery his lust for power has caused. At last he sees
its futility, and with it, the futility of that magic on
which he had risen to greatness:

> Ich bin nur durch die Welt gerannt;
> Ein jed' Gelüst ergriff ich bei den Haaren,
> Was nicht genügte, liess ich fahren,
> Was mir entwischte, liess ich ziehn.
> Ich habe nur begehrt und nur vollbracht,
> Und abermals gewünscht und so mit Macht
> Mein Leben durchgestürmt; erst gross und mächtig;
> Nun aber geht es weise, geht bedächtig.
> Der Erdenkreis ist mir genug bekannt,
> Nach drüben ist die Aussicht uns verrannt;
> Tor! wer dorthin die Augen blinzelnd richtet,
> Sich über Wolken seinesgleichen dichtet!
> Er stehe fest und siehe hier sich um;
> Dem Tüchtigen ist diese Welt nicht stumm.
> Was braucht er in die Ewigkeit zu schweifen!
> Was er erkennt, lässt sich ergreifen.
> Er wandle so den Erdentag entlang;
> Wenn Geister spuken, geh' er seinen Gang,
> Im Weiterschreiten find' er Qual und Glück,
> Er, unbefriedigt jeden Augenblick.

Four grey women approach, Want, Guilt, Need, Care.
Care alone can penetrate to him, entering his palace by
the keyhole; and Care breathes upon his eyes and he is
blind. Meanwhile at Mephistopheles's behest, grim
lemurs dig his grave; but to the blind Faust the sound
of pick and shovel means only the accomplishment of

his great task. The moment has at last come when he can bid the passing moment stay :

> Ja ! diesem Sinne bin ich ganz ergeben,
> Das ist der Weisheit letzter Schluss :
> Nur der verdient sich Freiheit wie das Leben,
> Der täglich sie erobern muss.
> Und so verbringt, umrungen von Gefahr,
> Hier Kindheit, Mann und Greis sein tüchtig Jahr.
> Solch ein Gewimmel möcht' ich sehn,
> Auf freiem Grund mit freiem Volke stehn.
> Zum Augenblicke dürft' ich sagen :
> Verweile doch, du bist so schön !
> Es kann die Spur von meinen Erdetagen
> Nicht in Äonen untergehn.—
> Im Vorgefühl von solchem hohen Glück
> Geniess' ich jetzt den höchsten Augenblick.

Faust sinks back dead. The moment of Mephistopheles's triumph has come. He summons his devils to seize Faust's soul as it emerges from his body. But now angels descend, do battle for its possession ; and victoriously bear it aloft.

Much has been written about the defeat of the ends of justice by Goethe's salvation of Faust. Mephistopheles is, of course, wrongly cheated out of the fruits of the wager he has won when Faust at last admits that the moment has arrived when he can bid the passing moment stay. Faust is only saved by virtue of the old poet's optimistic caveat : the good cannot and must not perish : as the angels sing :

> Gerettet ist das edle Glied
> Der Geisterwelt vom Bösen :
> " Wer immer strebend sich bemüht,
> Den können wir erlösen."

Indeed, had not this been proclaimed in no uncertain terms by God Himself in the Prologue in Heaven ? One might have preferred that other ending which Goethe is credited with having once contemplated, a scene where God should pardon both Mephistopheles and His erring servant Faust, and all have ended in beatified conciliation. But one thing is plain : an ending other than conciliatory was to Goethe's mind unthinkable. God will not and cannot let His servant fall ; and he sends His angels—in a scene which made a peculiar appeal to Ruskin—to scatter roses, thus discomfiting and defeating the powers of evil. Evil ? But what is evil ? Can evil have any substance at all in God's world ? To Goethe evil is but the steppingstone to the good, as Mephistopheles is the servant of God. And who actually is this Mephistopheles ? In early robust days he had been a very conventional and very human devil ; then he came to be a kind of elemental spirit, an emissary of the Earth Spirit ; then one of God's heavenly hierarchy. Once again, he is sublimated into an abstraction, who assumes at will the guises of heathen antiquity. With each successive transformation he becomes a paler effigy of his former self ; more and more the allegorical embodiment of an idea. And as the great drama closes, all guises are suddenly, as it were, stripped from him, and he seems to stand out as the arch-enemy of man—Time itself. Not evil is the great antagonist in *Faust*, but all-conquering Time. " The clock stands still ; the pointer falls."

In the grandiose Dantesque close of his poem Goethe, the " great heathen ", has, it is often claimed, become a convert to the Roman Catholic faith. The angels, " bearing the immortal part of Faust ", rise ever higher through a spiritual world as purely Catholic as that of any mediæval mystery. But might it not be fairer to say that this close, so far from indicating doctrinary narrowness, is a tribute to the old poet's wideness— in the best sense catholicism—of mind ? In these last years so many of the antitheses that had accompanied Goethe through life were resolved into harmony. There is no antagonism for him now between Protestant and Catholic, between Christianity and heathendom, between Greek and German, between Classic and Romantic ; just as in his own self the two souls that had fought for supremacy were at rest.   Least of all is there apostasy in this German Faust, who had passed through the purgatory of suffering and renunciation, who had dwelt in Arcady with Helen, when he at last ascends through saints and angels guided by the Eros who had initiated him into life, led by " Una Poenitentium, formerly called Gretchen ", to the feet of the Divine Mother in whom the heavenly and the earthly love are one and indivisible.

The last act of *Faust* is a fit allegorical close to a great allegorical life ; in its final words the symbol is resolved into perfect harmony.

> Alles Vergängliche
> Ist nur ein Gleichnis ;
> Das Unzulängliche
> Hier wird's Ereignis ;
> Das Unbeschreibliche
> Hier ist's getan ;
> Das Ewig-Weibliche
> Zieht uns hinan.

This *Faust* is then a tremendous effort to harmonize the world, the most wonderful, perhaps, in all literature ; the last great achievement of one whose mission all through his years was, rightly regarded, to bring conciliation and peace into a troubled world.   But it is admittedly difficult for us moderns to acquire the right focus for its complete appreciation.   The Second Part of *Faust* suffers, as a work of creative genius, and must always suffer in comparison with the intensely human First Part.   It is a poem of shadowy, schematic personalities, bandying shadowy and allegorical thoughts. Faust himself has been sublimated into a symbol ; Mephistopheles has become an abstraction ; in neither does any more the blood run red.   Helena, too, is but a shadow ; never could this Helena, this embodiment of supreme beauty, have " launched a thousand ships and burnt the topless towers of Ilium ".   There is indeed no human interest at all in this Second Part ; its actions are not human actions subject to human motives, but happenings in a world of fantasies, of classic phantoms and symbols. And yet, frankly accepting it as allegory, what a world it is, this world of the Second *Faust*! Can a more resplendent panorama be found anywhere in the literature of the world?

Faust is the most heterogeneous of all Goethe's works; it is a thing of broken ends, unconvincing joins, tantalizingly fragmentary, full of unsolved poetic problems. Goethe's dilatory inability to finish his drama in one mood and at one period of his life has brought confusion upon its theme, which no interpretative ingenuity can reduce to order. There is no real unity in the ever-changing, ever-growing figures of Faust and Mephistopheles; and there is as little unity of idea and problem in the great poem as there is in its form and style. A thing of inconsistencies, broken ends, unfulfilled promises, it is just perhaps in this incompleteness, in this lack of classic perfection and rounded smoothness, that its inexhaustible fascination lies. *Faust* would assuredly have been a more satisfying work of art had it been the product of a single period of the poet's life; but instead, it has become something much more precious: the spiritual essence of his whole life, the receptacle of his highest wisdom—a world-poem reflecting in its many facets the thought of one of the richest minds in the history of our race and of the momentous epoch of human evolution of which he was a part.

Chapter VII

GOETHE'S CONTRIBUTIONS TO SCIENCE

It was George Henry Lewes who first drew general
attention to Goethe's achievements in the field of
science; and since his time—especially in the last
quarter of the nineteenth century, when the barometer
of Goethe's reputation was rapidly rising—there has
been a tendency to attach perhaps undue weight to
this side of his activities. More particularly was it
claimed in the days when the Darwinian theory of
the origin of species provided a widely accepted solution to the mystery of life, that Goethe had anticipated
Darwin: the great biologist Ernst Haeckel was eloquent above all others in proclaiming Goethe a pioneer
of the theory of biological evolution. It is more possible to-day to arrive at a just estimate of the value
and the shortcomings of Goethe's contributions to
science.

The natural sciences played a very large part in
Goethe's intellectual life; he took himself very seriously as a scientist, and certainly with more justification than as a critic of painting and sculpture or with
his own drawings, where he rarely rose beyond the
level of the talented amateur. It is, indeed, no idle
claim to say that Goethe was the last of the great
minds of our race to be at home in both poetry and
science, which the nineteenth century, with its enormous strides in scientific discovery, was to separate
by so wide a gulf and often bring into irreconcilable
antagonism. In this respect Goethe was a true son
of the eighteenth century, when no hard and fast line

had yet been drawn between the mentality of the scientific observer and that of the poet, and when our own Royal Society still claimed as its domain both the empirical sciences and the world of the spirit. Science, philosophy and poetry then still lived in mutually helpful comradeship, poetry, the eldest sister, being the predominant partner. Imagination, disguised as hypothesis, invaded and fertilized the field of scientific fact; not, as in later times, when science came of age, and in the arrogance of its materialism deprived the imagination of the wings to soar. This pleasant amity was maintained down to the Romantic age, and with admittedly beneficial results : all our modern science stands deep in its debt to the interpretations of Romanticism.

The beginnings of Goethe's interest in science date back to a very early period. As a boy, he was filled with a Rousseau-like awe and fascination before the wonders of natural phenomena. In Leipzig as a young student, he was tempted to attend lectures on scientific subjects, notably electricity; and after his return to Frankfort as an invalid, he devoted himself to experiments with crucibles and retorts which have left their mark on the early *Faust*. Again, in Strassburg, where his intimate friends were students of medicine, he found in a still higher degree than in Leipzig relaxation from the dullness of jurisprudence by attending lectures on chemistry, anatomy and medicine. It will be remembered, too, with what interest he followed Lavater's investigations into the connexion between human character and physical characteristics, and how he contributed to Lavater's work on physiognomy. Even in these contributions may be traced a foreshadowing of that line of thought which was ultimately to find expression in his theory of the skull as the highest development of the vertebræ of the spinal column.

Goethe's systematic preoccupation with scientific

studies dates, however, only from his Weimar years. His practical concern with the mines of Ilmenau turned his attention to geology and mineralogy, and his first scientific essay is one *Über den Granit*—more poetry, it is true, than science—which he wrote on his expedition to the Harz Mountains to study the working of the mines there in 1777. Further stimulus came from Goethe's other activities for the Weimar state: his thoughts were turned to botany by his supervision of agriculture, horticulture and forestry, and more particularly, by his interest in the garden of his own house "Am Stern," and in the laying out of the Weimar park. In the longest of the journeys which he undertook from Weimar before his sojourn in Italy, that to Switzerland in 1779–80, we find him engrossed by the geological problems of the Alps; and in his official concern for the development of the university of Jena he always showed a greater interest in the professors of science than in those of the humanities.

Goethe's attitude to science never, however, belied the poet; he was led, in the first instance, to study its problems by that holy reverence for nature which had been instilled into him in early years by Rousseau; and Spinoza had taught him to see in nature the "living garment of God". The phenomena he saw around him, if they were thus a manifestation of Deity, could be no blind or accidental happenings. Everywhere Goethe sought and found continuity, gradual and law-governed development and progress: nature for him abhorred cataclysms as it abhors a vacuum; the universe he could not see otherwise than a divinely ordained and harmonious whole into which it was man's highest privilege and happiness to fit himself. This is the great thought that lies behind all Goethe's scientific thinking and guided him in his contributions to scientific discovery; and it is a thought which may be seen dimly emerging from the old Leibnizian

" Théodicée " and taking shape in the evolutional conception of Goethe's first great teacher Herder.

These preconceived ideas of the working of nature presented perhaps something of an obstacle where Goethe's study of geology was concerned; for here it was still difficult, in the rudimentary state of knowledge in the eighteenth century, to arrive at wise deductions from observation, and experiment was naturally impossible. It explains, too, why Goethe's contributions to that science are of least value to later generations. But his interest in it remained with him through life : his mineralogical collections were to the last one of his chief cares, and converted the great house on the Frauenplan into a veritable museum. We have seen how it was a geological problem—the controversy between Cuvier and St. Hilaire as to whether the structure of the globe was due to the agency of fire or water—which engrossed him in 1830, and was more momentous in his eyes than the political revolution in Paris of that year. This, Goethe's last passionate appeal, was for the synthetic and gradual aqueous process which St. Hilaire maintained against the theory of igneous cataclysms of Cuvier.

Of much greater significance than his geological theories was Goethe's contribution to the science of anatomy, or rather osteology ; for his interest in anatomy was restricted to the skeleton of man and the higher animals. With the help of the Jena professor, Justus Christian Loder, he mastered in 1781 the structure of the human frame ; and even thus early caught a glimpse of the value of comparison in interpreting the organic world. In 1784 he made the discovery that the intermaxillary bone which is to be found in mammals, is also present in a rudimentary form in man. The importance of this apparently trifling discovery lies in the fact that the absence of the bone had been hitherto held as a convincing proof of the break in continuity between man and the lower animals and of his exclusive position in nature. Goethe's views are set down in his first anatomical treatise : *Versuch aus der vergleichenden Knochenlehre, dass der Zwischenknochen der oberen Kinnlade dem Menschen mit den übrigen Tieren gemein sei* (*Essay in Comparative Osteology, showing that the Intermaxillary Bone of the Upper Jaw is common to Man and the other Animals*). This treatise may well be regarded as a foundation-stone of the new science of comparative anatomy which Goethe outlined in a later essay, *Entwurf einer Einleitung in die vergleichende Anatomie* (1795). The chance examination of a sheep's skull which he found on the Lido at Venice in 1790, suggested to him, as by a flash of intuition, another great, and more greatly daring, idea in support of his claim for anatomical continuity. He saw the skull in the light of a highly developed modification of the last six vertebræ of the mammalian spine. This thought is explained in the short essay, *Versuch über die Gestalt der Tiere* (1790).

In the science of botany Goethe was an equally adventurous pioneer. His mode of approach is essentially the same as in his anatomical studies. Here, too, he will prove that the infinite variety of nature may be reduced to unity, and her isolated phenomena to interlinked continuity of development. In his *Versuch, die Metamorphose der Pflanzen zu erklären*, published in 1790, he set out the theory that all forms of plant structure are but modifications of the leaf, the first cotyledons being the primal structure from which develop leaf and petal, stamen and pistil; the central stem of the typical " Urpflanze " throws out leaves and branches, as the vertebral column of animals throws out its appendages which make up the body; and as the uppermost vertebræ unite to form the crowning organ of the animal, its head, so at its highest point the stem of the plant bears flower and fruit.

It is not to be denied that, in these biological studies,

Goethe had at least a presentiment of that theory of organic evolution which Darwin was to set forth a generation and more later. There is a foreshadowing of Darwinism in an aphorism like the following :

> Nature can attain to whatever she sets out to achieve only by means of a gradual succession. She makes no leaps. She could not, for instance, make a horse, if it had not been preceded by all the other animals, as a kind of ladder by which she ascended to the structure of the horse.

And again :

> Nature, in order to arrive at man, institutes a long prelude of beings and forms which are, it is true, deficient in a great deal that is essential to man. But in each is manifest a tendency which points to the next form above it.

But we are hardly justified in drawing the conclusion that Goethe was a Darwin before Darwin. He himself closed the door on any speculation that might have led to an *Origin of Species* :

> When the earth [he said] had arrived at a certain point of maturity, mankind came into being everywhere where the land permitted of it. To pursue this thought further, as has been done, I hold to be a useless occupation which we may well leave to those who are fond of busying themselves with insoluble problems.

Apart from this attitude to the problem, Goethe's approach to it differed essentially from Darwin's. He was less concerned than the great English scientist in building up a theory from patiently accumulated facts ; rather he sought ratification for a preconceived idea ; for an endeavour to impose upon the phenomena of life the great Spinozistic conception of the ' one in all ". When Goethe explained his " Urpflanze " to Schiller, he was taken aback by his friend's acute observation : " That is an idea, not an experience." In all his scientific speculation Goethe went out from the idea ;

observation and experiment were directed to a degree that would not be countenanced by modern science to supporting and establishing the hypothesis.

Goethe had a greater pride in his investigations and theories in another field of science where both contemporaries and posterity have refused to give him the credit they allow his biological work, namely, in the science of optics. Goethe, however, was not interested in the science of light as a whole, but, unfortunately, only with the phenomena of colour. His studies in this field date from the early nineties, when his interest in the matter was kindled by casual observation of the effect of a prism on a ray of light : the first fruits of his observations he set down in his *Beiträge zur Optik* of 1791. Newton had explained the action of the prism to the satisfaction of the scientific world on the basis of his undulatory theory of light : waves of white light passing through the glass medium were subjected to graduated hindrances in their progress ; to these hindrances the constituent elements of white light reacted in varying ways, the result being the range of coloured light we call the spectrum. These coloured rays could then be gathered together again with the aid of a lens, the result being the original white light. This appeared to be the most convincing proof that colourless light was no homogeneous element, but a mingling of the entire range of colours. Newton's demonstration was reinforced by a convincing array of mathematical proof. Goethe, satisfied that certain features of the phenomenon did not bear out this theory, and still more, feeling that the theory ran counter to the thought that was so dear to his heart, namely, that behind the infinite variety of nature lay simplicity, unity and continuity, insisted that white light must be homogeneous, and propounded a new theory in accordance with which colour was merely the consequence of varying admixtures of light and darkness.

Obviously this is again an illustration of Schiller's remark about Goethe's theory of botanical morphology : it was primarily an idea, not a logical deduction from experience. All Goethe's experimenting and observing, spread over many years, the results of which fill the large work *Zur Farbenlehre*, are dominated by the desire to prove this theory of colour. At the same time the patience and thoroughness of his investigations deserve all honour : nowhere is he more of a true scientist than here. Not merely did he experiment, within the strictly optical field, with the action and reactions of colours ; but he also recorded observations on the distribution of colour in the animal and vegetable world, the use of colour by the great artists ; he even, to further his ends, embarked on the study of astronomy. But it was the theory, not the method, where, in the eyes of the scientific world, brought up in unquestioning confidence in Newton, his work was at fault. Goethe was no mathematician ; it was the one science with which his great brain was unable to cope ; and as Newton's optical theory was built upon mathematics, any confutation of it must be preceded by an examination of Newton's mathematical premisses. This Goethe was unable to do ; and he solved the difficulty, unscientifically enough, by ignoring it, and substituting a simpler quite unmathematical theory of his own.

When *Zur Farbenlehre* appeared in two volumes in 1810, it met with a very chill reception. Goethe was moved to a quite un-Goethelike anger; it was the bitterest pill he ever had to swallow. He expressed his resentment with a violence such as the lack of appreciation of his purely literary works had never evoked ; and on Newton the great charlatan he vented his wrath with the virulence of a Voltaire. How deep the wound must have penetrated is seen from a remark he made to Eckermann years later :

> As for what I have done as a poet, I take no pride in it whatever. Excellent poets have lived at the same time; more excellent poets have lived before me, and will come after me. But that in my century I am the only man who knows the truth in the difficult science of colour—of that I say, I am not a little proud.

That, outside the professional world of physicists, there were men of eminence like Schopenhauer who ranged themselves on his side, was but small consolation.

In point of fact, Goethe did suffer an injustice; for *Zur Farbenlehre* is a monumental production; it would be difficult to point to another scientific treatise written in those birth-years of modern science which is more worthy of our respect to-day. Moreover, it is introduced by an admirable and judicious review of the history of optics, to which, it is true, contemporaries were willing to accord a grudging praise, and which has received still more from modern critics. We feel as we re-read the work to-day, that to condemn it outright merely because Goethe shirked the refutation of the theory he opposed, was to ignore its many virtues and its contribution to the advance of knowledge by observation and experiment. It may be, as has been suggested, that in our twentieth century, when Newton's authority no longer stands where it did, a more indulgent eye may be cast on what a hundred and twenty years ago was only regarded as a lamentable aberration of a great mind.

The writings which have just been discussed by no means cover all Goethe's interest in the natural sciences; there were, in fact, few fields in which he was not interested; he had an open and receptive mind for nature in all her manifestations. In particular, meteorology claimed a large share of his attention; one volume of his scientific works is largely taken up with observations on cloud-formation and the possibilities of weather forecasting, matters in which contemporary English writers had led the way.

German writers of our time like to discuss Goethe's scientific "Methodenlehre". But it is doubtful whether this can carry us very far; Goethe never in his own mind formulated a consistent plan of scientific method. In his approach to science there was, however, always a philosophical or metaphysical element—and that long before his intercourse with Schiller had brought him to look with a more friendly eye on abstract thinking; he approached scientific problems with certain fixed presuppositions. To Spinoza he owed in early years that pantheism which lay behind all his conception of the physical world; and this pantheism was deepened and strengthened in later life by the one thinker among his contemporaries with whom he stood in intimate sympathy, Schelling. But Goethe was at no time a metaphysician; living in the most philosophic age of the world's history, he held himself aloof from its philosophy; was merely the interested onlooker. At most, he culled a little from this thinker and that, as he felt it could be useful to his own personal needs; but he had no faith in metaphysical systems. In the spirit of the century in which his best years were passed he never lost touch with its scepticism and common sense. Enough for him was to know where the problems lay; he recognized the limits of the human understanding, and refused to dogmatize or entertain dogmas about what in his view transcended the power of the mind to penetrate. "Man is not born to solve the problems of the world, but rather to discover where the problems lie, and then to keep within the limits of what he can know." It may be questioned whether such dogmatic distinction between the knowable and the unknowable was to the advantage of Goethe as a scientific thinker; it certainly closed avenues to him which later generations have explored and whereby they have widened our knowledge. But, on the other hand, the admission that there was an unknowable was an effective protest against the tyranny of scientific materialism and the mechanical interpretation of the universe. To the scientists of the later nineteenth century, grown arrogant with the rapid advance of knowledge and discovery, such a protest had no meaning; to them the " facts " of which the mind could take cognizance were the sum of knowledge. But here again, our twentieth century approaches the mysteries of science in another and less confident spirit, and in admitting transcendentalism into scientific thinking it may be the more ready to appreciate sympathetically the wisdom of Goethe.

To many of us to whom Goethe is, above all things, the great poet, there is a dark side to Goethe's scientific pursuits. Did they not place hindrances in the way of his poetic activity? It may have been that he only turned to science when poetic inspiration left him in the lurch; but it may also have been that science was at times responsible for that failing inspiration and led to his neglect of that function for which he was supremely gifted. We look to Goethe, not for scientific discovery, an activity with which many other minds were as able—and perhaps better able—to cope with successfully, but to more precious discoveries in the realm of the spirit and the imagination. May we not thus cherish something of a grudge that his immersion in scientific pursuits took up so very large a share in his life?

CHAPTER VIII

CONCLUSION

EVERY new generation in the past hundred years has felt the need of defining its attitude to Goethe; and the history of his fame has been a succession of varying attitudes towards him, a probing and questioning on the part of his readers as to whether he means the same thing to them as he did to their fathers. What, then, does Goethe mean to us to-day? Ignoring all attempts to establish absolute æsthetic values, and leaving the literary historian, armed with his trained critical sense and his historic perspective, to establish Goethe in his particular niche in the Valhalla of poetry, let us ask the more personal question: Do we still feel Goethe to be a poet of the present? How far is he still able to move us with his visions of poetic beauty? How far has he the power to add to our spiritual stature, to be a guide and a teacher to us? May we still turn to him in the twentieth century, as Carlyle turned to him a hundred years ago, in our doubts and perplexities, find in him a comforter and consoler in dark days?

The question of the living power of a great poet of the past is, of course, not the same thing as that of his literary achievement and eminence. We all recognize the greatness of Homer and Virgil, of Dante and Cervantes, of Shakespeare; and we do seek refuge with them, as in a kind of Golden Age, from the fever and the fret of our modern life; but it is rare that they can afford us a solution to immediate spiritual perplexities. They may fill our minds

with visions of pure beauty and sublime imaginings ;
but when it is a question of the intimate difficulties
that beset us, poets of a remote past cannot enter into
our particular problems.   They are too far away, too
much denizens of other worlds than ours, to give us
what we look for.   Does Goethe, whose life lies
nearer to our own time, also stand nearer to us, near
enough to be a living guide ?

It is perhaps a proof of Goethe's essential " live-
ness " that we have not yet reached objective finality
in our judgment of him ; that we still cannot speak
dispassionately of him.   He is an object of reverence,
and even passionate reverence, to some, while by others
he is repudiated and scorned.   We are still in the
stage of debating about him ; and thinking men in
all lands feel the necessity of putting to themselves
the question : Was Goethe really so great a poet as
we are told he was ?   Is he still great ?   Wherein
lies his claim to greatness ?   This need of re-estimat-
ing Goethe, of constantly revising our judgment of
him, is, on the whole, a hopeful sign.   As long as
this is our attitude to a writer of the past, he has
assuredly not ceased to be a living force in our intellectual life.

If we pass in review what has been said about
Goethe in the past hundred years, we meet with a
very wide range of opinion.   Amongst ourselves, we
have Carlyle's fervid Romantic interpretation of him
and his earnest appeal : " Close thy Byron, open thy
Goethe ! " balanced by the irreverent attitude of minds
like De Quincey's ; we have George Henry Lewes's
still fascinating biography ; and the sane and considered
estimates—tinged, it is true, with the Victorian passion for ethical ideals—of men like Matthew Arnold,
John Seeley, Edward Dowden.   Again, we cannot
neglect to take note of the steadfast loyalty to him
of his own people during the last forty years.   Indeed,
at no time in the history of German intellectual life

—not even in the wild years of fermentation when, with such splendid munificence, Goethe flung out the masterpieces of his youth into the " seed-field of time " —has he been held in such high esteem in his own land as in the last fifty years. The celebration of the hundred and fiftieth anniversary of his birth in 1899 formed an extraordinary contrast to the lukewarm celebration of 1849, when the esteem in which Goethe was held was at its lowest ebb. That year, 1899, no doubt, brought his fame in Germany to a kind of culmination. Down to the Great War this enthusiasm showed no signs of abatement; and from the abundant literature on him which has appeared since 1914, it would seem that Goethe, the spiritual leader of his people in their prosperity, has been a no less trusted leader to them in their adversity.

Goethe has left us much poetry of the highest order of beauty; but no other of the great minds of our race has bequeathed to us so much that falls disappointingly short of the highest achievement. As the years move on, the number of Goethe's creations that are acknowledged to be irreproachably great seems to diminish. It is not always easy to stand up to traditional opinion and be absolutely honest in our attitude to his work; but it will be generally admitted that in the brief hundred years that have passed since Goethe closed his eyes in Weimar, his works have not enjoyed the hoped-for immunity from the ravages of time; in this respect he has suffered more than many less gifted and less universal European writers. Only a very small proportion of all the hundred and fifty volumes that now comprise his collected literary remains bear upon them the stamp of eternity. Indeed, it might be questioned whether there is more than one sphere of imaginative creation in which Goethe achieves sustained and matchless supremacy, that of the lyric. Apart from his shorter poems, we have the great world-drama of *Faust*; there are the two classic dramas

Iphigenie auf Tauris and *Torquato Tasso*, the epic idyll of *Hermann und Dorothea*; and a plea must be made for that novel of Goethe's youth, which is too readily scoffed at by our modern intellectuals as a maudlin love-story : *Werthers Leiden*. But in the field of the prose epic and in the medium of prose Goethe was always less successful than when he wrote in verse. Who could compare *Wilhelm Meister* as an imaginative creation—significant as it is in the evolution of German fiction—with our own splendid *Tom Jones*? And the epic of his own youth, *Dichtung und Wahrheit*? Again, is it not too often lumbering in its style and too tedious in its leisurely irrelevancies to be an unmixed pleasure to the modern reader?

Such is a fair statement of the twentieth-century attitude among ourselves to Goethe the creative artist. That so great a mind as his should have given us so few masterpieces beyond all reproach is, no doubt, partly accounted for by the fact that in his writings he was an incorrigible procrastinator. Had he possessed the perseverance which his friend Schiller showed in so high a degree, that determination to weld the iron while it still glowed, instead of constantly having to heat it up afresh; had he wrestled with his " daimon " as Jacob with the angel, until he had found blessedness, he would certainly have left us more masterpieces which would be for us veritable " possessions for ever ".

But there is perhaps another reason for the discrepancy between Goethe's genius and his creations; and this reason is only dimly beginning to emerge in our time from the many discussions of the dualism or " polarity " of Goethe's nature. This dualism, it is true, gave Goethe that supreme balance of mind —a balance in which he has never been surpassed by any man—and made him so helpful and inspiring as a spiritual leader. But it is very questionable whether such polarity is a gain to the artist. There is no disintegrating polarity of the Goethean kind in Homer or Dante, in Sophocles or Shakespeare. In Goethe's breast were always two souls, and that not merely in the sense expressed by Faust in the often quoted lines :

> Zwei Seelen wohnen, ach, in meiner Brust,
> Die eine will sich von der andern trennen ;
> Die eine hält, in derber Liebeslust,
> Sich an die Welt mit klammernden Organen ;
> Die andre hebt gewaltsam sich vom Dust
> Zu den Gefilden hoher Ahnen—

but in every sense. Supreme achievement in the realm of the imagination can only be attained in single-ness of heart and soul ; to the artist with two conflicting souls in his breast it is rarely given to touch the very highest.

It was something of an admission of this disparity between Goethe's genius and his achievement when, at the revival of Goethe study and enthusiasm forty years ago, the parole went forth that greater than all his works was the life that Goethe lived ; his writings, we were told, should not be enjoyed and interpreted as art-works standing by themselves and justifying themselves, but rather as life-documents, as " frag-ments of a great confession ". That this view is now being discredited and a more objective attitude to Goethe's poetry insisted upon—Benedetto Croce's stimulating volume of some years ago was in this respect a clearing of the air—seems one of the significant advances of the Goethe criticism of our time. Real æsthetic values are always independent of subjective interest ; a work of art must stand or fall by its own merit.

But the fact remains that Goethe's life—by far the most fully documented life in literary annals—is a very precious heritage to after-generations. We saw how even the poet's youth, far back in the eighteenth century, has a freshness and fascination that seems as of yesterday. We still feel as Goethe felt ; no veil of time has descended between his way of looking at life and the world and ours ; Goethe's youth still holds the mirror up to an ideal in us, an ideal of joy in life, in nature, in love.   Then came the Weimar years, at first an immediate continuation of that early time of overflowing, ebullient genius ; Goethe—the Goethe of *Iphigenie, Egmont, Wilhelm Meisters Theatralische Sendung*—is still the directly inspired writer of genius, the " maker " and creator.   But with the maturing years a change came over him ; he ceased to be satisfied merely to obey the behest of his genius, and to give unthinkingly of his plenitude ; he became increasingly obsessed with the problems of his own life, his poetic mission, and responsibilities to his genius.   Possibly —indeed probably—these problems were forced upon Goethe by dissatisfaction with the narrowness of his sphere in Weimar, which at first promised so much, and was subsequently to appear to him so constricting. At last in 1787 he wrenched himself free ; for a year and a half in Italy he was completely his own master. And then the prison-bars of German provinciality closed upon him once more, never to let him free again.   Slowly but surely the pettiness of the old life ate into his soul ; and he who in Italy had discovered that he was " really born for poetry ", ceased to be in the high sense a poet at all.   The divine afflatus in great measure evaporated ; and the greatest spirit in Europe petrified into a German " Geheimrat "— pompous, magisterial, dictatorial.   Goethe ceased to create—to create naïvely and imaginatively ; the artist in him mortified ; he became a mere shadow of the inspired, instinctive genius of early days.   His prose became reflective, tediously informative ;   and his poetry apophthegmatic and subtle, even when it dealt with lyric and emotional things.   The light that shines on even so perfectly constructed a masterpiece as *Hermann und Dorothea*, is a light reflected through prisms ; it is no longer the pure clear sunshine of heaven that floods the pages of *Werther* and the early inspirations. It has flattered the German mind in the past that a poet—and one without noble blood in his veins—should have been lifted up into the spheres in which Goethe moved, have become the intimate of a reigning duke and his minister of state; but we outsiders who are insensitive to the glamour of such patronage must be pardoned if we see it all from another angle. Was it not rather a tragedy that the mightiest poetic mind of his age should have been ground down in so obsequious an activity? And Goethe himself knew it and felt it.

But there are always compensations in the ways of God to man. In this period of artistic abdication Goethe grew mightily in wisdom; no longer the inspired creator, he became the wisest of men, the exemplar and the prophet of his time. More self-reliant, more balanced, more confidence-inspiring this wisdom grew as his great life drew to a close. But like all the precious things in life, Goethe's balance of mind was no easy acquisition. He had his full share of the artist's sensitiveness; he was handicapped all his life by a sensitiveness to the other sex, which, apart from the disturbance it brought into his own personal life, coloured and narrowed down the issues of his poetry. It prevented Goethe seeing the great ethical problems of history, when he dealt with these poetically, apart from narrow issues of personal emotion; he was as little able as the great French tragic poets of the seventeenth century to eliminate the "love-interest" from his drama, although it never appears in quite so conventionally baroque a form. His great creations from *Götz* to *Faust* are trivialized—as our own Shakespeare's never are—by this dominating sex-complex. His whole long life was a persistent struggle with emotional cross-currents that threatened to dominate and thwart his genius; but from this struggle he emerged strong and self-reliant; he acquired freedom and balance.

Goethe's attainment of life-wisdom was, indeed, no blessing that dropped into his lap, but the issue of a long and bitter struggle. And this is what makes it precious to us. Not happiness, but sorrow, was the ultimate reward. We have seen how Goethe's life, in spite of a " success " such as few men of letters ever attain, went down in renunciation and loneliness ; and from this sorrow Goethe's life-wisdom rose great and pure. As to his own Faust, the night only brought greater clearness :

> Die Nacht scheint tiefer tief hereinzudringen,
> Allein im Innern leuchtet helles Licht.

That " Entsagung " which, in early days, had been but a purple fringe on the bright garment of life, became its main texture, and Goethe entered into the " Sanctuary of Sorrow ".

Thus if we are to define what makes Goethe an asset to our modern life, it is to be sought, less in the artistic qualities of his work as a whole, or any individual work, than in his personality, his universality and balance. That very polarity which was so disturbing a factor in his work as an artist only added to the completeness as a man, as the artist of his own life. This it was that " so mixed the elements in him that Nature might stand up and say to all the world : this was a man ". There is no greater optimist in the world's literature than Goethe ; and the significance of his optimism lay in the fact that it was no mere satisfaction that life had treated him kindly. Rather had he wrestled with the dark powers through " kummervolle Nächte ", through nights of tears, wrestled with them, and defied them. Like his Scottish disciple, Carlyle, he had attained the " Everlasting Yea " only after passing through the Valley of the Shadow, the " Everlasting No ". Goethe learned slowly and in constant struggle to see life steadily and see it whole, learned to believe in the goodness of the world. To him the words of *Genesis* said all that was to be said : " And God saw everything, and behold it was very good."

The great problem of evil, which men have tormented themselves with since the world began, lost all its terrors in the radiant confidence of this optimism. Goethe stood before it as the little children in Maeterlinck's *Oiseau bleu* before the mystery of death : " There *is* no death ! " For Goethe there is no evil ; there can be no evil, for God's world is good. What we with our limited understandings call evil is but a darker thread in the weft of life ; something that is only the good in a disguise that we are unable to penetrate. Evil is the servant of the good, as Mephistopheles is the servant of God. What else, indeed, is the ultimate teaching of *Faust* ?

It is in this buoyant faith in the goodness of the world that Goethe, this great interpreter of life, envisaged the problem of human endeavour. No man ever spoke wiser words to the perplexed seeker after a right interpretation of his individual problems than he. The first demand made upon every man is that he make the utmost of the gift of life. Learn the meaning of the " Know thyself " of the wise ancients, or, as Carlyle bluntly interpreted it : " Know what thou canst work at ! " And once thy sphere of activity is clear devote thyself to it with all thy might—not in overleaping ambition, but in wise limitation ; for " in der Beschränkung zeigt sich erst der Meister ". In steady, unabated effort lies salvation. Once man lets this zeal—the " holy earnestness " of *Wilhelm Meister*—flag ; the moment he is tempted to say to the passing moment : " Stay, thou art so fair ! " he is lost. Our Victorian moralists used to look askance at this life-philosophy of Goethe as something unworthy and selfish, as mere egoism. But they had forgotten the wise reminder of the poet that every man must be an egoist if he will not become one. And wherein lies the highest activity of man? Assuredly not in egoistic self-culture, but rather in race-service. Such is the goal to which Faust ultimately attains. Goethe's altruism is no mere vaguely exercised philanthropy, but an altruism in the interests of the great entity humanity, renunciation in the service of the race.

Goethe's optimism was a fatalistic optimism; his belief in the ultimate rightness of all happenings—whether they may appear to our limited minds as good or evil—led him gently, but inevitably on to the path of fatalism. He accepted life, as he counsels us to accept life, as it comes; not to revolt against it, or to rebel. He saw how some men were born to dark unhappy fates; others to success and glory. To the former his advice is to bear with fortitude, without complaint or regret, the life-burden put upon their shoulders; to the latter to fulfil the duties that are ascribed to them without exultation or pride. Even when supreme geniuses like Raphael, Mozart and Byron are cut off in their prime before their work is accomplished, Goethe still sees in it a wise ordinance of Providence, whereby " something is still left to be done in a world that is calculated to last a long time ". We must look upon life, not from the narrow window of our ego, but from the wide standpoint of human solidarity and human progress. Every man has his " God-given hest ", and that " God-given hest " must be fulfilled, for good or for evil; for it belongs to the divine scheme of things; it is dependent on genius, temperament, aspiration and desires which are not really ours, but the consequence of mysterious, inexplicable laws of inheritance. Goethe accepted the world as the fulfilment of infinite wisdom, manifesting itself in an endless chain of cause and effect. We can only " wait " in patience—" abwarten ", a little word that was very often on his lips in his last years,—steadfastly fulfil, according to our lights, our share in the world scheme. Thus Goethe's optimistic faith did not escape the danger to which all optimism is exposed, the tendency to merge into determinism.

We cannot thus close our eyes to the limitations which his optimism brought with it. We see it even in little things, in the conduct of his own life. He may have given a wise and philosophic justification of his doctrine of evil ; but it led him to refuse to countenance manifestly evil things, to shrink from them. This is apparent in Goethe's reluctance to face suffering, his abhorrence of asceticism and death. And it is reflected in his poetry. One might recall how, once the period of transcendent genius in Goethe's life was over, he sedulously avoided tragedy. *Egmont* is, in spirit, no tragedy ; *Iphigenie* had in it elements of tragedy which Goethe passed by ; and who but this inveterate optimist would have called the unhappy Tasso back from the shades, and refuse to show us the unfathomable tragic pity and fear that his life evokes ? The " Storm and Stress " *Faust* was tragic ; indeed, nothing could be more tragic ; but all the later development of the poem was, as we have seen, calculated to soften and erase its tragic effect. And perhaps, after all, this " Divine Comedy " of the modern world would have left a deeper mark on the minds of men had Faust ended in the grip of Mephistopheles, than kneeling, redeemed by the " woman soul ", beatified at the feet of the Virgin. The highest literature of the world is always tragic. But no ! Goethe said : God's world is good. The good must triumph. There is no evil !

Thus there are serious shadows on Goethe's optimistic wisdom. We have frankly to recognize in it the wisdom of an age, of which Goethe was the great completer and perfecter. His was the last and highest word in the progress of eighteenth-century thought—the end, as Leibniz had been the beginning ; he had put the crown on that splendid ideal of the " education of mankind " which had occupied the century's noblest minds. His ultimate mission to his age was, it might be said, to bring harmony into a Europe whose optimism had suffered many a buffet from the Lisbon earthquake of 1755 to the French Revolution and Napoleon. But there came a time, not long after Goethe closed his eyes, when new problems arose which Goethe's philosophy was powerless to solve. In his wise foresight he anticipated much ; but what he did not foresee was the wave of withering pessimism that swept over Europe towards the middle of the nineteenth century. Here renunciation, " Entsagung ", on which Goethe's own life-wisdom had been reared, took on another form which his optimism was but ill equipped to meet. And as time has gone on, other developments have supervened, not dreamt of in Goethe's philosophy. The old problem of good and evil has assumed new and terrible forms, which make us feel that, after all, " der Weisheit letzter Schluss " has no finality, but like the horizon moves always onward in front of the wanderer.

Even for our twentieth century, which looks back on the pessimism of Schopenhauer as a night that has passed, can one say that Goethe's ripe wisdom is likely to appeal, or, indeed, should appeal, to young ardent souls looking forward into life ? It may be consoling to the weary, the storm-tossed, the unfortunate to be told : Heaven is closed for us ; earth's narrow circle is all that is ours ; let us make the best of it ; let us frame our lives and our activities so that we may bring the best that is in us to fruition within these limitations. But to those who are facing life courageously may this not seem only quietism, only an evasion of responsibility ? Goethe's philosophy is no philosophy for the rebel, the pioneer into the unknown, the adventurer on uncharted seas. And it is only by daring greatly, by rebelling, that the world moves forward. Nor is his wisdom a consolation to the defiant soul that goes down in tragedy before the life-mystery ; for Goethe had nothing in him of the stuff of which martyrs are made ; he could not envisage life tragically. But, after all, it is not the ripe conclusions of his wisdom that we have to learn from him. Optimism may be the ultimate consummation of wisdom ; but ready-made optimism benefits no one, or, indeed, theories of any kind for the conduct of life. We have ourselves to fight out our own salvation ; to acquire our own wisdom ; we must, in Goethe's own words, " daily conquer our life anew ". His example teaches us how he grappled with his own problem ; and how he fought through to that spiritual equilibrium and "inner freedom" which are the most precious things in life. Thus, in the end, it is not Goethe's optimism by which his value for us moderns is to be gauged ; but the example that lies open to us in his works, of how he, opposed and disillusioned by " earth-spirits ", wrestled with them and overthrew them, ultimately attaining to peace and harmony. Goethe's greatest lesson is how to live so that our life-wisdom be justified of itself.

BIBLIOGRAPHICAL NOTES

R OUND no other poet has accumulated so vast a library of biography, criticism and commentary as round Goethe. The magnitude of this literature may be estimated from the bibliography, which occupies more than fifteen hundred pages, in the *Grundriss zur Geschichte der deutschen Literatur* of Karl Goedeke; the volumes of this work concerned with Goethe appeared in a third edition, Dresden, 1910–13.

The standard edition of Goethe's Works, to which the references in these notes are made, is : *Goethes Werke*, herausgegeben im Auftrage der Grossherzogin Sophie von Sachsen, Weimar, 1887–1919. It is in four divisions : *Werke*, 55 vols. ; *Naturwissenschaftliche Werke*, 13 vols. ; *Tagebücher*, 15 vols. ; *Briefe*, 50 vols. Each section is provided with an exemplary index. There are, of course, many other editions, which, when they aim at completeness, usually number 40 volumes. Of the more recent the following may be mentioned : *Jubiläums-Ausgabe*, herausgegeben von E. von der Hellen, Stuttgart, 1902–12 ; *Propyläen-Ausgabe*, Munich, 1909 ff. ; that in the *Goldene Klassiker-Bibliothek*, Berlin, 1909 ff. ; *Festausgabe*, herausgegeben von R. Petsch (with excellent commentaries), 18 vols., Leipzig, 1926–7. Still more numerous are the editions of selected works. That in six volumes, edited for the Goethe-Gesellschaft by Erich Schmidt, Weimar, 1909–10, was re-issued in 1924.

Editions of selected Letters have been published by E. von der Hellen, 6 vols., Stuttgart, 1901–13, and Ph. Stein, Berlin, 1902–25. Also, together with letters to Goethe, by R. M. Meyer, *Goethe und seine Freunde im Briefwechsel*, 3 vols., Berlin, 1909–10.

Goethe's Conversations have been collected by W. von Biedermann, 11 vols., Leipzig, 1889–91 ; 2nd ed., by F. von Biedermann, 5 vols., 1909–11.

There is as yet no uniform or satisfactory edition of even the chief works of Goethe in English translation ; the publication of such an edition has long been in the programme of the English Goethe Society. Meanwhile, there are 14 volumes allotted to the poet's works in the *Standard Library*, formerly Bohn's *Standard Library*, published by Messrs. George Bell & Sons. These translations are, however, mostly of very old date, and—notably of the prose works—very inadequate.

The first Biography of Goethe on a large scale was the English one by George Henry Lewes, London, 1855 (now in the *Everyman Library*), which enjoyed a long popularity both at home and in Germany. The more important general works are : H. Grimm, *Goethe-Vorlesungen*, 2 vols., Berlin, 1877 ; 8th ed., 1923 ; English translation by S. H. Adams, Boston, 1880 ; H. Düntzer, *Goethes Leben*, Leipzig, 1880 ; 2nd ed., 1883 ; English translation by T. W. Lyster, London, 1883 ; A. Baumgartner, *Goethe : sein Leben und seine Werke*, 3 vols., Freiburg, 1885–6 ; 4th ed., 2 vols., 1923–5 (from a Catholic standpoint); A. Bielschowsky, *Goethe : sein Leben und seine Werke*, 2 vols., Munich, 1895–1903 ; 42nd ed., 1922 ; new revised ed., by W. Linden, 1928 ; English translation by W. A. Cooper, 3 vols., New York, 1905–8 ; K. Heinemann, *Goethe*, Leipzig, 1895 ; 3rd ed., 1916 ; R. M. Meyer, *Goethe*, Berlin, 1894 ; 4th ed., 1913 ; F. Gundolf, *Goethe*, Berlin, 1916 ; 12th ed., 1925 ; G. Brandes, *Goethe*, German translation, Berlin, 1922 ; P. Hume Brown, *Life of Goethe*, 2 vols., London, 1920 ; B. Croce, *Goethe*, Bari, 1919 : English translation, London, 1923 ; W. Bode, *Goethes Leben*, 8 vols., Berlin, 1917 ff. ; E. Ludwig, *Goethe : Geschichte eines Menschen*, 3 vols., Stuttgart, 1920–1 ; latest cheap ed. in one vol., 1931 ; English translation, abbreviated, by E. Colburn Mayne, 2 vols., London, 1924 ; H. W. Nevinson, *Goethe : Man and Poet*, London, 1931.

Of works dealing with particular aspects of Goethe's life and work the following may be mentioned : J. Minor and A. Sauer, *Studien zur Goethe-Philologie*, Vienna, 1880 ; W. Scherer, *Aufsätze über Goethe*, Berlin, 1886 ; 2nd ed., 1900 ; W. von Biedermann, *Goethe-Forschungen*, 3 vols., Leipzig, 1879–99 ; A. Schöll, *Goethe in Hauptzügen seines Lebens und Wirkens*, Berlin, 1882 ; V. Hehn, *Gedanken über Goethe*, Berlin, 1887 ; 7th ed., 1909 ; Sir John Seeley, *Goethe after Sixty Years*, London, 1894 ; E. Dowden, in *New Studies in Literature*, London, 1895 ; E. Rod, *Essai sur Goethe*, Paris, 1898 ; M. Morris, *Goethe-Studien*, 2 vols., Berlin, 1897–8 ; 2nd ed., 1902 ; W. Bode, *Goethes Lebenskunst*, Berlin, 1903 ; and *Stunden mit Goethe*, 6 vols., Berlin, 1905–10 ; R. Steiner, *Goethes Weltanschauung*, Weimar, 1897 ; E. A. Boucke, *Goethes Weltanschauung auf historischer Grundlage*, Stuttgart, 1907 ; H. Siebeck, *Goethe als Denker*, Stuttgart, 1902 ; 2nd ed., 1905 ; Chr. Schrempf, *Goethes Lebensanschauung in ihrer geschichtlichen Entwicklung*, 2 vols., Weimar, 1905–7 ; H. Loiseau, *L'Évolution morale de Goethe*, Paris, 1911 ; K. J. Obenauer, *Goethe in seinem Verhältnis zur Religion*, Jena, 1921 ; H. A. Korff, *Die Lebensidee Goethes*, Leipzig, 1925 ; E. Maas, *Goethe und die Antike*, Berlin, 1912 ; G. P. Gooch, *The Political Background of Goethe's Life*, in *Publications of the English Goethe Society*, N.S., iii, London, 1926.

H. G. Gräf, *Goethe über seine Dichtungen*, 9 vols., Frankfort, 1901–14; J. W. Braun, *Goethe im Urteil seiner Zeitgenossen*, 3 vols., Berlin, 1883–5; H. Amelung, *Goethe als Persönlichkeit: Berichte und Briefe von Zeitgenossen* (Supplement to the *Propyläen-Ausgabe*), Munich, 1914–25. Useful commentaries to Goethe's chief works by H. Düntzer in *Erläuterungen zu den Klassikern*.

J. M. Carré, *Goethe en Angleterre*, 2 vols., Paris, 1920; E. Oswald, *Goethe in England and America; Bibliography*, 2nd ed., London, 1909; F. Baldensperger, *Goethe en France*, 2 vols., Paris, 1904–7.

The *Goethe-Jahrbuch*, published by the Goethe-Gesellschaft, 34 vols., Frankfort, 1880–1913; continued as *Jahrbuch der Goethe-Gesellschaft*. *Chronik des Wiener Goethe-Vereins*, Vienna, 1887 ff. *Publications of the English Society*, 11 vols., London, 1880–1910; new series, 1924 ff.

PART I

CHAPTER I.

Dichtung und Wahrheit, Books i–viii. S. Schultze, *Der junge Goethe: ein Bild seiner inneren Entwicklung*, Halle, 1893–4; J. Kühn, *Der junge Goethe im Spiegel seiner Dichtung*, Heidelberg, 1912.

F. Ewart, *Goethes Vater*, Hamburg, 1899; *Briefe der Frau Rat Goethe*, herausgegeben von A. Köster, 2 vols., Leipzig, 1904; 6th ed., 1923; K. Heinemann, *Goethes Mutter*, 8th ed., Leipzig, 1909; P. Bastier, *La mère de Goethe*, Paris, 1902; G. Witkowski, *Cornelia, die Schwester Goethes*, Frankfort, 1902; 2nd ed., 1924.

E. Mentzel, *Der Frankfurter Goethe*, Frankfort, 1900.

W. von Biedermann, *Goethe und Leipzig*, 2 vols., Leipzig, 1865; J. Vogel, *Goethes Leipziger Studentenjahre*, 4th ed., Leipzig, 1922; *Goethes Briefe an Leipziger Freunde*, herausgegeben von O. Jahn, Leipzig, 2nd ed., 1867; English translation by R. Slater, London, 1866.

Der junge Goethe, herausgegeben von M. Bernays, 3 vols., Leipzig, 1875; new ed. by M. Morris, 6 vols., Leipzig, 1909–12, a complete collection of Goethe's writings and letters between 1765 and 1775. *Annette, Werke*, xxxvii, pp. 11 ff.; *Die Laune des Verliebten* and *Die Mitschuldigen, Werke*, ix. Both plays have been translated by E. A. Bowring, Bohn's *Standard Library*. A. Döll, *Goethes Mitschuldigen*, Halle, 1909.

P. 8: Bettina von Arnim, *Goethes Briefwechsel mit einem Kind*, Berlin, 1835, ii, pp. 249 f.; P. 13: Letter from Moors, August 12, 1766 (O. Jahn, *op. cit.*, p. 63).

BIBLIOGRAPHICAL NOTES

CHAPTER II.

Dichtung und Wahrheit, Books ix–xi. R. Weissenfels, *Goethe im Sturm und Drang*, i, Halle, 1894.

H. Düntzer, *Herder und der junge Goethe in Strassburg*, in *Zur Goetheforschung, Neue Beiträge*, Stuttgart, 1891, pp. 77 ff.; E. Traumann, *Goethe der Strassburger Student*, Leipzig, 1910; 2nd ed., 1923.

J. Froitzheim, *Friederike Brion, nach geschichtlichen Quellen*, Gotha, 1893; A. Metz, *Friederike Brion*, Munich, 1911; A. Bielschowsky, *Friederike und Lili*, 2nd ed., Munich, 1906.

P. 22 : *Briefe*, i, p. 224; P. 25 : *Zum Schäkespears Tag, Werke*, xxxvii, p. 130; P. 26 : *Heidenröslein, Werke*, i, p. 16; P. 27 : *Dichtung und Wahrheit*, Book x, *Werke*, xxvii, pp. 351 ff.; P. 28 : *Briefe*, i, pp. 251 f.; Pp. 30 f. : *Willkommen und Abschied* and *Mailied, Werke*, i, pp. 68 f. (p. 382), 72 f.; P. 32 : *Die neue Melusine, Werke*, xxv, 1, pp. 131 ff.; P. 33 : *Faust*, i, ll. 2038 f.

CHAPTER III.

Dichtung und Wahrheit, Book xii.

Frankfurter Gelehrte Anzeigen vom Jahre 1772, herausgegeben von B. Seuffert, Heilbronn, 1883; M. Morris, *Goethes und Herders Anteil an dem Jahrgang 1772 der Frankfurter Gelehrten Anzeigen*, Stuttgart, 1899; 2nd ed., 1915; *Von deutscher Art und Kunst*, ed. by E. Purdie, Oxford, 1924.

J. H. Merck, *Schriften und Briefwechsel*, herausgegeben von K. Wolff, 2 vols., Leipzig, 1909; G. Zimmermann, *J. H. Merck, seine Umgebung und Zeit*, Frankfort, 1871.

W. Herbst, *Goethe in Wetzlar*, Gotha, 1881; H. Glöel, *Goethes Wetzlarer Zeit*, Berlin, 1911; *Goethe und Lotte*, Berlin, 1922; J. C. Kestner, *Goethe und Werther, Briefe*, herausgegeben von A. Kestner, Stuttgart, 1854; 3rd ed., 1910.

P. 38 : *Wandrers Sturmlied, Werke*, ii, pp. 67 ff.; Pp. 40 ff. : A. Kestner, *op. cit.*, pp. 40 ff.; P. 45 : *Prometheus, Werke*, ii, pp. 76 ff.

CHAPTER IV.

Götz von Berlichingen, Werke, viii; the earlier version in xxxix. *Götz von Berlichingen in dreifacher Gestalt*, herausgegeben von J. Bächtold, Freiburg, 1882; Edited with English notes by J. A. C. Hildner, Boston, 1910. The translation by Sir Walter Scott in Bohn's *Standard Library*.

H. Düntzer, *Götz von Berlichingen* in *Erläuterungen der Klassiker*, xi, 6th ed., Leipzig, 1900. P. Hagenbring, *Goethes Götz von Berlichingen : Erläuterung und literarische Würdigung*, i, Halle, 1911; H. Meyer-Benfey, *Goethes Götz von Berlichingen*, Weimar, 1930.

330

The *Lebensbeschreibung des Herrn Gözens von Berlichingen*, herausgegeben von F. von Steigerwald, has been reprinted by A. Leitzmann, Halle, 1916.

Die Leiden des jungen Werthers, Werke, xix. Herausgegeben von M. Hecker und F. A. Hünich, Leipzig, 1922. *The Sorrows of Werther* has been translated six times into English, the earliest (1779) from the French; the last and best is by W. Rose, with introduction and notes, London, 1929.

Die Leiden des jungen Goethe, erläutert von H. Düntzer, in *Erläuterungen der Klassiker*, iii, 2nd ed., Leipzig, 1880. E. Schmidt, *Richardson, Rousseau und Goethe*, Jena, 1875; 2nd ed., Leipzig, 1902; H. Smith, *Goethe and Rousseau*, in *Publications of the English Goethe Society*, N.S., iii, London, 1926, pp. 31 ff.; W. Rose, *From Goethe to Byron*, London, 1924. J. W. Appel, *Werther und seine Zeit*, Leipzig, 1855; 4th ed., Oldenburg, 1896. On the world-wide popularity of *Werther* and the many translations and imitations see Goedeke's *Grundriss*, iv, 3rd ed., pp. 163 ff., where the bibliography occupies fifty-eight pages.

P. 58 : Letter to Lavater, *Briefe*, ii, p. 156.

CHAPTER V.

Dichtung und Wahrheit, Books xiii–xx.

Goethe und Lavater : Briefe und Tagebücher, herausgegeben von H. Funck (*Schriften der Goethe-Gesellschaft*, xvi), Weimar, 1901.

F. E. Graf Dürckheim, *Lili's Bild, geschichtlich entworfen*, 2nd ed., Munich, 1894; F. Servaes, *Goethes Lili*, 2nd ed., Bielefeld, 1920.

Goethes Schweizerreise 1775, herausgegeben von K. Koetschau und M. Morris (*Schriften der Goethe-Gesellschaft*, xxii), Weimar, 1907.

P. 62 : Letter to Kestner, *Briefe*, ii, p. 104; *Faust*, i, ll. 3432 ff., *Werke*, xiv, pp. 173 f.; P. 64: *Diné zu Coblenz, Werke*, ii, p. 267; Pp. 65 f.: *An Belinden, Werke*, i, p. 71 ; P. 67: *An Lili*, *ibid.*, iv, p. 204; Pp. 68 f.: *Dichtung und Wahrheit, Werke*, xxix, pp. 184, 192.

CHAPTER VI.

Clavigo and *Stella, Werke*, xi. Erläutert von H. Düntzer, *Erläuterungen der Klassiker*, xiii, 2nd ed., Leipzig, 1878; G. Grempler, *Goethes Clavigo*, Halle, 1911. Translations of *Clavigo* by E. A. Bowring in Bohn's *Standard Library*, and by Members of the Manchester Goethe Society, London, 1897. *Stella* was translated in 1798, and anonymously, London, 1890.

Goethes Faust in ursprünglicher Gestalt nach der Göchhausenschen Abschrift, herausgegeben von E. Schmidt, Weimar, 1887; also in *Werke*, xxxix, pp. 217 ff. There is an English translation by

W. H. Van der Smissen, in his *Goethe's Faust done into English Verse*, Toronto and London, 1926, pp. 377 ff. J. Collin, *Untersuchungen über Goethes Faust in seiner ältesten Gestalt*, Frankfort, 1896 ; J. Minor, *Goethes Faust : Entstehungsgeschichte und Erklärung*, i, Stuttgart, 1901. For the general literature on Goethe's *Faust* see below, notes to Part ii, chapter viii. In the present chapter and Part ii, chapter viii, I have drawn largely on my Introduction to *Goethe's Faust, Part i*, translated by G. M. Cookson (*Broadway Translations*), London, 1927. P. 74 : *Dichtung und Wahrheit*, x, *Werke*, xxvii, pp. 320 f. P. 77 : *Werke*, xxxix, p. 251. For the other data bearing on the composition of *Faust*, see O. Pniower, *Goethes Faust : Zeugnisse und Excurse zu seiner Entstehungsgeschichte*, Berlin, 1899.

PART II
Chapter I.

P. Kühn, *Weimar*, 2nd ed., Leipzig, 1919 ; W. Bode, *Das Leben in Altweimar*, 3rd ed., Weimar, 1922 ; W. Bode, *Der Weimarische Musenhof, 1756–81*, Berlin, 1917 ; W. Bode, *Amalie, Herzogin von Sachsen-Weimar*, 3 vols., 2nd ed., Berlin, 1909 ; H. Wahl, *Karl August von Weimar : sein Leben in Briefen*, Weimar, 1928 ; *Briefwechsel des Grossherzogs Karl August mit Goethe*, 2 vols., Weimar, 1863 ; herausgegeben von H. Wahl, 3 vols., Berlin, 1915–18.

H. Düntzer, *Goethes Eintritt in Weimar*, Leipzig, 1883 ; A. Diezmann, *Goethe und die lustige Zeit in Weimar*, Weimar, 1905 ; A. Schöll, *Goethe als Staats- und Geschäftsmann*, in *Goethe in Hauptzügen seines Lebens*, Berlin, 1882.

Goethe's *Tagebücher*, i. H. Düntzer, *Goethes Tagebücher der sechs ersten Weimarischen Jahre*, Leipzig, 1889 ; W. Bode, *Goethes Leben im Garten am Stern*, 2nd ed., Berlin, 1910.

Goethes Schweizerreisen, herausgegeben von H. Wahl, Gotha, 1921.

Goethes Briefe an Charlotte von Stein, herausgegeben von A. Schöll ; 3rd ed. herausgegeben von J. Wahle, 2 vols., Frankfort, 1899–90 ; herausgegeben von J. Petersen, 3 vols., 2nd ed., Leipzig, 1923 ; W. Bode, *Charlotte von Stein*, Berlin, 1909 ; E. Höfer, *Goethe und Charlotte von Stein*, 8th ed., Berlin, 1923.

Goethes lyrische Dichtungen der ersten Weimarischen Jahre, herausgegeben von R. Kögel, Basel, 1896.

P. 94 : The Duke's letter to Fritsch, C. von Beaulieu-Marconnay, *Anna Amalia, Carl August und Minister von Fritsch*, Weimar, 1874, p. 157 ; P. 96 : *Torquato Tasso*, Act ii, sc. i, ll. 928 ff. ; P. 98 : To Charlotte von Stein, *Briefe*, iv, pp. 66 f. ; P. 99 : *Gesang der Geister*, *Werke*, ii, p. 56 ; to Charlotte von Stein, *Briefe*, iv,

p. 120; P. 102: *Werke*, iv, pp. 97 f.; P. 103: To Charlotte von Stein, *Briefe*, v, p. 80; to Lavater, *ibid.*, iv, p. 299; P. 106: *Über allen Gipfeln, Werke*, i, p. 98; *Das Göttliche, ibid.*, ii, pp. 83 f.

CHAPTER II.

Egmont, Werke, viii. Herausgegeben von H. Jantzen, Leipzig, 1914; ed. with English notes by J. T. Hatfield, Boston, 1904. English translation by Anna Swanwick in Bohn's *Standard Library*. E. Zimmermann, *Goethes Egmont*, Halle, 1909; L. Kleiber, *Studien zu Goethes Egmont*, Berlin, 1913.

Iphigenie auf Tauris, Werke, x. *Iphigenie auf Tauris in vierfacher Gestalt*, herausgegeben von J. Bächtold, Freiburg, 1883; edited with English notes by K. Breul, Cambridge, 1899; 2nd ed., 1904; Erläutert von H. Düntzer, *Erläuterungen der Klassiker*, xi, 7th ed., Leipzig, 1899; English translation by Anna Swanwick in Bohn's *Standard Library*.

K. Fischer, *Goethes Iphigenie auf Tauris*, 3rd ed., Heidelberg, 1900; C. Steinweg, *Das Seelendrama in der Antike und seine Weiterentwicklung bis auf Goethe und Wagner*, Halle, 1924; J. G. Robertson, *Goethe's Iphigenie auf Tauris: Some New Points of View*, in *Publications of the English Goethe Society*, N.S., i, London, 1924, pp. 25 ff. Part of the present chapter is an abbreviation of this article. The criticism of C. Schrempf, to which I am indebted, will be found in his *Goethes Lebensanschauung in ihrer geschichtlichen Entwicklung*, ii, Stuttgart, 1907, pp. 226 ff.

P. 109: *Dichtung und Wahrheit, Werke*, xxix, pp. 174 f.; Pp. 119 f.: The quotations from De La Touche are from Act ii, sc. iv; Act iii, sc. i and the last scene; Pp. 119 f.: *Iphigenie*, Act iii, sc. ii, ll. 1266 ff.; P. 120: *Ibid.*, Act iii, sc. iii, ll. 1355 ff.; P. 121: *So im Handeln, Werke*, iv, p. 277; P. 122: *Iphigenie*, Act v, sc. ii, ll. 1916 ff.; P. 123: *Ibid.*, Act iv, sc. v, ll. 1716 f.; P. 124: *Ibid.*, Act iv, sc. v, ll. 1726 ff.

CHAPTER III.

Italienische Reise, Werke, xxx–xxxii. Herausgegeben von G. von Grävenitz, Leipzig, 1912. English translation by A. J. W. Morrison in Bohn's *Standard Library*.

Tagebücher, i, pp. 143 ff., and *Briefe*, viii, from which the quotations on pp. 130 ff. are taken. *Tagebücher und Briefe Goethes aus Italien an Frau von Stein und Herder*, herausgegeben von E. Schmidt (*Schriften der Goethe-Gesellschaft*, ii), Weimar, 1886.

H. Grimm, *Goethe in Italien*, in *Fünfzehn Essays*, 3rd ed., Berlin, 1884; *Mit Goethe in Italien*, herausgegeben von J. Vogel, Berlin, 1908; J. Haarhaus, *Auf Goethes Spuren in Italien*, 3 vols., Leipzig, 1896–98; J. Vogel, *Aus Goethes römischen Tagen*, Leipzig, 1905;

C. H. Herford, *Goethe's Italian Journey* (*Studies in European Literature*, *Taylorian Lectures*, Oxford, 1900).

CHAPTER IV.

Fragments of *Nausikaa*, *Werke*, x, pp. 97 ff. G. Kettner, *Nausikaa*, Berlin, 1912.

Torquato Tasso, *Werke*, x. Ed. by J. G. Robertson, Manchester, 1918. The present chapter is largely an abbreviation of the Introduction to this edition. Cp. also *Publications of the English Goethe Society*, N.S., v, London, 1928, pp. 46 ff. English translation by Anna Swanwick in Bohn's *Standard Library*.

K. Fischer, *Goethes Torquato Tasso*, 3rd ed., Heidelberg, 1900; E. Castle, *Tasso-Probleme*, in *Zeitschrift für die österreichische Gymnasien*, lviii, 1907, pp. 97 ff.; E. Rueff, *Zur Entstehungsgeschichte von Goethes Tasso*, Marburg, 1910.

Römische Elegien, *Werke*, i, pp. 231 ff. Herausgegeben von A. Leitzmann, Bonn, 1912. English translation by E. A. Bowring in *Goethe's Poems*, Bohn's *Standard Library*.

P. 144: Ampère in *Le Globe*, iii, 1826, pp. 97 ff.; P. 149: F. von Biedermann, *Goethes Gespräche*, iii, pp. 393 ff.; Pp. 150, 151, 152, 154: The quotations from *Tasso* are respectively: Act iii, sc. iv, ll. 2112 ff., Act v, sc. v, ll. 3426 ff., 3448 ff., Act i, sc. iii, ll. 536 ff.; P. 155: *Römische Elegien*, No. vii, *Werke*, i, p. 242.

CHAPTER V.

C. A. H. Burkhardt, *Das Repertoire des Weimarischen Theaters unter Goethes Leitung*, Hamburg, 1891; J. Wahle, *Das Weimarische Hoftheater unter Goethes Leitung* (*Schriften der Goethe-Gesellschaft*, vi), Weimar, 1892.

Goethes Briefwechsel mit seiner Frau, herausgegeben von H. G. Gräf, Frankfort, 1916; 2nd ed., 1923; E. Federn, *Christiane von Goethe*, 4th ed., Munich, 1920.

Campagne in Frankreich and *Belagerung von Mainz*, *Werke*, xxxiii. English translations of both works by L. Dora Schmitz in Bohn's *Standard Library*. G. Roethe, *Goethes Kampagne in Frankreich*, Berlin, 1919.

E. Dowden, *Goethe and the French Revolution*, in *New Studies in Literature*, London, 1895, pp. 181 ff.; G. P. Gooch, *German Literature and the French Revolution*, London, 1920, pp. 174 ff.

Venetianische Epigramme, *Werke*, i, pp. 305 ff. English translation in *Goethe's Poems* (*Standard Library*). The quotations in the text (pp. 164 f.) are from Nos. 4, 96, 34.

Goethes Briefwechsel mit Heinrich Meyer, herausgegeben von M. Hecker, 3 vols. (*Schriften der Goethe-Gesellschaft*, xxxii–xxxiv), Weimar, 1917–22.

Der Grosskophta and *Der Bürgergeneral*, *Werke*, xvii.

Pp. 156 f. : Letter to the Duke, March 17, 1788, *Briefe*, viii, pp. 357 ff. ; P. 160: *Gefunden, Werke*, i, p. 25 ; Pp. 162 f. : Letters to Charlotte von Stein, *Briefe*, ix, pp. 123 f., 127.

CHAPTER VI.

Briefwechsel zwischen Schiller und Goethe, herausgegeben von W. Vollmer, 2 vols., Stuttgart, 1881 ; herausgegeben von H. G. Gräf und A. Leitzmann, 3 vols., Leipzig, 1912 ; *Selections from the Correspondence between Schiller and Goethe*, ed. by J. G. Robertson, Boston, 1898. *Correspondence between Schiller and Goethe*, translated by L. Dora Schmitz, 2 vols., London, 1877–9 : *Goethe und Schiller in Briefen von Heinrich Voss*, herausgegeben von H. G. Gräf, Leipzig, 1896.

Unterhaltungen deutscher Ausgewanderten, Werke, xviii. *Xenien*, herausgegeben von E. Schmidt und B. Suphan (*Schriften der Goethe-Gesellschaft*, viii), Weimar, 1893 ; also *Werke*, v. 1, pp. 203 ff. ; *Literarischer Sansculottismus, Werke*, 1, pp. 196 ff. ; E. Boas, *Schiller und Goethe im Xenienkampf*, 2 vols., Stuttgart, 1851.

Pp. 173 ff. : Letters from Schiller to Körner, *Schillers Briefe*, herausgegeben von F. Jonas, Stuttgart, 1892–6, ii, pp. 115 ff., 218 ff., 249, iii, p. 113 ; P. 177 : Schiller's letter to Goethe, *ibid.*, iii, pp. 472 ff. ; P. 182 : To Zelter, June 1, 1805, *Briefe*, xix, p. 8 ; P. 183 : *Epilog zu Schillers Glocke, Werke*, xvi, p. 166.

CHAPTER VII.

Wilhelm Meisters Lehrjahre, Werke, xxi–xxiii. English translation by Thomas Carlyle, London, 1824. *Wilhelm Meisters Theatralische Sendung*, herausgegeben von H. Maync, Stuttgart, 1911 ; also now *Werke*, li, lii. W. Wundt, *Goethes Wilhelm Meisters Lehrjahre und die Entwicklung des modernen Lebensideals*, Berlin, 1913 ; E. Wolff, *Mignon*, Munich, 1909 ; A. Matthes, *Mignon, Goethes Herz*, Leipzig, 1900 ; H. Funk, *Die schöne Seele : Bekenntnisse, Schriften und Briefe der Susanna von Klettenberg*, Leipzig, 1911.

Hermann und Dorothea, Werke, l. English translation by E. A. Bowring in *Goethe's Poems* (Bohn's *Standard Library*). Erläutert von H. Düntzer, *Erläuterungen der Klassiker*, i, 9th ed., Leipzig, 1906 ; ed. with English notes by C. A. Buchheim, Oxford, 1901. W. von Humboldt, *Ästhetische Versuche über Hermann und Dorothea*, Brunswick, 1799 ; 4th ed., 1882 ; V. Hehn, *Über Goethes Hermann und Dorothea*, 3rd ed., Stuttgart, 1913.

Die natürliche Tochter, Werke, x. G. Kettner, *Goethes Natürliche Tochter*, Berlin, 1912.

Pp. 187 f. : *Kennst du das Land, Werke*, xxi, p. 233 ; also i, p. 161 ; P. 189 : On *Hamlet, ibid.*, Book iv, chap. xiii, *ibid.*, pp. 72 ff. ; P. 191 : Book v, chap. iii, *ibid.*, xxii, p. 149 ; P. 194 :

To Eckermann, January 18, 1825, F. von Biedermann, *Goethes Gespräche*, iii, p. 157; P. 200: *Hermann und Dorothea*, vi, ll. 4 ff., 76 ff. *Werke*, 1, pp. 232, 234 f.

CHAPTER VIII.

Faust, Erster Teil, Werke, xiv. *Urfaust, Fragment und die Ausgabe von 1808 im Paralleldruck*, herausgegeben von H. Lebede, Berlin, 1912. Herausgegeben von G. Witkowski, 7th ed., Leipzig, 1924; von R. Petsch, Leipzig, 1924; and many earlier editions. Ed. with English notes by Calvin Thomas, 2 vols., Boston, 1892, 1901; and by J. Goebel, New York, 1907. *Faust, ein Fragment*, von W. L. Holland, Heilbronn, 1882. There are between forty and fifty translations of the First Part of *Faust* into English. Of these the versions of Anna Swanwick (1850), revised ed., 1893, and Bayard Taylor (1871) still, on the whole, maintain their supremacy.

Das Volksbuch vom Dr. Faust, herausgegeben von R. Petsch, Halle, 1911; *Die Faust-Dichtung vor, neben und nach Goethe*, herausgegeben von K. G. Wendringer, 4 vols., Berlin, 1914; *Gestaltungen des Faust: die bedeutendsten Werke seit 1587*, herausgegeben von N. W. Geissler, 3 vols., Munich, 1927.

K. Fischer, *Goethes Faust nach seiner Entstehung, Idee und Komposition*, 3 vols., 5th ed., Heidelberg, 1904; J. Minor, *Goethes Faust: Entstehungsgeschichte und Erklärung*, 2 vols., Stuttgart, 1901; E. Traumann, *Goethes Faust nach Entstehung und Inhalt erklärt*, 2 vols., 2nd ed., Munich, 1919–20; O. Pniower, *Goethes Faust: Zeugnisse und Excurse zu seiner Entstehungsgeschichte*, Berlin, 1899; G. Lowes Dickinson and F. Melian Stawell, *Goethe's Faust*, London, 1928.

P. 206: *Werke*, xxxii, pp. 288 f.; P. 211: *Schillers Briefe*, herausgegeben von F. Jonas, iv, p. 72; Goethe, *Briefe*, x, p. 209; P. 212: *Ibid.*, xii, p. 167; Schiller's letter, *ed. cit.*, v, pp. 205 f.; P. 213: *Briefe*, xv, p. 214; Pp. 215–17: *Faust*, i, ll. 300 ff.; 1692 ff.

PART III

CHAPTER I.

O. Harnack, *Goethe in der Epoche seiner Vollendung*, 2nd ed., Leipzig, 1901.

A. Fischer, *Goethe und Napoleon*, 2nd ed., Frauenfeld, 1900. For Goethe's own account of his interview Napoleon, see *Werke*, xxxvi, pp. 269 ff.; for Talleyrand's statement, *Goethe-Jahrbuch*, xiii, 1892, pp. 252 ff.

K. Th. Gaedertz, *Goethes Minchen*, 2nd ed., Bremen, 1889; K. Fischer, *Goethes Sonettenkranz*, Heidelberg, 1896.

Bettinas Leben und Briefwechsel mit Goethe, herausgegeben von

R. Steig und F. Bergemann, 2nd ed., Leipzig, 1927; Bettina von Arnim, *Goethes Briefwechsel mit einem Kind*, herausgegeben von J. Fränkel, 3 vols., Jena, 1906. English translation, London, 1838.

CHAPTER II.

Die Wahlverwandtschaften, Werke, xx. English translation by R. D. Boylan, in Bohn's *Standard Library*. Erläutert von H. Düntzer, *Erläuterungen der Klassiker*, x, 2nd ed., Leipzig, 1878. O. F. Walzel, *Goethes Wahlverwandtschaften im Rahmen ihrer Zeit*, in *Goethe-Jahrbuch*, xxvii, 1906, pp. 166 ff.; C. Semler, *Goethes Wahlverwandtschaften und des Dichters sittliche Weltanschauung*, Hamburg, 1886; A. F. Poncet, *Les Affinités électives*, Paris, 1910.

Pandora, Werke, i, pp. 295 ff. It has not been translated into English. U. von Wilamowitz-Möllendorff, *Goethes Pandora*, in *Goethe-Jahrbuch*, xix, 1898; E. Cassirer, *Goethes Pandora*, in his *Idee und Gestalt*, Berlin, 1921.

P. 247 : *Pandora*, ll. 1081 ff.

CHAPTER III.

Dichtung und Wahrheit, Werke, xxvi–xxix. English translation by J. Oxenford, London, 1850; revised by M. Steele Smith, 2 vols., London, 1908. K. Jahn, *Dichtung und Wahrheit : Vorgeschichte, Entstehung, Kritik, Analyse*, Halle, 1908; K. Alt, *Studien zur Entstehungsgeschichte von Dichtung und Wahrheit*, Weimar, 1898.

Goethe und Österreich : Briefe und Erläuterungen, herausgegeben von A. Sauer, 2 vols. (*Schriften der Goethe Gesellschaft*, xvii, xviii), Weimar, 1902–4.

Des Epimenides Erwachen, Werke, xvi, pp. 331 ff. It has not been translated.

E. von den Hagen, *Goethe als Herausgeber von Kunst und Altertum*, Berlin, 1912; G. Böhlich, *Goethes Propyläen*, Stuttgart, 1915; K. Vollbehr, *Goethe und die bildende Kunst*, Leipzig, 1895.

Goethes Briefwechsel mit S. Boisserée, 2 vols., Stuttgart, 1862.

J. G. Robertson, *Goethe und Byron* (*Publications of the English Goethe Society*, N.S., ii), London, 1925.

P. 257 : *Westöstlicher Divan, Werke*, vi, p. 162 ; P. 262 : *Der 6 Juni, 1816, Werke*, iv, p. 61.

CHAPTER IV.

Westöstlicher Divan, Werke, vi, vii. English Translation by E. A. Bowring, in Bohn's *Standard Library; West-Eastern Divan*, translated by E. Dowden, London, 1914. K. Burdach, *Goethes Westöstlicher Divan*, in *Vorspiel*, iii, Halle, 1926.

Goethes Briefwechsel mit Marianne von Willemer, herausgegeben von M. Hecker, 4th ed., Leipzig, 1922.

Wilhelm Meisters Wanderjahre, Werke, xxiv, xxv. English Translation as far as Book iii, chap. ix, by Thomas Carlyle, London, 1824. See above, Notes to Part ii, chap. vii.

P. 264: *Werke*, vi, p. 5; P. 265: *Ibid.*, p. 168; P. 271: *Werke*, xxv, 1, p. 190.

CHAPTER V.

F. Norman, *Henry Crabb Robinson and Goethe (Publications of the English Goethe Society*, N.S., vi, viii), London, 1930–1.

Aus Ottilie von Goethes Nachlass, herausgegeben von W. von Öttingen, 2 vols. (*Schriften der Goethe-Gesellschaft*, xxvii, xxviii), Weimar, 1912–13. W. Bode, *Goethes Sohn*, Berlin, 1918.

H. Sauer, *Goethe und Ulrike*, Reichenberg, 1925. *Trilogie der Leidenschaft, Werke*, iii, pp. 17 ff.

Goethe und die Romantik: Briefe mit Erläuterungen, herausgegeben von C. Schüddekopf und O. Walzel, 2 vols. (*Schriften der Goethe-Gesellschaft*, xiii, xiv), Weimar, 1898–9.

Goethes und Carlyles Briefwechsel, herausgegeben von H. Oldenberg, Berlin, 1887; English ed., by C. E. Norton, London, 1887; O. Baumgarten, *Carlyle und Goethe*, Tübingen, 1906; *Goethes Briefwechsel mit Zelter*, herausgegeben von M. Hecker, 2 vols., Leipzig, 1913–15.

J. P. Eckermann, *Gespräche mit Goethe*, herausgegeben von H. H. Houben, Leipzig, 1926; English translation by J. Oxenford, London, 1850; J. Petersen, *Die Entstehung der Eckermannschen Gespräche und ihre Glaubwürdigkeit*, Frankfort, 1926; H. H. Houben, *J. P. Eckermann: sein Leben für Goethe*, 2 vols., Leipzig, 1925–8. F. Soret, *Zehn Jahre bei Goethe, 1822–32*, herausgegeben von H. H. Houben, Leipzig, 1929. *Goethes Gespräche mit dem Kanzler Müller*, herausgegeben von C. A. H. Burkhardt, 3rd ed., Stuttgart, 1904.

CHAPTER VI.

Faust, Zweiter Teil, Werke, xv. English Translations by Anna Swanwick, Bayard Taylor and others; see above Notes to Part ii, chap. viii; also for general literature on *Faust*.

G. Witkowski, *Die Handlung im zweiten Teil von Faust*, 3rd ed., Leipzig, 1916; V. Valentin, *Über die klassische Walpurgisnacht und die Helenadichtung*, Leipzig, 1901.

Pp. 288 ff.: *Werke*, xv, pp. 173 ff.; P. 292: Act i, ll. 4679 ff.; P. 297: Act v, ll. 11433 ff.; P. 298: Act v, ll. 11573 ff., 11934 ff.; P. 300: Act v, ll. 12104 ff.

CHAPTER VII.

Goethes naturwissenschaftliche Schriften, Section ii of the Weimar edition, 13 vols. Herausgegeben von R. Steiner, 3 vols. (*Deutsche Nationalliteratur*, cxiv–cxvi), Stuttgart, 1885–97.

R. Magnus, *Goethe als Naturforscher*, Leipzig, 1906 ; E. Barthel, *Goethes Wissenschaftslehre in ihrer modernen Tragweite*, Bonn, 1922 ; W. Jablowski, *Vom Sinn der Goetheschen Naturforschung*, Berlin, 1927. *Goethes Metamorphosen der Pflanzen*, herausgegeben von A. Hansen, 2 vols., Giessen, 1907 ; *Zur Farbenlehre*, herausgegeben von G. Ipsen, Leipzig, 1926. The latter work was translated into English by Sir Charles L. Eastlake, *Goethe's Theory of Colours*, London, 1840 ; M. Semper, *Die geologischen Studien Goethes*, Leipzig, 1914 ; W. von Wasielewski, *Goethe und die Deszendenzlehre*, Frankfort, 1903.

CHAPTER VIII.

P. 317 : *Faust*, i, ll. 1112 ff. ; P. 320 : *Faust*, ii, ll. 11499 ff.

CHRONOLOGICAL LIST OF GOETHE'S WORKS

	Written	First Published
I.—1765–75		
Poetische Gedanken über die Höllen-fahrt Jesu Christi . . .	1764	1766
Annette.	1766–67	1897
Die Laune des Verliebten. Ein Schäferspiel	1767–68	1806
Neue Lieder in Melodien gesetzt .	1767–69	1769
Die Mitschuldigen. Ein Lustspiel .	1768–69	1787
Sesenheimer Lieder and Volkslieder.	1770–71	1775–89 and later
Zum Schäkespears Tag . . .	1771	1854
Geschichte Gottfriedens von Ber-lichingen, dramatisiert. . .	1771–72	1833
Von deutscher Baukunst . .	1772	1772
Briefe des Pastors zu*** ; Zwo wich-tige biblische Fragen . . .	1772	1773
Contributions to the Frankfurter Gelehrte Anziegen . . .	1772–73	1772–73
Götz von Berlichingen. Ein Schau-spiel	1773	1773
Jahrmarktsfest zu Plundersweilern .	1773	1774
Ein Fastnachtsspiel vom Pater Brey	1773	1774
Satyros, oder der vergötterte Wald-teufel. Drama	1773	1817
Prometheus. Drama (fragment) .	1773	1830
Des Künstlers Erdewallen. Drama	1773	1774
Götter, Helden und Wieland. Eine Farce.	1773	1774
Der ewige Jude (fragment of an epic)	1774	1836
Des Künstlers Apotheose. Drama .	1774	1879
Clavigo. Ein Trauerspiel . .	1774	1774
Die Leiden des jungen Werthers .	1773–74	1774
Erwin und Elmire . . .	1773–74	1775

340

	Written	First Published
Gedichte an Lili Schönemann	1775	1775 and later
Stella. Ein Schauspiel für Liebende	1775	1776
Claudine von Villa Bella . .	1774–75	1776
Hanswursts Hochzeit . . .	1775	1836
Faust, in its earliest form (Urfaust) .	1773–75	1887

II.—1776–90

	Written	First Published
Hans Sachsens Poetische Sendung .	1776	1776
Die Geschwister. Ein Schauspiel .	1776	1787
Lila. Ein Schauspiel mit Gesang .	1777	1790
Harzreise im Winter . . .	1777	1789
Der Triumph der Empfindsamkeit .	1777–78	1787
An den Mond	1778	1789
Briefe aus der Schweiz . . .	1779	1796
Gesang der Geister über den Wassern	1779	1789
Iphigenie auf Tauris. Ein Schauspiel (in prose)	1779	1854
Jery und Bätely. Ein Singspiel .	1779	1780
Die Vögel. Nach Aristophanes .	1781	1787
Das Neueste von Plundersweilern .	1781	1817
Elpenor. Ein Trauerspiel (fragment)	1781	1806
Auf Miedings Tod	1782	1782
Die Fischerin. Ein Singspiel . .	1782	1782
Ilmenau	1783	1815
Über den Granit	1784	1877
Die Geheimnisse (fragment of an epic)	1784–85	1789
Scherz, List und Rache. Ein Singspiel	1784	1790
Egmont. Ein Trauerspiel . .	1775–87	1788
Wilhelm Meisters Theatralische Sendung	1776–85	1911
Iphigenie auf Tauris (final form) .	1786–87	1787
Künstlers Apotheose. Drama .	1788	1789
Nausikaa. Ein Trauerspiel (fragment)	1786–87	1827
Torquato Tasso. Schauspiel . .	1780–81, 1788–89	1790
Das römische Carneval . . .	1788	1808
Römische Elegien	1788–89	1795
Faust. Ein Fragment . . .	1775, 1787	1790
Versuch, die Metamorphose der Pflanzen zu erklären	1785–86, 1790	1790
Venetianische Epigramme . .	1790	1796
Schriften (in eight volumes) . .		1787–90

III.—1791–1805

	Written	First Published
Beiträge zur Optik . . .		1791–92
Der Grosskophta. Ein Lustspiel .	1790–91	1792
Reise der Söhne Megaprazons (fragment)	1792	1837
Der Bürgergeneral. Ein Lustspiel .	1792	1793
Reineke Fuchs, in zwölf Gesängen .	1792–93	1793
Die Aufgeregten. Ein politisches Drama (unfinished) . . .	1794	1817
Das Mädchen von Oberkirch. Ein Trauerspiel (fragment). . .	1793	1895
Wilhelm Meisters Lehrjahre . .	1790–95	1795–96
Unterhaltungen deutscher Ausgewanderten	1794–95	1795
Das Märchen.	1795	1795
Der Zauberflöte zweiter Teil. Dramatisches Märchen (fragment) .	1795	1802
Entwurf einer allgemeinen Einleitung in die vergleichende Anatomie .	1795–96	1820
Xenien (with Schiller) . . .	1795–96	1797
Benvenuto Cellini. Nach dem Italienischen	1796–97	1796–97
Vier Jahreszeiten	1796	1797
Ballads (Alexis und Dora ; Der neue Pausias ; Der Zauberlehrling ; Der Schatzgräber ; Die Braut von Korinth ; Der Gott und die Bajadere)	1796–97	1797
Hermann und Dorothea . .	1796–97	1797
Achilleis (fragment) . . .	1797–99	1808
Euphrosyne ; Das Blümlein Wunderschön	1798	1799
Neue Schriften (in seven volumes) .		1792–1800
Weissagungen des Bakis. . .	1798	1800
Propyläen. Eine periodische Schrift		1798–1800
Der Sammler und die Seinen . .	1798–99	1799
Mahomet. Ein Trauerspiel nach Voltaire	1799	1802
Tancred. Ein Trauerspiel nach Voltaire	1800	1802
Paläophron und Neoterpe. Ein Festspiel	1800	1802
Die guten Frauen (Die guten Weiber)	1800	1802
Was wir bringen. Vorspiel . .	1802	1802

342

	Written	First Published
Die natürliche Tochter. Trauerspiel	1799–1803	1803
Rameaus Neffe. Ein Dialog von Diderot	1804	1805
Winckelmann und sein Jahrhundert.	1804–05	1805
Epilog zu Schillers Glocke	1805	1805

IV.—1806–32

	Written	First Published
Vorspiel zur Eröffnung des Weimarischen Theaters	1807	1816
Faust. Erster Teil	1797–1805	1808
Pandora. Ein Festspiel	1807–08	1808
Sonette	1807–08	1815
Zur Farbenlehre	1801–10	1810
Die Wahlverwandtschaften. Ein Roman	1808–09	1809
Werke (published by Cotta, Tübingen) thirteen volumes		1806–10
Philipp Hackert	1807–11	1811
Shakespeares Romeo und Julia	1811	1841
Die Wette. Lustspiel	1812	1837
Die wandelnde Glocke	1813	1815
Des Epimenides Erwachen	1814	1814
Aus meinem Leben. Dichtung und Wahrheit, I–III	1808–14	1811–14
Italienische Reise	1786–88, 1813–17	1816–17
Zweiter römischer Aufenthalt	1787–88, 1817–29	1829
Werke (published by Cotta, Tübingen) twenty volumes		1815–19
Prolog zur Eröffnung des Berliner Theaters	1821	1821
Campagne in Frankreich	1792, 1820–21	1822
Belagerung von Mainz	1793, 1821–22	1822
Tag- und Jahreshefte	1819–25	1830
Shakespeare und kein Ende	1815	1826
Westöstlicher Divan	1814–18	1819
Zur Naturwissenschaft überhaupt		1817–24
Trilogie der Leidenschaft	1823–24	1827
Gedichte (collected in the Ausgabe letzter Hand)		1827

343

	Written	First Published
Novelle.	1826–27	1828
Correspondence with Schiller (1794– 1805).		1828–29
Über Kunst und Altertum. Six volumes		1816–32
Zahme Xenien	1820–21	1820, 1827
Maximen und Reflexionen . .		1833
Wilhelm Meisters Wanderjahre, complete	1807, 1827–28	1833
Aus meinem Leben. Dichtung und Wahrheit. Vol. IV . . .	1824–31	1833
Faust. Zweiter Teil . . .	1800–32	1832
Werke. Vollständige Ausgabe letzter Hand (publ. by Cotta, Tübingen). Forty volumes		1827–31
Nachgelassene Werke (publ. by Cotta, Tübingen). Twenty volumes .		1832–42

INDEX

345

347

INDEX

GOETHE'S WORKS

INDEX

349